Other Books and Series by Jeff Bowen

Applications for Enrollment of Chickasaw Newborn Act of 1905
Volumes I thru VII

Cherokee Intermarried White 1906 Volume I thru X

Applications for Enrollment of Creek Newborn Act of 1905 Volume I & II

Visit our website at **www.nativestudy.com** to learn more about these and other books and series by Jeff Bowen

APPLICATIONS FOR ENROLLMENT OF CREEK NEWBORN ACT OF 1905 VOLUME III

TRANSCRIBED BY
JEFF BOWEN

NATIVE STUDY
Gallipolis, Ohio
USA

Other Books and Series by Jeff Bowen

1901-1907 Native American Census Seneca, Eastern Shawnee, Miami, Modoc, Ottawa, Peoria, Quapaw, and Wyandotte Indians (Under Seneca School, Indian Territory)

1932 Census of The Standing Rock Sioux Reservation with Births And Deaths 1924-1932

Census of The Blackfeet, Montana, 1897- 1901 Expanded Edition

Eastern Cherokee by Blood, 1906-1910, Volumes I thru XIII

Choctaw of Mississippi Indian Census 1929-1932 with Births and Deaths 1924-1931   Volume I
Choctaw of Mississippi Indian Census 1933, 1934 & 1937, Supplemental Rolls to 1934 & 1935 with Births and Deaths 1932-1938, and Marriages 1936-1938 Volume II

Eastern Cherokee Census Cherokee, North Carolina 1930-1939
Census 1930-1931 with Births And Deaths 1924-1931 Taken By Agent L. W. Page Volume I
Eastern Cherokee Census Cherokee, North Carolina 1930-1939
Census 1932-1933 with Births And Deaths 1930-1932 Taken By Agent R. L. Spalsbury   Volume II
Eastern Cherokee Census Cherokee, North Carolina 1930-1939
Census 1934-1937 with Births and Deaths 1925-1938 and Marriages 1936 & 1938 Taken by Agents R. L. Spalsbury And Harold W. Foght Volume III

Seminole of Florida Indian Census, 1930-1940 with Birth and Death Records, 1930-1938

Texas Cherokees 1820-1839 A Document For Litigation 1921

Choctaw By Blood Enrollment Cards 1898-1914 Volumes I thru XVII

Starr Roll 1894   (Cherokee Payment Rolls) Districts: Canadian, Cooweescoowee, and Delaware Volume One
Starr Roll 1894 (Cherokee Payment Rolls) Districts: Flint, Going Snake, and Illinois   Volume Two
Starr Roll 1894 (Cherokee Payment Rolls) Districts: Saline, Sequoyah, and Tahlequah; Including Orphan Roll   Volume Three

Cherokee Intruder Cases Dockets of Hearings 1901-1909 Volumes I & II

Indian Wills, 1911-1921 Records of the Bureau of Indian Affairs Books One thru Seven;
Native American Wills & Probate Records 1911-1921

Other Books and Series by Jeff Bowen

Turtle Mountain Reservation Chippewa Indians 1932 Census with Births & Deaths, 1924-1932

Chickasaw By Blood Enrollment Cards 1898-1914 Volume I thru V

Cherokee Descendants East An Index to the Guion Miller Applications Volume I
Cherokee Descendants West An Index to the Guion Miller Applications Volume II (A-M)
Cherokee Descendants West An Index to the Guion Miller Applications Volume III (N-Z)

Applications for Enrollment of Seminole Newborn Freedmen, Act of 1905

Eastern Cherokee Census, Cherokee, North Carolina, 1915-1922, Taken by Agent James E. Henderson   Volume I (1915-1916)
   Volume II (1917-1918)
   Volume III (1919-1920)
   Volume IV (1921-1922)

Complete Delaware Roll of 1898

Eastern Cherokee Census, Cherokee, North Carolina, 1923-1929, Taken by Agent James E. Henderson   Volume I (1923-1924)
   Volume II (1925-1926)
   Volume III (1927-1929)

Applications for Enrollment of Seminole Newborn Act of 1905 Volumes I & II

North Carolina Eastern Cherokee Indian Census 1898-1899, 1904, 1906, 1909-1912, 1914 Revised and Expanded Edition

1932 Hopi and Navajo Native American Census with Birth & Death Rolls (1925-1931) Volume 1 - Hopi
1932 Hopi and Navajo Native American Census with Birth & Death Rolls (1930-1932) Volume 2 - Navajo

Western Navajo Reservation Navajo, Hopi and Paiute 1933 Census with Birth & Death Rolls 1925-1933

Cherokee Citizenship Commission Dockets 1880-1884 and 1887-1889 Volumes I thru V

Copyright © 2011
by Jeff Bowen

ALL RIGHTS RESERVED
No part of this publication may be reproduced
or used in any form or manner whatsoever
without previous written permission from the
copyright holder or publisher.

Originally published:
Baltimore, Maryland
2011

Reprinted by:

Native Study LLC
Gallipolis, OH
www.nativestudy.com
2020

Library of Congress Control Number: 2020917992

ISBN: 978-1-64968-082-2

Made in the United States of America.

This series is dedicated to the descendants of the Creek newborn listed in these applications.

DEPARTMENT OF THE INTERIOR.

Commissioner to the Five Civilized Tribes.

NOTICE.

Opening of Land Office at Wewoka,
IN THE SEMINOLE NATION, INDIAN TERRITORY.

Notice is hereby given that on Monday, September 4, 1905, the Commissioner to the Five Civilized Tribes will establish a land office at Wewoka, in the Seminole Nation, Indian Territory, for the purpose of allowing citizens and freedmen of the Seminole Nation to select allotments of land for their minor children enrolled under the Act of Congress approved March 3, 1905 (33 Stat. L 1060), and for the further purpose of allowing citizens and freedmen of the Seminole Nation, whose allotments are incomplete, to select additional land in order to bring the value of their allotments up to the standard of $309.09, as nearly as may be practicable.

Each child whose enrollment in accordance with the Act of March 3, 1905, has been duly approved by the Secretary of the Interior, is entitled to receive an alllotment of forty acres without regard to the character or value of the land selected.

Selection of allotments for minor children must be made by their citizen or freedmen parents or by a duly appointed guardian, or curator, or by a duly appointed administrator.

TAMS BIXBY,
Commissioner.

Muskogee, Indian Territory,
July 29, 1905.

This particular notice makes mention of the Act of 1905. The Creek and Seminole were closely related tribes. Both tribes' notices were like similar in nature.

DEPARTMENT OF THE INTERIOR,
Commission to the Five Civilized Tribes.

Closing of Citizenship Rolls
OF THE MUSKOGEE OR CREEK NATION.

WHEREAS, on June 13, 1904, the Secretary of the Interior, under the authority in him vested by the provisions of the act of Congress approved March 3, 1901, (31 Stat., 1058) ordered that September 1, 1904, be and the same is hereby fixed as the time when the rolls of the Muskogee or Creek Nation shall be closed:

Notice is hereby given that the Commission to the Five Civilized Tribes will, at its office in Muskogee, Indian Territory, up to and inclusive of September 1, 1904, receive applications for the enrollment of citizens and freedmen of the Muskogee or Creek Nation, and that after that date the application of no person whomsoever for enrollment as a citizen or freedman of said nation will be received by the Commission.

Commission to the Five Civilized Tribes,
TAMS BIXBY, Chairman,
T. B. NEEDLES,
C. R. BRECKINRIDGE,
Commissioners.

Muskogee, Indian Territory,
June 25, 1904.

A notice like this was printed in newspapers and posted throughout Indian Territory.

INTRODUCTION

This series concerns Applications for Enrollment of Creek Newborn, National Archive film M-1301 (Act of 1905), as described in the National Archives publication *American Indians*. It falls under the heading Applications for Enrollment of the Commission to the Five Civilized Tribes, 1898-1914, M-1301 and is transcribed from microfilm rolls 414-419. This shows the application forms filled out by individuals applying for enrollment in the Five Civilized Tribes under the Dawes Commission. These applications contain additional information that wasn't abstracted to the census cards that you find in series M-1186. This particular roll (Creek by Birth) contains its own series of numbers separate from M-1186. To find each party's roll number you would have to reference M-1186. On July 25, 1898, there was an Indian Territory Division created in the Office of the Department of Interior. This division was created because of the increased work caused by what was called the Curtis Act, named after Senator Charles Curtis. Basically, this law stated that the tribal rolls needed to be descriptive and pointed out that each tribal roll was without description and had to be redone. At this point there was such a struggle among the Creeks to accept that the Government was going to change their way of life, again, that their leaders were refusing to cooperate in handing over their census information. The Commission had found that enrolling the Creeks was a difficult task not only because the Creek feared what was coming but also because their tribal structure was consistent with being a confederacy with forty-four different bands whose tribesmen lived in different towns of which each had a king that was supposed to keep track of their citizenry. The Commission reported that there was very little evidence of any census that existed and what there was had been kept carelessly. There were attempts and tribal conflicts along the way, but the Curtis Act would make it so they had to do it again no matter what effort from the past. In 1899, Agent Wesley Smith educated Washington to the fact that it was difficult to verify Creek eligibility. The acts passed by the Creeks themselves concerning enrollment since 1893 had been strewn amongst the archives of the Creek Council in Muskogee, I.T., and there was no provision ever approved for the printing of the those enrollments. There was confusion and difficulty let alone the fact that surnames were practically unknown among the Creek. But there was no confusion on March 9, 1905, when the Commission stated they would come to seven towns in the Creek Nation and accept applications that had to be made on a standardized blank form and contain a notarized affidavit from the mother and the attending doctor or midwife. A few by mail, but most of them were offered to a field party led by Commissioner Needles. The Commission took in applications for 2,410 children by the deadline of midnight, May 2, 1905.

This series contains applications and correspondence from 1,171 of those claimants. Realizing there were over 2,400 applicants originally, it is understood that not all were accepted. Also included are names of doctors, lawyers, mid-wives, and others who attended to the Creek Nation before and during this time in history.

Jeff Bowen
Gallipolis, Ohio
NativeStudy.com

Applications for Enrollment of Creek Newborn
Act of 1905   Volume III

BIRTH AFFIDAVIT.

DEPARTMENT OF THE INTERIOR.
COMMISSION TO THE FIVE CIVILIZED TRIBES.

IN RE APPLICATION FOR ENROLLMENT, as a citizen of the CREEK Nation, of Louisa McKellop , born on the 31st day of May , 1902

Name of Father: Peter McKellop   a citizen of the   Creek   Nation.
Name of Mother: Betsey McKellop   a citizen of the   Creek   Nation.

Postoffice   Coweta, Ind. Ter.

AFFIDAVIT OF MOTHER.

UNITED STATES OF AMERICA, Indian Territory,
    WESTERN   DISTRICT.

    I, Betsey McKellop , on oath state that I am 26 years of age and a citizen by birth , of the Creek Nation; that I am the lawful wife of Peter McKellop , who is a citizen, by birth of the Creek   Nation; that a female child was born to me on 31st day of May , 1902 , that said child has been named Louisa McKellop, and is now living.

                                               her
Witnesses To Mark: Betsey x McKellop
  { RB Bush   mark
  { A Schooles

Subscribed and sworn to before me this 25th day of April , 1905.

    My Commission Expires   J.E. Jerome
    Jan. 13 1909   Notary Public.

AFFIDAVIT OF ATTENDING PHYSICIAN OR MID-WIFE.

UNITED STATES OF AMERICA, Indian Territory,
    WESTERN   DISTRICT.

    I, Jenny Berryhill , a midwife , on oath state that I attended on Mrs. Betsey McKellop , wife of Peter McKellop on the 22 day of May , 1902 ; that there was born to her on said date a female child; that said child is now living and is said to have been named Louisa McKellop
                                               her
                                       Jennie x Berryhill
Witnesses To Mark: mark
  { S.H. Henderson
  { W.H. Bush

Applications for Enrollment of Creek Newborn
Act of 1905   Volume III

Subscribed and sworn to before me this 25 day of April, 1905.

                                                  J.E. Jerome

My Commission Expires   Notary Public.
Jan. 13, 1909

BIRTH AFFIDAVIT.

DEPARTMENT OF THE INTERIOR.
COMMISSION TO THE FIVE CIVILIZED TRIBES.

IN RE APPLICATION FOR ENROLLMENT, as a citizen of the CREEK Nation, of Louisa McKellop, born on the 31 day of May, 1902

Name of Father:	Peter McKellop	a citizen of the	Creek	Nation.
Name of Mother:	Betsey McKellop	a citizen of the	Creek	Nation.

                            Postoffice   Coweta

AFFIDAVIT OF ~~MOTHER~~. father

UNITED STATES OF AMERICA, Indian Territory, ⎫
     WESTERN   DISTRICT. ⎭

    I, Peter McKellop, on oath state that I am 25 years of age and a citizen by blood, of the Creek Nation; that I am the lawful ~~wife~~ husband of Betsy McKellop, who is a citizen, by blood of the Creek Nation; that a female child was born to me on 31 day of May, 1902, that said child has been named Louisa McKellop, and is now living.

                                          Peter McKillop[sic]

Witnesses To Mark:

{

Subscribed and sworn to before me this 15 day of March, 1905.

                                            Edw C Griesel
                                            Notary Public.

Applications for Enrollment of Creek Newborn
Act of 1905   Volume III

BIRTH AFFIDAVIT.

DEPARTMENT OF THE INTERIOR.
COMMISSION TO THE FIVE CIVILIZED TRIBES.

IN RE APPLICATION FOR ENROLLMENT, as a citizen of the Creek Nation, of Allie B. Couch, born on the 11 day of Sept , 1904

Name of Father:	J.C. Couch	a citizen of the	US	Nation.
Name of Mother:	Amanda "	a citizen of the	Creek	Nation.

Postoffice   Wagoner

(child present)

AFFIDAVIT OF MOTHER.

UNITED STATES OF AMERICA, Indian Territory,
WESTERN   DISTRICT.

I, Amanda Couch, on oath state that I am 22 years of age and a citizen by blood , of the Creek Nation; that I am the lawful wife of JC Couch , who is a citizen, by ----- of the U.S. Nation; that a female child was born to me on 11 day of Sept. , 1904 , that said child has been named Allie B. Couch , and was living March 4, 1905.

Amanda Couch

Witnesses To Mark:

Subscribed and sworn to before me this 11 day of March, 1905.

Edw C Griesel
Notary Public.

AFFIDAVIT OF ATTENDING PHYSICIAN OR MID-WIFE.

UNITED STATES OF AMERICA, Indian Territory,
WESTERN   DISTRICT.

I, Mary E. Couch , a midwife , on oath state that I attended on Mrs. Amanda Couch , wife of J C Couch on the 11 day of Sept. , 1904 ; that there was born to her on said date a female child; that said child was living March 4, 1905; and is said to have been named Allie B. Couch

Her
Mary E. x Couch
mark

Witnesses To Mark:
{ M L Dubois
  EC Griesel

Applications for Enrollment of Creek Newborn
Act of 1905 Volume III

Subscribed and sworn to before me this 11 day of March, 1905.

                                                     Edw C Griesel
                                                    Notary Public.

BIRTH AFFIDAVIT.

DEPARTMENT OF THE INTERIOR.
COMMISSION TO THE FIVE CIVILIZED TRIBES.

IN RE APPLICATION FOR ENROLLMENT, as a citizen of the CREEK Nation, of Gertie May Couch, born on the 26 day of May, 1902

Name of Father: J.C. Couch	a citizen of the U.S.	Nation.
Name of Mother: Amanda "	a citizen of the Creek	Nation.

                               Postoffice   Wagoner

(Child present)

                                  AFFIDAVIT OF MOTHER.

UNITED STATES OF AMERICA, Indian Territory, ⎫
      WESTERN   DISTRICT.   ⎬

      I, Amanda Couch, on oath state that I am 22 years of age and a citizen by blood, of the Creek Nation; that I am the lawful wife of J.C. Couch, who is a citizen, by ----- of the U.S. Nation; that a female child was born to me on 26 day of May, 1902, that said child has been named Gertie May Couch, and is now living.

                                                Amanda Couch

Witnesses To Mark:

{

Subscribed and sworn to before me this 11 day of March, 1905.

                                                Edw C Griesel
                                                Notary Public.

                  AFFIDAVIT OF ATTENDING PHYSICIAN OR MID-WIFE.

UNITED STATES OF AMERICA, Indian Territory, ⎫
       Western   DISTRICT.   ⎬

      I, M. L. Dubose[sic], a midwife, on oath state that I attended on Mrs. Amanda Couch, wife of J C Couch on the 26 day of May, 1902; that there was born to her on

Applications for Enrollment of Creek Newborn
Act of 1905   Volume III

said date a female child; that said child is now living and is said to have been named Gertie May Couch

M.L. Dubois

Witnesses To Mark:
{

Subscribed and sworn to before me this 11 day of March, 1905.

Edw C Griesel
Notary Public.

COMMISSIONERS:
TAMS BIXBY,
THOMAS B. NEEDLES,
C.R. BRECKINBRIDGE.

WM. O. BEALL
Secretary

DEPARTMENT OF THE INTERIOR,
COMMISSIONER TO THE FIVE CIVILIZED TRIBES.

REFER IN REPLY TO THE FOLLOWING:

NC 153.

ADDRESS ONLY THE
COMMISSION TO THE FIVE CIVILIZED TRIBES.

Muskogee, Indian Territory, May 18, 1905.

Sissie Tiger,
    Fentress, Indian Territory.

Dear Sir[sic]:

    In the matter of the application for the enrollment of your minor child, Peggy Tiger, as a citizen of the Creek Nation, you are advised that the Commission requires the affidavit of the midwife or physician in attendance at the birth of said child.

    There is herewith enclosed a blank form of birth affidavit, and in executing same care should be exercised to see that all blanks are properly filled, all names written in full and in the event that the person signing the affidavit is unable to write, signature by mark must be attested by two witnesses. Each affidavit must be executed before a Notary Public and the notarial seal and signature of the officer must be attached to each separate affidavit.

Respectfully,

Tams Bixby

BC.   Chairman.

Applications for Enrollment of Creek Newborn
Act of 1905   Volume III

BIRTH AFFIDAVIT.

DEPARTMENT OF THE INTERIOR.
COMMISSION TO THE FIVE CIVILIZED TRIBES.

IN RE APPLICATION FOR ENROLLMENT, as a citizen of the Creek Nation, of Peggy Jimboy, born on the 14th day of June, 1904

Name of Father: Wiley Jimboy   a citizen of the   Creek   Nation.
Name of Mother: Sissie Tiger   a citizen of the   Creek   Nation.

Postoffice   Wetumka, I.T.

AFFIDAVIT OF MOTHER.

UNITED STATES OF AMERICA, Indian Territory,
Western   DISTRICT.

I, Sissie Tiger, on oath state that I am 19 years of age and a citizen by blood, of the Creek Nation; that ~~I am the lawful wife~~ the child of Wiley Jimboy, who is a citizen, by blood of the Creek Nation; that a female child was born to me on 14th day of June, 1904, that said child has been named Peggy Jimboy, and was living March 4, 1905.

Sissie Tiger

Witnesses To Mark:
{

Subscribed and sworn to before me this 3rd day of June, 1905.

Jeff T. Canard
Notary Public.

Com Ex Aug 2^d 1906

AFFIDAVIT OF ATTENDING PHYSICIAN OR MID-WIFE.

UNITED STATES OF AMERICA, Indian Territory,
Western   DISTRICT.

I, Pinar Tiger, a mid wife, on oath state that I attended on Mrs. Sissie Tiger, ~~wife of Wiley Jimboy~~ on the 14th day of June, 1904; that there was born to her on said date a female child; that said child was living March 4, 1905; and is said to have been named Peggie Jimboy

her
Pinar x Tiger
mark

Witnesses To Mark:
{ Roly Canard
  Simmer Canard

Applications for Enrollment of Creek Newborn
Act of 1905   Volume III

Subscribed and sworn to before me this 3rd day of June, 1905.

Jeff T. Canard
Notary Public.

Com Ex Aug 2d 1906

BIRTH AFFIDAVIT.

DEPARTMENT OF THE INTERIOR.
COMMISSION TO THE FIVE CIVILIZED TRIBES.

IN RE APPLICATION FOR ENROLLMENT, as a citizen of the CREEK Nation, of Peggy Jimboy, born on the 14 day of June, 1904

Name of Father:	Wiley Jimboy	a citizen of the	Creek	Nation.
Name of Mother:	Sissy Tiger	a citizen of the	"	Nation.

Postoffice   Fentress

Child Present Gr

AFFIDAVIT OF MOTHER.

UNITED STATES OF AMERICA, Indian Territory,
   WESTERN   DISTRICT.

I, Sissy Tiger, on oath state that I am 19 years of age and a citizen by blood, of the Creek Nation; that I am not the lawful wife of Wiley Jimboy, who is a citizen, by blood of the Creek Nation; that a female child was born to me on 14 day of June, 1904, that said child has been named Peggy Jimboy, and was living March 4, 1905.

Sissie Tiger

Witnesses To Mark:

Subscribed and sworn to before me this 13 day of March, 1905.

Edw C Griesel
Notary Public.

Applications for Enrollment of Creek Newborn
Act of 1905 Volume III

BIRTH AFFIDAVIT.

DEPARTMENT OF THE INTERIOR.
COMMISSION TO THE FIVE CIVILIZED TRIBES.

IN RE APPLICATION FOR ENROLLMENT, as a citizen of the CREEK Nation, of Joe Brown Williford , born on the 25 day of October , 1903

Name of Father:	M.M. Williford	a citizen of the	U. S.	Nation.
Name of Mother:	Lou Brown Williford	a citizen of the	Creek	Nation.

Postoffice   Fry

Child present J.D.

AFFIDAVIT OF MOTHER.

UNITED STATES OF AMERICA, Indian Territory,
WESTERN   DISTRICT.

I, Lou Brown Williford , on oath state that I am 24 years of age and a citizen by blood , of the Creek Nation; that I am the lawful wife of M. M. Williford , who is a citizen, by ----- of the U. S. Nation; that a male child was born to me on 25 day of October, 1903 , that said child has been named Joe Brown Williford , and is now living.

Mrs Lou Williford

Witnesses To Mark:

Subscribed and sworn to before me this 11th day of Mar. , 1905.

My Commission
Ex. July 25" 1907

(No signature given)
Notary Public.

BIRTH AFFIDAVIT.

DEPARTMENT OF THE INTERIOR.
COMMISSION TO THE FIVE CIVILIZED TRIBES.

IN RE APPLICATION FOR ENROLLMENT, as a citizen of the CREEK Nation, of Joe Brown Williford , born on the 25" day of October , 1903

Name of Father:	M.M. Williford	a non- a citizen of the	Creek	Nation.
Name of Mother:	Lou Williford	a citizen of the	Creek	Nation.

Postoffice   Fry, Ind. Ter.

Applications for Enrollment of Creek Newborn
Act of 1905   Volume III

Child present J.D.

AFFIDAVIT OF MOTHER.

UNITED STATES OF AMERICA, Indian Territory,
WESTERN   DISTRICT.

I, Mrs. Lou Williford , on oath state that I am 24 years of age and a citizen by Blood , of the Creek Nation; that I am the lawful wife of M. M. Williford , who is a non citizen, by ----- of the Creek Nation; that a male child was born to me on 25" day of October, 1903 , that said child has been named Joe Brown Williford, and is now living.

Mrs Lou Williford

Witnesses To Mark:
{ Frank L. Haymer
  J.D. Thomas

Subscribed and sworn to before me this 14" day of March , 1905.

Z.I.J. Holt

My commission expires May 9" 1907   Notary Public.

AFFIDAVIT OF ATTENDING PHYSICIAN OR MID-WIFE.

UNITED STATES OF AMERICA, Indian Territory,
Western District   DISTRICT.

I, Mrs. Ella Strawhun , a Mid-wife , on oath state that I attended on Mrs. Lou Williford , wife of M.M. Williford on the 25" day of October , 1903 ; that there was born to her on said date a male child; that said child is now living and is said to have been named Joe Brown Williford

Mrs Ella Strawhun

Witnesses To Mark:
{ Frank L. Haymer
  J.D. Thomas

Subscribed and sworn to before me this 14" day of March , 1905.

Z.I.J. Holt

My commission expires May 9" 1907   Notary Public.

Applications for Enrollment of Creek Newborn
Act of 1905 Volume III

BIRTH AFFIDAVIT.

DEPARTMENT OF THE INTERIOR.
COMMISSION TO THE FIVE CIVILIZED TRIBES.

IN RE APPLICATION FOR ENROLLMENT, as a citizen of the CREEK Nation, of McKinley Porter, born on the 26 day of Oct., 1904

Name of Father:	Lewis Porter	a citizen of the	Creek	Nation.
Name of Mother:	Elsie "	a citizen of the	Creek	Nation.

Postoffice   Porter, I.T.

(Child present) 4/6-05 M.

AFFIDAVIT OF MOTHER.

UNITED STATES OF AMERICA, Indian Territory,
    WESTERN   DISTRICT.

I, Elsie Porter, on oath state that I am 22 years of age and a citizen by blood, of the Creek Nation; that I am the lawful wife of Lewis Porter, who is a citizen, by blood of the Creek Nation; that a male child was born to me on 26" day of Oct, 1904, that said child has been named McKinley Porter, and is now living.

Elsie Porter

Witnesses To Mark:
{

Subscribed and sworn to before me this 6" day of April, 1905.

J. McDermott
Notary Public.

AFFIDAVIT OF ATTENDING PHYSICIAN OR MID-WIFE.

UNITED STATES OF AMERICA, Indian Territory,
    WESTERN   DISTRICT.

I, Sarah Thompson, a midwife, on oath state that I attended on Mrs. Elsie Porter, wife of Lewis Porter on the 26" day of Oct., 1904; that there was born to her on said date a *(blank)* child; that said child is now living and is said to have been named McKinley Porter

Sarah Thompson

Witnesses To Mark:
{

Applications for Enrollment of Creek Newborn
Act of 1905   Volume III

Subscribed and sworn to before me this 6" day of April, 1905.

J. McDermott
Notary Public.

BIRTH AFFIDAVIT.

DEPARTMENT OF THE INTERIOR.
COMMISSION TO THE FIVE CIVILIZED TRIBES.

IN RE APPLICATION FOR ENROLLMENT, as a citizen of the CREEK Nation, of McKinley Porter, born on the ----- day of October, 1904

Name of Father:	Lewis Porter	a citizen of the	Creek	Nation.
Name of Mother:	Elsie Porter	a citizen of the	Creek	Nation.

Postoffice   Porter, I.T.

AFFIDAVIT OF MOTHER.

UNITED STATES OF AMERICA, Indian Territory,
WESTERN   DISTRICT.

I, Mose Smith, on oath state that I am 39 years of age and a citizen by blood, of the Creek Nation; that I am the ~~lawful wife~~ step-father of Elsie Porter, who is a citizen, by blood of the Creek Nation; that a male child was born to me on ----- day of October, 1904, that said child has been named McKinley Porter, and is now living.

Mose Smith

Witnesses To Mark:
{

Subscribed and sworn to before me this 11th day of Mar, 1905.

My Commission   J. McDermott
Expires July 25" 1907   Notary Public.

Applications for Enrollment of Creek Newborn
Act of 1905   Volume III

BIRTH AFFIDAVIT.

DEPARTMENT OF THE INTERIOR.
COMMISSION TO THE FIVE CIVILIZED TRIBES.

IN RE APPLICATION FOR ENROLLMENT, as a citizen of the CREEK Nation, of Pleasant Porter, born on the 21 day of Feb., 1902

Name of Father:	Lewis Porter	a citizen of the	Creek	Nation.
Name of Mother:	Elsie "	a citizen of the	Creek	Nation.

Postoffice   Porter, I.T.

(Child present) 4/6-1905 M.

AFFIDAVIT OF MOTHER.

UNITED STATES OF AMERICA, Indian Territory, }
    WESTERN   DISTRICT. }

I, Elsie Porter, on oath state that I am 22 years of age and a citizen by blood, of the Creek Nation; that I am the lawful wife of Lewis Porter, who is a citizen, by blood of the Creek Nation; that a male child was born to me on 21st day of Feb, 1902, that said child has been named Pleasant Porter, and is now living.

Elsie Porter

Witnesses To Mark:
{

Subscribed and sworn to before me this 6" day of April, 1905.

J. McDermott
Notary Public.

AFFIDAVIT OF ATTENDING PHYSICIAN OR MID-WIFE.

UNITED STATES OF AMERICA, Indian Territory, }
    WESTERN   DISTRICT. }

I, Sarah Thompson, a midwife, on oath state that I attended on Mrs. Elsie Porter, wife of Lewis Porter on the 21st day of Feb, 1902; that there was born to her on said date a *(blank)* child; that said child is now living and is said to have been named Pleasant Porter

Sarah Thompson

Witnesses To Mark:
{

Applications for Enrollment of Creek Newborn
Act of 1905   Volume III

Subscribed and sworn to before me this 6" day of April, 1905.

J. McDermott
Notary Public.

BIRTH AFFIDAVIT.

DEPARTMENT OF THE INTERIOR.
COMMISSION TO THE FIVE CIVILIZED TRIBES.

IN RE APPLICATION FOR ENROLLMENT, as a citizen of the CREEK Nation, of Plesent[sic] Porter, born on the ----- day of February, 1902

Name of Father:	Lewis Porter	a citizen of the	Creek	Nation.
Name of Mother:	Elsie Porter	a citizen of the	Creek	Nation.

Postoffice   Porter, I.T.

AFFIDAVIT OF MOTHER.

UNITED STATES OF AMERICA, Indian Territory,
WESTERN   DISTRICT.

I, Mose Smith, on oath state that I am 39 years of age and a citizen by blood, of the Creek Nation; that I am the ~~lawful wife of~~ step-father of Elsie Porter, who is a citizen, by blood of the Creek Nation; that a male child was born to ~~me~~ her on ----- day of February, 1902, that said child has been named Plesent Porter, and is now living.

Mose Smith

Witnesses To Mark:
{

Subscribed and sworn to before me this 11th day of Mar, 1905.

My Commission   J. McDermott
Expires July 25" 1907   Notary Public.

NC 156.

Muskogee, Indian Territory, May 19, 1905.

Archie A. Gregory,
   Inola, Indian Territory.

Dear Sir:

Applications for Enrollment of Creek Newborn
Act of 1905   Volume III

In the matter of the application for the enrollment of your minor child, Frank Lee Gregory, as a citizen of the Creek Nation, you are advised that the Commission requires the affidavits of the mother and midwife or physician in attendance at the birth of said child.

There is herewith enclosed a blank form of birth affidavit, and in executing same care should be exercised to see that all blanks are properly filled, all names written in full and in the event that the person signing the affidavit is unable to write, signatures by mark must be attested by two witnesses. Each affidavit must be executed before a Notary Public and the notarial seal and signature of the officer must be attached to each separate affidavit.

Respectfully,

BC.   Chairman.

BIRTH AFFIDAVIT.

DEPARTMENT OF THE INTERIOR.
COMMISSION TO THE FIVE CIVILIZED TRIBES.

IN RE APPLICATION FOR ENROLLMENT, as a citizen of the CREEK Nation, of Frank Lee Gregory, born on the 10 day of Aug , 1903

Name of Father: Archie Gregory   a citizen of the   Creek   Nation.
Name of Mother: Florence   "   a citizen of the   U. S.   Nation.

Postoffice   Inola

Child Present Gr.

AFFIDAVIT OF MOTHER.

UNITED STATES OF AMERICA, Indian Territory,
    WESTERN   DISTRICT.

I, Archie Gregory, on oath state that I am 27 years of age and a citizen by blood , of the Creek Nation; that I am the lawful wife of Florence Gregory , who is a citizen, by ----- of the U. S. Nation; that a male child was born to me on 10 day of Aug. , 1903, that said child has been named Frank Lee Gregory , and was living March 4, 1905.

                                                Archie Gregory
Witnesses To Mark:

Subscribed and sworn to before me this 13 day of March , 1905.

                                                Edw C Griesel
                                                    Notary Public.

Applications for Enrollment of Creek Newborn
Act of 1905   Volume III

BIRTH AFFIDAVIT.

DEPARTMENT OF THE INTERIOR.
COMMISSION TO THE FIVE CIVILIZED TRIBES.

IN RE APPLICATION FOR ENROLLMENT, as a citizen of the Creek Nation, of Frank Lee Gregory, born on the 10th day of August, 1903

Name of Father:	Archie A Gregory	a citizen of the	Creek	Nation.
Name of Mother:	Florence L. Gregory	a citizen of the	U. S.	Nation.

Postoffice   Inola Ind Ter

AFFIDAVIT OF MOTHER.

UNITED STATES OF AMERICA, Indian Territory, }
WESTERN   DISTRICT. }

I, Florence L Gregory, on oath state that I am 24 years of age and a citizen by Birth, of the United States ~~Nation~~; that I am the lawful wife of Archie A. Gregory, who is a citizen, by Blood of the Creek Nation; that a male child was born to me on 10th day of August, 1903, that said child has been named Frank Lee Gregory, and was living March 4, 1905.

Florence L Gregory

Witnesses To Mark:
{

Subscribed and sworn to before me this 22nd day of May, 1905.

Com expires Sept 6-08   T J Rice
                              Notary Public.

AFFIDAVIT OF ATTENDING PHYSICIAN OR MID-WIFE.

UNITED STATES OF AMERICA, Indian Territory, }
Western   DISTRICT. }

I, Catherine F. Ingram, a Mid-wife, on oath state that I attended on Mrs. Florence L Gregory, wife of Archie A Gregory on the 10th day of August, 1903; that there was born to her on said date a male child; that said child was living March 4, 1905; and is said to have been named Frank Lee Gregory

Catherine F Ingram

Applications for Enrollment of Creek Newborn
Act of 1905   Volume III

Witnesses To Mark:
{

      Subscribed and sworn to before me this 22nd day of May, 1905.

Com expires Sept 6-08   T J Rice
                                               Notary Public.

                                                  NC 157.

                  Muskogee, Indian Territory, May 19, 1905.

Charles R. Cane,
      Wagoner, Indian Territory.

Dear Sir:

      In the matter of the application for the enrollment of your minor children, Robert Carr and Willie I. Cane, as a citizen of the Creek Nation, you are advised that the Commission requires the affidavits of the mother and midwife or physician in attendance at the birth of said children.

      There are herewith enclosed two blank forms of birth affidavits, and in executing same care should be exercised to see that all blanks are properly filled, all names written in full and in the event that the persons signing the affidavits are unable to write, signatures by mark must be attested by two witnesses. Each affidavit must be executed before a Notary Public and the notarial seal and signature of the officer must be attached to each separate affidavit.

                                       Respectfully,

BC.   Chairman.

NC-157.

                  Muskogee, Indian Territory, July 26, 1905.

Charlie R. Cane,
      Wagoner, Indian Territory.

Dear Sir:

      On March 13, 1905 you appeared before the Commission to the Five Civilized Tribes and made application for the enrollment of your son Robert Carl Cane as a citizen by blood of the Creek Nation and at that time submitted your affidavit and the affidavit of Minnie May, which set forth that said child was born February 4, 1904. Subsequently you filed with said Commission the affidavits of Mollie B. Cane, the mother of said child,

Applications for Enrollment of Creek Newborn
Act of 1905   Volume III

and Sarah Jane Ragan, the attending midwife at his birth, which set forth that said child was born on February 24, 1904.

You are requested to immediately inform this office as to which of the above dates, if either of them is the correct date of the birth of your said son Robert Carl Cane.

Respectfully,

Commissioner.

Copy

Wagoner, Indian Territory, 7-31-1905.

Honorable Tams Bixby,
    Muskogee, Indian Territory.

Dear Sir:

In answering your letter of July 26th to Charles R. Cane relative to his son Robert C. Cane I beg to say that the affidavits of Mollie B. Cane and the attending midwife at its birth state the correct date of his birth, namely February 24th.

Yours very truly,

RMS-RFB.   (Not signed.)

BIRTH AFFIDAVIT.

DEPARTMENT OF THE INTERIOR.
COMMISSION TO THE FIVE CIVILIZED TRIBES.

IN RE APPLICATION FOR ENROLLMENT, as a citizen of the CREEK Nation, of Willie R. Cane, born on the 5 day of Aug, 1902

Name of Father: Charles R. Cane   a citizen of the   Creek   Nation.
Name of Mother: Mollie B. Cane   a citizen of the U.S. Choctaw Nation.

Postoffice   Wagoner

Applications for Enrollment of Creek Newborn
Act of 1905 Volume III

Child Present Gr.

AFFIDAVIT OF ~~MOTHER~~. father

UNITED STATES OF AMERICA, Indian Territory,
    WESTERN   DISTRICT.

    I, Charles R. Cane , on oath state that I am 34 years of age and a citizen by blood , of the Creek Nation; that I am the lawful ~~wife~~ hus of Mollie B. Cane , who is a citizen, by ~~Creek~~ of the CreekUS[sic] Nation; that a male child was born to me on 5 day of Aug , 1902, that said child has been named Willie R Cane , and was living March 4, 1905.

                                                      Charlie R. Cane

Witnesses To Mark:
{

    Subscribed and sworn to before me this 13 day of March, 1905.

                                                      Edw C Griesel
                                                          Notary Public.

AFFIDAVIT OF ATTENDING PHYSICIAN OR MID-WIFE.

UNITED STATES OF AMERICA, Indian Territory,
    Western   DISTRICT.

    I, Minnie May , a assistant midwife , on oath state that I attended on Mrs. Mollie B. Cane , wife of Charles R. Cane on the 5 day of Aug , 1902 ; that there was born to her on said date a male child; that said child was living March 4, 1905; and is said to have been named Willie R. Cane

                                                      Minnie May

Witnesses To Mark:
{

    Subscribed and sworn to before me this 13 day of March, 1905.

                                                      Edw C Griesel
                                                        Notary Public.

Applications for Enrollment of Creek Newborn
Act of 1905   Volume III

BIRTH AFFIDAVIT.

DEPARTMENT OF THE INTERIOR.
COMMISSION TO THE FIVE CIVILIZED TRIBES.

IN RE APPLICATION FOR ENROLLMENT, as a citizen of the Creek Nation, of Robert Carl Cane , born on the 24 day of February , 1904

Name of Father: Charles R. Cane   a citizen of the Creek Nation.
Name of Mother: Mollie B Cane   a citizen of the United States ~~Nation~~.

Postoffice   Wagoner, Ind. Terr.

AFFIDAVIT OF MOTHER.

UNITED STATES OF AMERICA, Indian Territory,
Western Judicial   DISTRICT.

I, Mollie B. Cane , on oath state that I am 27 years of age and a citizen by blood , of the United States ~~Nation~~; that I am the lawful wife of Charles R. Cane , who is a citizen, by blood of the Creek Nation; that a male child was born to me on 24th day of February , 1904 , that said child has been named Robert Carl Cane , and was living March 4, 1905.

Mollie B. Cane

Witnesses To Mark:
{

Subscribed and sworn to before me this 23 day of May , 1905.

Rose M. Simpson
Notary Public.

AFFIDAVIT OF ATTENDING PHYSICIAN OR MID-WIFE.

UNITED STATES OF AMERICA, Indian Territory,
Western   DISTRICT.

I, Sarah Jane Ragan , a midwife , on oath state that I attended on Mrs. Mollie B. Cane , wife of Charley R. Cane on the 24th day of Feb. , 1904 ; that there was born to her on said date a male child; that said child was living March 4, 1905; and is said to have been named Robert Carl Cane

Sarah Jane Ragan

Witnesses To Mark:
{

Applications for Enrollment of Creek Newborn
Act of 1905   Volume III

Subscribed and sworn to before me this 22nd day of May, 1905.

                J.E. Jerome
                Notary Public.
        My Commission Expires Jan. 13, 1909

BIRTH AFFIDAVIT.

DEPARTMENT OF THE INTERIOR.
COMMISSION TO THE FIVE CIVILIZED TRIBES.

IN RE APPLICATION FOR ENROLLMENT, as a citizen of the Creek Nation, of Robert Carl Cane, born on the 4 day of Feb, 1904

Name of Father:	Charles R. Cane	a citizen of the Creek	Nation.
Name of Mother:	Mollie B Cane	a citizen of the US	Nation.

        Postoffice   Wagoner

Child Present Gr.

AFFIDAVIT OF MOTHER.

UNITED STATES OF AMERICA, Indian Territory, ⎱
    WESTERN   DISTRICT. ⎰

I, Charles R Cane, on oath state that I am 34 years of age and a citizen by blood, of the Creek Nation; that I am the lawful ~~wife~~ hus of Mollie B. Cane, who is a citizen, by ----- of the U.S. Nation; that a male child was born to me on 4 day of Feb, 1904, that said child has been named Robert Carl Cane, and was living March 4, 1905.

                Charlie R. Cane

Witnesses To Mark:
{

Subscribed and sworn to before me this 13 day of March, 1905.

                Edw C Griesel
                Notary Public.

AFFIDAVIT OF ATTENDING PHYSICIAN OR MID-WIFE.

UNITED STATES OF AMERICA, Indian Territory, ⎱
    Western   DISTRICT. ⎰

I, Minnie May, a asst midwife, on oath state that I attended on Mrs. Mollie B. Cane, wife of Charles R. Cane on the 4 day of Feb, 1904; that there was born to her

Applications for Enrollment of Creek Newborn
Act of 1905 Volume III

on said date a male child; that said child was living March 4, 1905; and is said to have been named Robert Carl Cane

                Minnie May

Witnesses To Mark:
{

  Subscribed and sworn to before me this 13 day of March, 1905.

                Edw C Griesel
                  Notary Public.

BIRTH AFFIDAVIT.
DEPARTMENT OF THE INTERIOR.
COMMISSION TO THE FIVE CIVILIZED TRIBES.

IN RE APPLICATION FOR ENROLLMENT, as a citizen of the Creek Nation, of William R. Cane, born on the 5th day of August, 1902

| Name of Father: | Charley R. Cane | a citizen of the Creek Nation. |
| Name of Mother: | Mollie B Cane | a citizen of the United States ~~Nation~~. |

         Postoffice Wagoner, Ind. Terr.

AFFIDAVIT OF MOTHER.

UNITED STATES OF AMERICA, Indian Territory, }
  Western   DISTRICT.

  I, Mollie B. Cane, on oath state that I am 27 years of age and a citizen by *(blank)*, of the United States ~~Nation~~; that I am the lawful wife of Charley R. Cane, who is a citizen, by blood of the Creek Nation; that a male child was born to me on 5th day of August, 1902, that said child has been named William R. Cane, and was living March 4, 1905.

               Mollie B. Cane

Witnesses To Mark:
{

  Subscribed and sworn to before me this 23rd day of May, 1905.

                Rose M. Simpson
                 Notary Public.

Applications for Enrollment of Creek Newborn
Act of 1905   Volume III

AFFIDAVIT OF ATTENDING PHYSICIAN OR MID-WIFE.

UNITED STATES OF AMERICA, Indian Territory, ⎫
    Western   **DISTRICT.** ⎭

    I, Minnie May , ~~a~~ *(blank)* , on oath state that I ~~attended~~ was present and assisted the mid-wife in attending on Mrs. Mollie B. Cane , wife of Charley R. Cane on the 5th day of August , 1902; that there was born to her on said date a male child; that said child was living March 4, 1905; and is said to have been named William R Cane

                                  Minnie May

Witnesses To Mark:
    {

    Subscribed and sworn to before me this 23 day of May, 1905.

                                    Rose M Simpson
                                    Notary Public.

BIRTH AFFIDAVIT.

DEPARTMENT OF THE INTERIOR.
COMMISSION TO THE FIVE CIVILIZED TRIBES.

    IN RE APPLICATION FOR ENROLLMENT, as a citizen of the CREEK Nation, of Maxie Howard , born on the 8 day of Aug , 1904

Name of Father:	H.B. Howard	a citizen of the U.S.	Nation.
Name of Mother:	Mattie "	a citizen of the Creek	Nation.

                        Postoffice   Coweta I.T.

(Child present) HGH

AFFIDAVIT OF MOTHER.

UNITED STATES OF AMERICA, Indian Territory, ⎫
    WESTERN   **DISTRICT.** ⎭

    I, Mattie Howard , on oath state that I am 23 years of age and a citizen by blood , of the Creek Nation; that I am the lawful wife of H.B. Howard , who is a citizen, by ----- of the U.S. Nation; that a female child was born to me on 8 day of Aug , 1904, that said child has been named Maxie Howard , and is now living.

                                  Mattie Howard

Witnesses To Mark:
    {

Applications for Enrollment of Creek Newborn
Act of 1905   Volume III

Subscribed and sworn to before me this 11 day of March , 1905.

My Commission   J. McDermott
Ex July 25" 1907   Notary Public.

AFFIDAVIT OF ATTENDING PHYSICIAN OR MID-WIFE.

UNITED STATES OF AMERICA, Indian Territory,
Western   DISTRICT.

I, Kizzie Lovett , a midwife , on oath state that I attended on Mrs. Mattie Howard , wife of H B Howard on the 8 day of Aug , 1904 ; that there was born to her on said date a female child; that said child is now living and is said to have been named Maxie Howard

                                                                                                    her
                                                                                    Kizzie x Lovett
Witnesses To Mark: mark
 Zera Ellen Parrish
 J McDermott

Subscribed and sworn to before me this 11 day of March, 1905.

                                                J. McDermott
                                                Notary Public.

BA-260-261-B

In regard to the discrepancy in the date of the birth of Lucy Hill, the correct year appears to be as 1901. In the absence of my original notes, I am unable to say whether the witnesses miscalled the year or the stenographer made an error in recording or transcribing his notes as same refer to the year when Lucy was born.

                                                JY Miller

BA-260-261-B

DEPARTMENT OF THE INTERIOR,
COMMISSION TO THE FIVE CIVILIZED TRIBES.

Muskogee, Indian Territory, March 13, 1905.

In the matter of the application for the enrollment of Lucy and Amanda Hill as Creeks.

Applications for Enrollment of Creek Newborn
Act of 1905   Volume III

Pollie Hill, being duly sworn, testified as follows (through Jesse McDermott, Official Interpreter):

EXAMINATION BY THE COMMISSION:
Q What is your name? A Pollie Hill.
Q What is your age? A 27.
Q What is your postoffice? A Hannah.
Q What is the name of your father? A James Hill.

Pollie Hill and James Hill are identified on Creek Indian card, field No. 2070, and their names are contained in the partial list of Creek citizens by blood, approved by the Secretary of the Interior March 28, 1902, Roll Nos. 6374 and 6373, respectively.

Q You have a child named Amanda Hill? A Yes sir.
Q When was Amanda born? A August 9, 1904.
Q Amanda is living, is she? A Yes sir.
Q Have you a child named Lucy Hill? A Yes sir.
Q When was Lucy born? A May 31.
Q What year? A 1900.
Q Lucy living? A Yes sir.
Q Who was present when Lucy was born? A Lasser.
Q Was she the midwife? A Yes sir.
Q Is she living? A Yes sir.
Q What is her postoffice? A Hannah.
Q Do you know what time children have to be born to file under the old law? A Yes sir.
Q What date was that? A May 25th.
Q You are sure that Lucy was born after that? A Yes sir.

Jim Hill, being duly sworn, testified as follows (through Jesse McDermott, Official Interpreter):

EXAMINATION BY THE COMMISSION:
Q What is your name? A Jim Hill.
Q What is your age? A About 43.
Q What is your postoffice? A Hannah.
Q Did you have children named Amanda and Lucy Hill? A Yes sir.
Q When was Amanda born? A August 9.
Q What year? A 1904.
Q When was Lucy born? A May 31, 1900.
Q Did you ever hold any official position in the Creek Nation? A Yes sir.
Q What position? A I am a member of the House of Representatives of the Creek Nation.
Q Were you a member of the House of Representatives in 1901? A From that time I have held the position that I hold now.
Q Do you remember when the last Creek treaty was passed? A May 25.
Q How long after that was Lucy born? A About five days.

Applications for Enrollment of Creek Newborn
Act of 1905   Volume III

Q You knew that Lucy was not entitled under the old laws? A Yes sir, that's why I didn't enroll.

INDIAN TERRITORY, Western District.
  I, J. Y. Miller, a stenographer to the Commission to the Five Civilized Tribes, do hereby certify upon oath that the above and foregoing is a true and complete translation of my notes as same appear in my stenographic report of this case.

              J Y Miller

Sworn and subscribed before me
 this the 24 day of April, 1905
              Zera E Parrish
                Notary Public.
My Com Expire Apl 11, 1909.

DEPARTMENT OF THE INTERIOR,
COMMISSION TO THE FIVE CIVILIZED TRIBES.
Eufaula, I. T., April 5, 1905.

  In the matter of the application for the enrollment of Lucy Hill as a citizen by blood of the Creek Nation.

    POLLY HILL, being duly sworn, testified as follows:

  Through Alex Posey Official Interpreter:

  BY COMMISSION:
Q What is your name? A Polly Hill.
Q How old are you? A Twenty-seven.
Q How old are you? A Twenty-seven.[sic]
Q What is your post office address? A Hanna.
Q Are you a citizen of the Creek Nation? Yes, sir.
Q To what town do you belong? A Tulsa Canadian.
Q Do you make application for the enrollment of your minor child, you are advised that the Commission requires further evidence as to the birth of said child. of your minor child, Lucy Hill, as a citizen by blood of the Creek Nation? A Yes, sir.
Q What is the name of her father? A James Hill.
Q Is he a citizen of the Creek Nation? A Yes, sir.
Q To what town does he belong? A Hillabee.
Q When was Lucy born? A May 31, 1901.
Q How do you fix the date of the child's birth? A By a record which we have at home.
Q Who made the record? A My husband, James Hill.
Q When did he make the record? A Right after the birth of the child.
Q Who attended on you at the birth [sic] Lucy? A Lussie Harjo.
Q Are you positive that your child, Lucy, was born May 31, 1901? A Yes, sir.

Applications for Enrollment of Creek Newborn
Act of 1905   Volume III

James HILL, being duly sworn, testified as follows:

Through Alex Posey Official Interpreter:

BY COMMISSION:
Q What is your name? A James Hill.
Q How old are you? A About forth-three.
Q What is you post office address? A Hanna.
Q Are you a citizen of the Creek Nation? A Yes, sir.
Q To what town do you belong? A Hillabee.
Q Have you a child named Lucy? A Yes, sir.
Q What is the name of the mother of that child? A Polly Hill.
Q Do you know when Lucy was born? A May 31, 1901.
Q Was there any record made of the child's birth? A I made a record of the child's birth about a month after she was born?
Q Have you that record? A It is at home.

Lussie Harjo, being duly sworn, testified as follows:

Through Alex Posey Official Interpreter:

BY COMMISSION:
Q What is your name? A Lussie Harjo.
Q How old are you? A About thirty.
Q What is your post office address? A Hanna.
Q Are you a citizen of the Creek Nation? A Yes, sir.
Q To what town do you belong? A Kialigee.
Q Do you know James and Polly Hill? A Yes, sir.
Q Do you know a child of theirs named Lucy Hill? A Yes, sir.
Q Do you know when that child was born? A The child was born the last of May.
Q Do you know what date? A I do not know.
Q Was it on the last day of May? A I attended on the mother at the time the child was born but I cannot swear as to the exact date. I only know that it was on the last of May.
Q Do you know whether or not a record was made of the child's birth? A No, sir.
Q How old is the child? A The child is going on five years old.

------:O:------

I, D. C. Skaggs, on oath state that thde[sic] above and foregoing is a full and true transcript of my stenographic notes as taken in said cause on said date.

DC Skaggs

Subscribed and sworn to before me this 21 day of July, 1905.

J McDermott
Notary Public.

Applications for Enrollment of Creek Newborn
Act of 1905 Volume III

BIRTH AFFIDAVIT.

DEPARTMENT OF THE INTERIOR.
COMMISSION TO THE FIVE CIVILIZED TRIBES.

IN RE APPLICATION FOR ENROLLMENT, as a citizen of the CREEK Nation, of Lucy Hill, born on the 31 day of May, 1901

Name of Father:　　James Hill　　　　　a citizen of the　　Creek　　Nation.
Name of Mother:　　Polly　"　　　　　　a citizen of the　　　"　　　Nation.

Postoffice　　Hanna

AFFIDAVIT OF MOTHER.

UNITED STATES OF AMERICA, Indian Territory,　}
　　WESTERN　　　　　DISTRICT.　　　　　　}

I, Polly Hill, on oath state that I am 27 years of age and a citizen by blood, of the Creek Nation; that I am the lawful wife of James Hill, who is a citizen, by blood of the Creek Nation; that a female child was born to me on 31 day of May, 1901, that said child has been named Lucy Hill, and is now living.

　　　　　　　　　　　　　　　　Polly Hill

Witnesses To Mark:
{

Subscribed and sworn to before me this 13 day of March, 1905.

　　　　　　　　　　　　J. McDermott
　　　　　　　　　　　　　　Notary Public.

　　　　　　　　　　　　father
AFFIDAVIT OF ~~ATTENDING PHYSICIAN OR MID-WIFE.~~

UNITED STATES OF AMERICA, Indian Territory,　}
　　Western　　　　　DISTRICT.　　　　　　}

I, James Hill, a m　　, on oath state that I attended on Mrs. *(blank)*, ~~wife~~ husband of Polly Hill on the 31 day of May, 1901; that there was born to her on said date a female child; that said child is now living and is said to have been named Lucy Hill.

　　　　　　　　　　　　　　　James Hill

Witnesses To Mark:
{

Applications for Enrollment of Creek Newborn
Act of 1905   Volume III

Subscribed and sworn to before me this 13 day of March, 1905.

                                          J McDermott
                                          Notary Public.

BIRTH AFFIDAVIT.

DEPARTMENT OF THE INTERIOR.
COMMISSION TO THE FIVE CIVILIZED TRIBES.

IN RE APPLICATION FOR ENROLLMENT, as a citizen of the Creek Nation, of Lucy Hill, born on the 31 day of May, 1901

Name of Father: James Hill   a citizen of the   Creek   Nation. Hillabee Town
Name of Mother: Polly "   a citizen of the   "   Nation. Tulsa Canadian Town

                            Postoffice   Hanna IT

AFFIDAVIT OF MOTHER.

UNITED STATES OF AMERICA, Indian Territory, }
    WESTERN   DISTRICT.

    I, Polly Hill, on oath state that I am 27 years of age and a citizen by blood, of the Creek Nation; that I am the lawful wife of James Hill, who is a citizen, by blood of the Creek Nation; that a female child was born to me on 31 day of May, 1901, that said child has been named Lucy Hill, and was living March 4, 1905.

                                          Polly Hill

Witnesses To Mark:

{

    Subscribed and sworn to before me this 5 day of April, 1905.

                                        Drennan C Skaggs
                                          Notary Public.

AFFIDAVIT OF ATTENDING PHYSICIAN OR MID-WIFE.

UNITED STATES OF AMERICA, Indian Territory, }
    Western   DISTRICT.

    I, Lussie Harjo, a midwife, on oath state that I attended on Mrs. Polly Hill, wife of James Hill on the 31 day of May, 1901; that there was born to her on said

Applications for Enrollment of Creek Newborn
Act of 1905   Volume III

date a *(blank)* child; that said child was living March 4, 1905; and is said to have been named Lucy Hill

Witnesses To Mark:
{

Subscribed and sworn to before me this 5 day of April , 1905.

                    Drennan C Skaggs
                    Notary Public.

BIRTH AFFIDAVIT.

DEPARTMENT OF THE INTERIOR.
COMMISSION TO THE FIVE CIVILIZED TRIBES.

IN RE APPLICATION FOR ENROLLMENT, as a citizen of the CREEK Nation, of Mandy Hill, born on the 9 day of Aug , 1904

Name of Father:	James Hill	a citizen of the	Creek	Nation.
Name of Mother:	Polly "	a citizen of the	"	Nation.

                    Postoffice   Hanna

(Child present)

AFFIDAVIT OF MOTHER.

UNITED STATES OF AMERICA, Indian Territory, }
       WESTERN   DISTRICT.

I, Polly Hill , on oath state that I am 27 years of age and a citizen by blood , of the Creek Nation; that I am the lawful wife of James Hill , who is a citizen, by blood of the Creek Nation; that a female child was born to me on 9 day of Aug. , 1904 , that said child has been named Mandy Hill , and is now living.

                    Polly Hill
Witnesses To Mark:
{

Subscribed and sworn to before me this 13 day of March , 1905.

                    J. McDermott
                    Notary Public.

Applications for Enrollment of Creek Newborn
Act of 1905 Volume III

father
AFFIDAVIT OF ~~ATTENDING PHYSICIAN OR MID-WIFE.~~

UNITED STATES OF AMERICA, Indian Territory, ⎫
    Western   DISTRICT.   ⎬
                                 ⎭

      I, James Hill , a m , on oath state that I attended on Mrs. *(blank)* , ~~wife~~ husband of Polly Hill on the 9 day of Aug , 1904 ; that there was born to her on said date a female child; that said child is now living and is said to have been named Mandy Hill.

                                             James Hill

Witnesses To Mark:
{

      Subscribed and sworn to before me this 13 day of March, 1905.

                                        J McDermott
                                              Notary Public.

BIRTH AFFIDAVIT.
DEPARTMENT OF THE INTERIOR.
COMMISSION TO THE FIVE CIVILIZED TRIBES.

      IN RE APPLICATION FOR ENROLLMENT, as a citizen of the Creek Nation, of Mandy Hill, born on the 9 day of Aug , 1904

Name of Father:	Jim Hill	a citizen of the	Creek	Nation.
Name of Mother:	Polley Hill	a citizen of the	Creek	Nation.

                            Postoffice   Hanna I.T.

AFFIDAVIT OF MOTHER.

UNITED STATES OF AMERICA, Indian Territory, ⎫
    Western   DISTRICT.   ⎬

      I, Polley Hill , on oath state that I am 28 years of age and a citizen by blood , of the Creek   Nation; that I am the lawful wife of Jim Hill , who is a citizen, by blood of the Creek   Nation; that a Female   child was born to me on 9 day of Aug. , 1904 , that said child has been named Mandy Hill , and was living March 4, 1905.

                                          Polly Hill

Witnesses To Mark:
{

Applications for Enrollment of Creek Newborn
Act of 1905   Volume III

Subscribed and sworn to before me this 27 day of July, 1905.

                                                L. G. McIntosh
                                                Notary Public.

AFFIDAVIT OF ATTENDING PHYSICIAN OR MID-WIFE.

UNITED STATES OF AMERICA, Indian Territory, }
    Western   DISTRICT.

I, Hannah Deere , a citizen acting midwife , on oath state that I attended on Mrs. Polly Hill , wife of Jim Hill on the 9 day of Aug , 1904 ; that there was born to her on said date a Female child; that said child was living March 4, 1905; and is said to have been named Mandy Hill

                                                Hannah Deere

Witnesses To Mark:
{

Subscribed and sworn to before me this 27 day of July, 1905.

                                                L. G. McIntosh
                                                Notary Public.

(The above affidavit was given again)

                                                               NC 160.

                              Muskogee, Indian Territory, May 19, 1905.

James Hill,
       Hanna, Indian Territory.

Dear Sir:

      In the matter of the application for the enrollment of your minor child, Mandy Hill, as a citizen of the Creek Nation, you are advised that the Commission requires the affidavit of the midwife or physician in attendance at the birth of said child.

      There is herewith enclosed a blank form of birth affidavit, and in executing same care should be exercised to see that all blanks are properly filled, all names written in full and in the event that the person signing the affidavit is unable to write, signature by mark must be attested by two witnesses. Each affidavit must be executed before a Notary Public and the notarial seal and signature of the officer must be attached to each separate affidavit.

Applications for Enrollment of Creek Newborn
Act of 1905   Volume III

Respectfully,

BC.

Chairman.

(The above letter given again)

NC-160

Muskogee, Indian Territory, July 26, 1905.

James Hill,
    Hanna, Indian Territory.

Dear Sir:

    On March 13, 1905 you appeared before the Commission to the Five Civilized Tribes and made application for the enrollment of your daughter Mandy Hill, born August 9, 1904, as a citizen by blood of the Creek Nation, and at that time submitted your affidavit and the affidavit of your wife, Polly Hill, as to the birth of said child.

    You are advised that it will be necessary for you to furnish this office with the affidavit of the attending physician or midwife as to the birth of said child; but in case no physician or midwife attended at the birth of said child it will be necessary for you to file the affidavits of two disinterested witnesses as to the birth of said child who know when said child was born and whether or not she was living March 4, 1905 March 4, 1905.

    You should give this matter your prompt attention.

Respectfully,

Commissioner.

H C
Env

262
BA 622B.

DEPARTMENT OF THE INTERIOR,
COMMISSION TO THE FIVE CIVILIZED TRIBES.
MUSKOGEE, INDIAN TERRITORY, MARCH 13, 1905.

-ooOoo-

    In the matter of the application for the enrollment of Rena Johnson as a citizen by blood of the Creek Nation.

Applications for Enrollment of Creek Newborn
Act of 1905 Volume III

ROBERT H. JOHNSON, being duly sworn, testified as follows:

EXAMINATION BY COMMISSION:
Q What is your name? A Robert H. Johnson.
Q How old are you? A 32.
Q What is your postoffice address? A Weer.
Q Are you a citizen of the Creek Nation? A I am.

Witness is identified on Creek Indian Card, Field Number 212, and his name is contained in the partial list of Creek citizens by blood, approved by the Secretary of the Interior March 13, 1902, Roll Number 722.

Q Have you a child named Rena? A I have.
Q When was Rena born? A March 15, 1902.
Q What is the name of her mother? A Annie.
Q Is she a citizen of the Creek Nation? A Seminole.
Q If it should be found that your child, Rena Johnson, has rights in both Nations in which Nation do you desire to have her enrolled? A I would like to have her enrolled in the Creek Nation.
Q Is Rena's mother living? A No, she is dead.
Q When did she die? A last 16th day of July three years ago—no, it will be three years ago this coming July.
Q How old was Rena when her mother died? A Rena was born the 15th day of March and her mother died July 16th of the same year.
Q Is Rena living? A Yes, sir.
Q Who was present when Rena was born? A Just me and Annie.
Q Didn't you have a doctor or midwife? A No---just me and Annie.

Witness is notified that it would be advisable for him to have Rena brought before the Commission at some early date.

Zera Ellen Parrish, being sworn on her oath states that as a stenographer for the Commission to the Five Civilized Tribes she reported the above case and that this is a full, true and correct transcript of her stenographic notes in same.

Zera Ellen Parrish

Subscribed and sworn to before me this 15 day of March, 1905.

Edw C Griesel
Notary Public.

Applications for Enrollment of Creek Newborn
Act of 1905 Volume III

NC 161.
OCH.

DEPARTMENT OF THE INTERIOR,
COMMISSIONER TO THE FIVE CIVILIZED TRIBES.

In the matter of the application for the enrollment of Rena Johnson, as a citizen by blood of the Creek Nation.

D E C I S I O N.

The record in this case shows that on March 13, 1905, application was made, in affidavit form, for the enrollment of Rena Johnson, as a citizen by blood of the Creek Nation, under the provisions of the act of Congress approved March 3, 1905 (33 Stats., 1048), and that testimony was offered in support thereof on said date. Supplemental affidavits were filed November 23, 1905, and January 24, 1907.

The evidence and the records of this office show that said Rena Johnson is the child of Annie Johnson, a citizen of the Seminole Nation, and Robert F. Johnson, whose name appears upon a schedule of citizens by blood of the Creek Nation approved by the Secretary of the Interior March 13, 1902, opposite number 722.

The evidence further shows that said Rena Johnson was born March 15, 1902, and that said child was living March 4, 1905 March 4, 1905.

The records of this office show that Rena Johnson is not enrolled as a citizen of the Seminole Nation, and that no application has been made for her enrollment as such.

It is therefore, ordered and adjudged that said Rena Johnson is entitled to be enrolled as a citizen by blood of the Creek Nation under the provisions of the act of Congress approved March 3, 1905 (33 Stat. L., 1048), and the application for her enrollment as such is accordingly granted.

Tams Bixby Commissioner.

Muskogee, Indian Territory.
FEB 2- 1907

AFFIDAVIT OF TWO DISINTERESTED WITNESSES.

United States of America, (
Western District, (ss.
Indian Territory. (

We, the undersigned, on oath state that we are personally acquainted Annie Johnson the lawful wife of Robert F Johnson; that there was born to her a female child on or about the 15 day of March, 1902; that the said child has been named Rena Johnson and was living March 4, 1905.

We further state that we have no interest in this case.

Applications for Enrollment of Creek Newborn
Act of 1905   Volume III

Witness to mark.

Charley Simmons

Johnson Martin

Subscribed and sworn to before me,
this 23 day of January, 1904.

                                                   J. McDermott

My Com   Notary Public.
Exp. July 25" 1908

Indian Territory,   :
                    ss.
Western District.   :

    I, Robert F. Johnson, being first duly sworn according to law deposes and says that he is a Citizen of the Creek Nation and of lawful age; that he was the husband of Annie Childers Johnson a Seminole Indian; that they were living at the time of the birth of Arena Johnson one mile north of Weer, Indian Territory, that I have made application some time ago for the enrollment of the said Arena Johnson, that she was born on the 15th day of March, 1902 that she is the daughter of Annie Childers Johnson; that at the time of the birth of the said Arena Johnson there was no one except my self with the said Annie C. Johnson; that the said Arena Johnson is the identical child who was born to the said Annie Childers Johnson on the 15th day of March, 1902: that I am the lawful father of the said Arena Johnson; that the said Arena Johnson is now living at Henrietta, Indian Territory, with to[sic] Indian[sic] by the [sic] John and Sile[sic] Perryman; that the facts herein stated are true of my own knowledge; that Annie Childers Johnson died some few weeks after the birth of Arena Johnson.

Robert F. Johnson

Subscribed and sworn to before me this 19th day of Nov. 1905.

B J Beavers
Notary Public.

My commission expires December 19, 1908

Indian Territory,   :
                    ss.
Western District.   :

    I, Johnson Martin, being first duly sworn according to law deposes and says that I am a citizen of the Creek Nation and a resident of Coweta, Indian Territory, that I am personally acquainted with Robert F. Johnson and Arena Johnson and knew the said

Applications for Enrollment of Creek Newborn
Act of 1905 Volume III

Robert F. Johnson when his wife was Annie Childers Johnson was living and was personally acquainted with the said Annie Childers Johnson; that the said Arena Johnson was born on the 15th day of March 1902, that he was not present at the time of the birth but saw the mother and child together a short time after the birth of the said Arena Johnson; that this affiant was the father of a child who was born two days previous to the birth of the said Arena Johnson; that this affiant was living near the home of the Johnsons at the time; that the mother, Annie Childers Johnson died some three months after the birth of the child, Arena Johnson; that the said Annie Johnson was living with Robert F. Johnson at the time and had been living together as husband and wife; that he has known the said Robert F. Johnson and Arena Johnson ever since the time heretofore a state and that this affiant verily believes the facts herein stated to be true to the best of his knowledge and thehe[sic] is in no wise interested, directly or indirectly in the application of Arena Johnson for enrollment:
               Johnson Martin
               ~~Robert F. Johnson~~

Sworn and Subscribed to before me this 18th day of November, 1905.

               BJ Beavers
My commission expires December 19, 1908.

  I BJ Beavers hereby certify that the signature made above and erased was made by Johnson by mistake, thinking and intending to sign his own affidavit and *(illegible)* certify.
  Wherefore I am Notary Public witnessed before the aforesaid District and Territory.

               BJ Beavers
               Notary Public

Indian Territory, :
       ss.
Western District. :

  I, Charley Simmons being first duly sworn, according to law, deposes and says that he is a citizen of the Creek nation[sic] and that he has known Robert F. Johnson and Annie Childers Johnson, deceased for some years; that the said Robert F. Johnson and Annie Childers Johnson were living together until the death of Annie C. Johnson as husband and wife; that the said Arena Johnson was born about the 15th of March, 190?; that it was born at about the time of the birth of the child born to Johnson Martin; that he saw the child, Arena Johnson, with the mother the day after its birth and is certain to the best of his knowledge and circumstances surrounding the case that the said Arena Johnson was the child of Annie C. Johnson; that he has known the said Arena Johnson and Robert F. Johnson since that time and that the facts herein stated he verily believes to be true to the best of his knowledge and belief.
               Charley Simmons

Applications for Enrollment of Creek Newborn
Act of 1905 Volume III

Sworn and subscribed to before me this 18th day of November, 1905.

>BJ Beavers
>Notary Public.

My commission expires Dec. 19, 1908.

NC-161.

Muskogee, Indian Territory, May 27, 1905.

Robert H[sic]. Johnson
>Weer, Indian Territory.

Dear Sir:

    In the matter of the application for the enrollment of your minor child, Rena Johnson, as a citizen of the Creek Nation, you are advised that the Commission requires the affidavit of two disinterested witnesses, furnishing proof that Annie Johnson was the mother of said child, giving the date of her death.

>Respectfully,

>Chairman.

NC.161.

Muskogee, Indian Territory, July 14, 1905.

Commissioner to the Five Civilized Tribes,
>Seminole Enrollment Division,
>>Muskogee, Indian Territory.

Gentlemen:

    March 11, 1905, application was made to the Commission to the Five Civilized Tribes for the enrollment of Rena Johnson, born March 15, 1902, as a citizen by blood of the Creek Nation. It is stated in said application that the father of said child is Robert F. Johnson, a citizen of the Creek Nation, and that the mother is Annie Johnson, a citizen of the Seminole Nation.

    You are requested to inform the Creek Enrollment Division as to whether application has been made for the enrollment of said Rena Johnson, as a citizen of the Seminole Nation, and if so, what disposition has been made of the same.

>Respectfully,

>Commissioner.

Applications for Enrollment of Creek Newborn
Act of 1905   Volume III

DEPARTMENT OF THE INTERIOR,
COMMISSIONER TO THE FIVE CIVILIZED TRIBES.

Muskogee, Indian Territory, July 18, 1905.

Chief Clerk,
    Creek Enrollment Division.

Dear Sir:

    Receipt is acknowledged of your letter of July 14, 1905 (NC-161) stating that an application was made to the Commission to the Five Civilized Tribes for the enrollment of Rena Johnson, born March 15, 1902, child of Robert F. Johnson, a citizen of the Creek Nation, and Annie Johnson, a citizen of the Seminole Nation, as a citizen by blood of the Creek Nation and requesting to be informed as to whether an application has been made for the enrollment of said Rena Johnson as a citizen of the Seminole Nation.

    In reply to your letter you are advised that it does not appear from an examination of the records of this office that any application was made to the Commission to the Five Civilized Tribes for the enrollment of said Rena Johnson as a citizen of the Seminole Nation.

    Respectfully,

    Tams Bixby   Commissioner.

NC-161

Muskogee, Indian Territory, December 11, 1905.

Robert F. Johnson,
    Weer, Indian Territory.

Dear Sir:

    There are on file at this Office affidavits executed by you relative to the birth of your minor child, born March 15, 1902. The name of said child is variously given in your affidavits as "Rena" Johnson and "Arena" Johnson.

    In order that this discrepancy may be corrected, there is herewith enclosed a blank form of birth affidavit, which you are requested to execute, giving the correct name of said child, and return affidavit, when executed, to this Office in the enclosed envelope.

    There are also on file at this Office the affidavits of Charley Simmons and Johnson Martin relative to the birth of said Rena (or Arena) Johnson. Said affidavits are defective inasmuch as the affiants failed to state whether or not said Rena (or Arena) Johnson was living March 4, 1905. There are herewith enclosed two blank forms of birth

Applications for Enrollment of Creek Newborn
Act of 1905   Volume III

affidavits, which you are requested to cause said Johnson Martin and Charley Simmons to execute and return when executed to this Office.

These matters should receive your immediate attention.

Respectfully,

Acting Commissioner.

1 B A
Dis

N.C.161

Muskogee, Indian Territory, July 5, 1906.

Robert F. Johnson,
　　Weer, Indian Territory.

Dear Sir:

There are on file in this office affidavits executed by you relative to the birth of your minor child, born March 15, 1902. The name of said child is variously given in your said affidavits as Rena and Arena Johnson.

In order that this discrepancy may be corrected there is herewith inclosed[sic] a blank form of birth affidavit which you are requested to execute, giving the correct name of said child and return same to this office in the inclosed[sic] envelope.

There are also on file the affidavits of Charley Simmons and Johnson Martin relative to the birth of said child. Said affidavits are defective inasmuch as the affiants fail to state whether or not said child was living March 4, 1905. There is inclosed[sic] a blank form for disinterested witnesses which you are requested to cause said parties to execute and when so executed to return to this office.

As a former letter from this office to you in this matter has received no response, you are requested to give this letter your immediate attention.

Respectfully,

Commissioner.

BA
Dis.
Env.

Applications for Enrollment of Creek Newborn
Act of 1905   Volume III

N.C.161

Muskogee, Indian Territory, January 7, 1907.

Jesse McDermott,
    Clerk in Charge Creek Enrollment Field Party,
        Earlsboro, Oklahoma Territory.

Dear Sir:

    Enclosed you will find copies of testimony and affidavits in the matter of the application of Rena Johnson for enrollment as a citizen of the Creek Nation.

    Robert F. Johnson, the father of said applicant, is identified as a citizen of the Creek Nation wherein in his affidavit filed March 13, 1905, he states that he is a Seminole freedman.

    In the supplemental affidavits the said Rena Johnson is variously called Rena and Aurena[sic] Johnson.

    It is requested that you have new affidavits executed in proper form and for that purpose blanks are enclosed herewith.

                                        Respectfully,

AG-7-1   Commissioner.

NBC 161.

Muskogee, Indian Territory, March 7, 1907.

Robert F. Johnson,
    Weer, Indian Territory.

Dear Sir:

    You are hereby advised that on March 2, 1907, the Secretary of the Interior approved the enrollment of your minor child, Rena Johnson, as a citizen by blood of the Creek Nation, and that the name of said child appears upon the roll of new born citizens by blood of the Creek Nation, enrolled under the Act of Congress approved March 3, 1905, as number 1227.

    This child is now entitled to an allotment and application therefor should be made without delay to the Creek Land Office, Muskogee, Indian Territory.

                                        Respectfully,

                                                   Commissioner.

Applications for Enrollment of Creek Newborn
Act of 1905 Volume III

BIRTH AFFIDAVIT.

DEPARTMENT OF THE INTERIOR.
COMMISSION TO THE FIVE CIVILIZED TRIBES.

 IN RE APPLICATION FOR ENROLLMENT, as a citizen of the Creek Nation, of Rena Johnson, born on the 15 day of March, 1902

Name of Father:	Robert F. Johnson	a citizen of the	Creek Nation.
Name of Mother:	Annie " (d)	a citizen of the	Seminole Nation.

      Postoffice Weer

AFFIDAVIT OF MOTHER.

UNITED STATES OF AMERICA, Indian Territory,
 Western   DISTRICT.

 I, Robert F. Johnson, on oath state that I am 32 years of age and a citizen by freedman, of the Creek Nation; that I am the lawful ~~wife~~ husband of Annie Johnson, who is a citizen, by freedman of the Seminole Nation; that a female child was born to me on 15 day of March, 1902, that said child has been named Rena Johnson, and is now living.

           Robert F. Johnson

Witnesses To Mark:
 Seal

 Subscribed and sworn to before me this 13 day of March, 1905.

          Edw C?[sic] Griessel[sic]
          Notary Public.

BIRTH AFFIDAVIT.

DEPARTMENT OF THE INTERIOR.
COMMISSION TO THE FIVE CIVILIZED TRIBES.

 IN RE APPLICATION FOR ENROLLMENT, as a citizen of the CREEK Nation, of Rena Johnson, born on the 15 day of March, 1902

Name of Father:	Robert F. Johnson	a citizen of the	Creek Nation.
Name of Mother:	Annie " (d)	a citizen of the	Seminole Nation.

      Postoffice Weer

Applications for Enrollment of Creek Newborn
Act of 1905   Volume III

AFFIDAVIT OF MOTHER.

UNITED STATES OF AMERICA, Indian Territory, }
WESTERN   DISTRICT.

I, Robert F. Johnson, on oath state that I am 32 years of age and a citizen by Freedman, of the Creek Nation; that I am the lawful ~~wife~~ husb of Annie Johnson, who is a citizen, by Freedman of the Seminole Nation; that a female child was born to me on 15 day of March ,1902 , that said child has been named Rena Johnson, and is now living.

                                  Robert F. Johnson

Witnesses To Mark:
{

Subscribed and sworn to before me this 13 day of March, 1905.

                                  Edw C Griesel
                                  Notary Public.

BIRTH AFFIDAVIT.

DEPARTMENT OF THE INTERIOR.
COMMISSION TO THE FIVE CIVILIZED TRIBES.

IN RE APPLICATION FOR ENROLLMENT, as a citizen of the CREEK Nation, of Clemmie Russell, born on the 8 day of July, 1901

| Name of Father: | James Russell | a citizen of the | U.S. | Nation. |
| Name of Mother: | Mary A.   " | a citizen of the | Creek | Nation. |

                            Postoffice   Redfork

(Child present)

AFFIDAVIT OF MOTHER.

UNITED STATES OF AMERICA, Indian Territory, }
WESTERN   DISTRICT.

I, Mary Russell, on oath state that I am 31 years of age and a citizen by blood, of the Creek Nation; that I am the lawful wife of James Russell, who is a citizen, by ----- of the U.S. Nation; that a female child was born to me on 8 day of July, 1901, that said child has been named Clemmie Russell, and was living March 4, 1905.

                                  Mary A. Russell

Witnesses To Mark:
{

Applications for Enrollment of Creek Newborn
Act of 1905   Volume III

Subscribed and sworn to before me this 13 day of March , 1903.

          Edw C Griesel
            Notary Public.

BIRTH AFFIDAVIT.

DEPARTMENT OF THE INTERIOR.
COMMISSION TO THE FIVE CIVILIZED TRIBES.

  IN RE APPLICATION FOR ENROLLMENT, as a citizen of the Creek Nation, of Clemmie Russell, born on the 8th day of July , 1901

Name of Father:	James Russell	a citizen of the	U.S.	Nation.
Name of Mother:	Mary A "	a citizen of the	Creek	Nation.

       Postoffice **RED FORK, I.T.**

     AFFIDAVIT OF ~~MOTHER~~. father

UNITED STATES OF AMERICA, Indian Territory, ⎫
  Western   DISTRICT. ⎭

  I, James W. Russell, on oath state that I am 34 years of age and a citizen by birth , of the U.S. Nation; that I am the lawful ~~wife~~ husband of Mary A. Russell , who is a citizen, by blood of the Creek Nation; that a female child was born to me on 8th day of July , 1901 , that said child has been named Clemmie Russell , and is now living.

          James W. Russell

Witnesses To Mark:

  Subscribed and sworn to before me this 16th day of March, 1905.

My Commission expires Oct 19, 1907.   Allen Henry
            Notary Public.

    AFFIDAVIT OF ATTENDING PHYSICIAN OR MID-WIFE.

UNITED STATES OF AMERICA, Indian Territory, ⎫
  Western   DISTRICT. ⎭

  I, Sarah Berryhill , a mid-wife , on oath state that I attended on Mrs. Mary A. Russell , wife of James W. Russell on the 8th day of July , 1901 ; that there was born to

Applications for Enrollment of Creek Newborn
Act of 1905   Volume III

her on said date a female child; that said child is now living and is said to have been named Clemmie Russell

Sarah Berryhill

Witnesses To Mark:
{

Subscribed and sworn to before me this 16th day of March, 1905.

My Commission expires Oct 19, 1907.   Allen Henry
Notary Public.

NC 165.

DEPARTMENT OF THE INTERIOR,
COMMISSION TO THE FIVE CIVILIZED TRIBES.
MUSKOGEE, I.T. MAY 23, 1905.

In the matter of the application for the enrollment of John Boyd Combs, as a citizen by blood of the Creek Nation.

Katie Combs being duly sworn, testified as follows:

Examination by the Commission:
Q What is your name? A Katie Combs.
Q What is your age? A I don't know exactly how old I am.
Q Well about? Witness appears to be about 25.
Q What is your post office address? A Checotah.
Q Have you some new born children? A Sir.
Q Have you some new born children –children who were born in the last four years?
A Yes sir.
Q What are their names? Pearl and John Boyd Combs.
Q Pearl Combs living? A Yes sir.
Q And is that John Boyd you have in your arms? A Yes sir.
Q When was Pearl Combs born? A I don't know exactly.
Q You don't? A No sir.
Q When was John Boyd Combs born? A The 3rd of March, on Friday.
Q You don't remember the date on which Pearl was born? A No sir.
Q How many years difference in the ages of the two? A She is just two years old.
Q You can't remember when she was born? A No sir.
Q Don't you know the year? A No sir.
Q Don't know the month ~~nea?~~ the year, do you? A No sir.
Q Did you ever know the month or day on which Pearl was born? A I didn't pay any attention to it.
Q Didn't pay any attention? A No sir.
Q Who was present when this child was born—was anybody present? A I don't know anything about it.

Applications for Enrollment of Creek Newborn
Act of 1905   Volume III

Q Were'nt[sic] you conscious—you weren't so sick you couldn't see, could you? A (No answer)
Q Who was there? A Mrs. Gardner and Miss McQueen.
Q What is Mrs. Gardner's first name? A Ella Gardner.
Q What is Miss McQueen's first name? A Sage McQueen.
Q What was she doing there? A She was there to wait on ~~her~~. me
Q Is that all that were there? A Yes sir.
Q No men were present? A No sir.
Q How old is this child John Boyd Combs? A I told you a while ago.
Q No you didn't, you told me when he was born, I asked you how old is he? A About two months old.
Q Is he just two months old, or is he more than two months or less than two months old? A Two months.
Q Just exactly two months? A Yes sir.
Q What day of the month is today? A I don't know.
Q What month is this, do you know? A No sir, I don't know.
Q Do you know what day of the week is today? A Today is Tuesday I guess.
Q Well, is this January, March, May or June, or what month? You just simply know it is Tuesday? A No answer).

--------oOo------

John W. Combs, being duly sworn, testified as follows:

By Commission:
Q What is your name? A J.W. Combs.
Q What is your age? A About fifty years old.
Q What is your post office address? A Checotah.
Q You are a citizen of the United States, are you? A Yes sir.
Q Are you the father of John Boyd Combs? A Yes sir.
Q Have you also a child just older than this child? A Yes sir, Pearly.
Q When was Pearly born? A I don't know exactly, she is something like three years old.
Q When was John Boyd Combs born? A The 3rd of March, this year 1905.
Q This year? A Yes sir.
Q You remember the year month and day of which John Boyd Combs was born but you don't remember the date of the birth of Pearly. A I just figured on this, that the time for the roll of new born children to be closed, and it was just the day before the time was up that this child was born, that is why I remember the date of birth of John Boyd.
Q Well, now, Mr. Combs I will ask you what time in the day was it this child was born? A I don't remember that either. I had been to town and had just got back and found my woman sick. I got work she was sick and hurried home.
Q So the child was born when you got there? A No sir, it was born after I got home, it was born in the evening.
Q Well now, how long had the child been born before you actually saw it? A Probably 10 or 12 minutes, something like that.
Q You are sure it wasn't as much as an hour? A No sir.
Q Now what time of the the[sic] day was it that you actually saw this child? A The 3rd day of March when I got back there from town, I got word that my wfie[sic] was

Applications for Enrollment of Creek Newborn
Act of 1905   Volume III

complaining and I hurried back home, it was like something about 2 or 3 o'clock in the evening.
Q You are sure it was born before sundown? A Yes sir.
Q On the day before the inauguration of the President? A Yes sir.
Q Do you know what day of the month today is? A I don't know, just along about the 23rd or 24th.
Q You know the month do you? A I believe I do. I believe it is May.
Q How old is this child now? A Well now I would have to figure on that.
Q If you have to figure on it there isn't any use to ask the question? A I don't know.

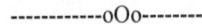

Ella Gardner, being duly sworn, testified as follows:

By Commission.
Q Do you sometime sign your name E.M. Gardner? A Yes sir.
Q Do you know Mrs. Katie Combs? A Yes sir.
Q How long have you known her? A Six months.
Q Do you know her husband? A Yes sir.
Q What is his name? A Wesley Combs.
Q He signs his name as John W. Combs sometimes, doesn't he? A Yes sir.
Q How old are you? A 25.
Q What is your post office address? A Checotah.
Q Have you any occupation? A No sir.
Q Do you know a child of these people by the name of Pearl Combs? A I know the child but don't know anything about her age.
Q Do you know a child of theirs by the name of John Boyd Combs? A Yes sir.
Q Were you present when the child was born? A Yes sir.
Q When was it born, was it in the night time or day time? A day time.
Q What what[sic] time? A Two o'clock in the evening.
Q What day? A 3rd of March on Friday.
Q What makes you remember this Mrs. Gardner? A Cuase[sic] I was there and there aint any use for anybody to forget anything like that.
Q Were you ever present at any any[sic] births besides this? A Yes sir.
Q Can you tell the dates of those other births? A I can tell----
Q Can you tell about how many children you have assisted at the birth? A Yes, about ten I guess.
Q Can you tell me the date of the birth- the day or month on which any of those children were born? A One.
Q What is the name of that one? A I know the child but it isn't named.
Q Whose child is it? A Thomas---
Q Mr. Thomas, do you know his first name? A No sir.
Q Is he a citizen of the Creek Nation? A No sir.
Q Is she? A No sir.
Q White people were they? A Yes sir.
Q When was that child born? A About a week before this child was born.

Applications for Enrollment of Creek Newborn
Act of 1905 Volume III

Q Can you tell the day of the week or month on which any of these other children were born? A No sir. I aint been with anybody since John Boyd was born.
Q And of those other eight children –you can't tell the month or day of the week on which any of them were born? A I can't tell the month and day of the children.
Q Do you live with these people? A No sir, I live near them in a tent.
Q That is the reason why you remember the date of the birth of this child so well, when you assisted with this one. A Yes sir, this is the reason I remember.
Q Do you know when a child would have to be born in der to come in under this new law? A No sir.
Q Well that has nothing to do with fixing the date of the birth of this child in your mind? A No sir.
Q Who was in the house at the time this child was born besides you and the mother? A Miss McQueen.
Q Weren't any man present? A No sir.

Katie Combs being recalled, testified as follows:

Q What hour of the day was this child born, Mrs. Combs, do you know? A 4 o'clock in the evening.
Q Did you make any kind of a record os[sic] this child's birth? A No sir.

John W. Combs, recalled, testified as follows:

Q You say you remember the date of the birth of this child because it was born the day before the time run out; that is how it happens you remember it? A Yes sir.
Q You understand the law with reference to new born children? A Yes sir.
Q Did you talk to your wife and the midwife about this before you came up here?
A Yes we talked about the age of the child, and also made an affidavit to that effect. Another reason why I remember so well its age, was, that it was born just in time to get on the roll as the day after that the time run out.
Q Can you remember the day, month and the year on which they made out that affidavit about that child? A Why I thonk[sic] so.
Q What date was it? A I think it was no, I can't remember the date they made the affidavit out.
Q You stated a minute ago that you remembered the date of the birth of said child, because you made an affidavit to that affect? A Well because we talked about it, --it was just the day before the law went out.
Q You didn't put down in a book the date of the birth of said child? A No sir.

Q Why, didn't you say you knew the law, and you say you know it was born right close to the time the law went out, and still you didn't think enough of it to put it down in a book or make a record of some kind? A No, I didn't put it down.
Q That would have helped you remember it.

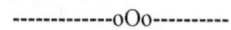

Applications for Enrollment of Creek Newborn
Act of 1905   Volume III

Sabra McQueen, being duly sworn, testified as follows P[sic]

Q What is your name? A Sabra McQueen.
Q How old are you? A About 44 year old past.
Q What is your post office address? A Checotah.
Q Do you live near Mrs. Combs? A Yes sir.
Q Who else was present? A Mrs. Gardner.
Q Are you sure that Mrs. Gardner was present when the child was born? A My eyes seen her.
Q Was that all that were there? A Just me and her.
Q Now can you tell what hour of the day or what time of the day was it that your eyes seen her and this child for the first time in this world? A The 3rd day of March. What year do you call this, I can't read or write.
Q This is 1905? A Well, 1905, was on this day this child was born to this woman.
Q Do you know what day today is? A My old folks said today was Tuesday.
Q What day of the month? A I think I am not sure, that this is the 23rd day of May.
Q Did your folks tell you this also? A No sir. I looked at the almanac.
Q How do you know this is the 23rd day of May? A Because I looked at the almanac last night. I can tell that much.
Q Did you look at the almanac to see what day this child was born? A Yes sir.
Q Did you have to light a lamp to look at the almanac to see what date it was? A No sir.
Q It was born in the day time? A Yes sir.
Before breakfast or before dinner or what? A Just kinder betwixt and between *(illegible)* 12 anw o'clock.
Q Are you sure it wasn't born after one o'clock? A Yes, sir, I am sure it wasn't born after.
Q Are you sure it wasn't born after one o'clock? A I looked at the clock, they had a clock on the mantle piece and I looked to see what time it was.
Q Have you any other reason for remembering that it was March 3rd, besides the fact that you were there and that you looked at the clock at the birth of said child? I just tried to see how many children Santa Claus would let me catch this year.
Q How many did he let you catch this year? A I have caught about 12 or 13.
Q Since last Santa Claus' Christmas? A Yes sir.
Q These 12 or 13 children you have caught were they citizens? A No sir, white people and negros.
Q This is the only citizen child you have caught? A Yes sir, the only one this year.
Q Well aunty I want you to tell me—can you remember the dates of the birth of the 12 or 13 Santa Claus' children you have caught? A Yes sir.
Q Noa[sic] you tell them all? A Pretty near all.

Q How can you remember all these dates.[sic] Well, because I mark them down at home in my almanac, I put a straight mark down opposite the date.
Q Have you got this child marked down? A Yes sir.
Q When did you mark it down.[sic] That same evening I went home after it was born. Do you remember what you put down about this child? I just marked a straight mark oposite[sic] the date it was born.
Q Was this the last child you caught? A Yes, sir, the only citizen one.

Applications for Enrollment of Creek Newborn
Act of 1905 Volume III

Lona Merrick, being duly sworn, states that the above and foregoing is a true and correct transcript of her stenographic notes as taken on said date in said cause.

Lona Merrick

Subscribed and sworn to before me this 23 day of May, 1905.

Edw C Griesel
Notary Public.

N.C. 165. I.D.

DEPARTMENT OF THE INTERIOR,
COMMISSIONER TO THE FIVE CIVILIZED TRIBES.

In the matter of the application for the enrollment of John Boyd Combs as a citizen by blood of the Creek Nation.

DECISION.

The record in this case shows that on March 15, 1905, the affidavit of Katie Combs relative to the birth of her minor child, John Boyd Combs, was filed with the Commission to the Five Civilized Tribes at Muskogee, Indian Territory, which said affidavit is considered as an application for the enrollment of said John Boyd Combs as a citizen by blood of the Creek Nation. Further proceedings were had May 23, 1905.

The evidence shows that said John Boyd Combs was born March 3, 1905, and that he was living at the date of the last proceedings herein.

The evidence further shows that said John Boyd Combs is the child of John W. Combs, a non citizen, and of Katie Combs, and an examination of the records of this office shows that the name of Katie Combs is contained in the partial list of citizens by blood of the Creek Nation approved by the Secretary of the Interior March 13, 1902, roll No. 1617.

It is, therefore, ordered and adjudged that said John Boyd Combs is entitled to be enrolled as a citizen by blood of the Creek Nation in accordance with the provisions of the act of Congress March 3, 1905 (Public No. 212), and the application for his enrollment as such is accordingly granted.

Tams Bixby Commissioner.

Muskogee, Indian Territory.
FEB 2- 1907

Applications for Enrollment of Creek Newborn
Act of 1905   Volume III

BIRTH AFFIDAVIT.

DEPARTMENT OF THE INTERIOR.
COMMISSION TO THE FIVE CIVILIZED TRIBES.

IN RE APPLICATION FOR ENROLLMENT, as a citizen of the Creek Nation, of Pearl Combs, born on the 3^d day of October, 1902

Name of Father:	John W. Combs	a citizen of the United States Nation.
Name of Mother:	Katie Combs	a citizen of the Creek Nation.

Postoffice   Checotah I.T.

AFFIDAVIT OF MOTHER.

UNITED STATES OF AMERICA, Indian Territory,
Western   DISTRICT.

I, Katie Combs, on oath state that I am 25 years of age and a citizen by Blood, of the Creek Nation; that I am the lawful wife of John W. Combs, who is a citizen, by *(blank)* of the United States Nation; that a Female child was born to me on 3^d day of October, 1902, that said child has been named Pearl Combs, and is now living.

Witnesses To Mark:
{ Minnie Combs
  Nettie Combs

her
Katie x Combs
mark

Subscribed and sworn to before me this 14th day of March, 1905.

My Commission Expires   J.B. Morrow
July 1st 1906   Notary Public.

AFFIDAVIT OF ATTENDING PHYSICIAN OR MID-WIFE.

UNITED STATES OF AMERICA, Indian Territory,
Western   DISTRICT.

I, D. M. Pate, a Physician, on oath state that I attended on Mrs. Katie Combs, wife of John W. Combs on the 3^d day of October, 1902; that there was born to her on said date a Female child; that said child is now living and is said to have been named Pearl Combs

D.M. Pate M.D.

Witnesses To Mark:
{

Applications for Enrollment of Creek Newborn
Act of 1905 Volume III

Subscribed and sworn to before me this 28 day of March, 1905.

My Commission Expires July 1, 1906.   J.B. Morrow
                                                                Notary Public.

BIRTH AFFIDAVIT.

DEPARTMENT OF THE INTERIOR.
COMMISSION TO THE FIVE CIVILIZED TRIBES.

IN RE APPLICATION FOR ENROLLMENT, as a citizen of the Creek Nation, of John Boyd Combs, born on the 3^d day of March, 1905

Name of Father: John W. Combs   a citizen of the United States Nation.
Name of Mother: Katie Combs   a citizen of the   Creek   Nation.

                         Postoffice   Checotah Ind. Ter.

AFFIDAVIT OF MOTHER.

UNITED STATES OF AMERICA, Indian Territory, ⎫
         Western   DISTRICT.   ⎭

I, Katie Combs, on oath state that I am 25 years of age and a citizen by Blood, of the Creek Nation; that I am the lawful wife of John W. Combs, who is a citizen, by *(blank)* of the United States Nation; that a male child was born to me on 3^d day of March, 1905, that said child has been named John Boyd Combs, and is now living.

                                             her
                                     Katie x Combs
Witnesses To Mark: mark
   { Minnie Combs
   { Nettie Combs

Subscribed and sworn to before me this 14th day of March, 1905.

My Commission Expires   J.B. Morrow
July 1st 1906   Notary Public.

Applications for Enrollment of Creek Newborn
Act of 1905   Volume III

AFFIDAVIT OF ATTENDING PHYSICIAN OR MID-WIFE.

UNITED STATES OF AMERICA, Indian Territory,
    Western   DISTRICT.

    I, E.M. Gardner, a midwife, on oath state that I attended on Mrs. Katie Combs, wife of John W. Combs on the 3^d day of March, 1905; that there was born to her on said date a male child; that said child is now living and is said to have been named John Boyd Combs

                                        E M Gardner

Witnesses To Mark:

    Subscribed and sworn to before me this 14th day of March, 1905.

                                        J.B. Morrow
                                              Notary Public.

                                              NC 163.

                    Muskogee, Indian Territory, May 19, 1905.

John W. Combs,
    Checotah, Indian Territory.

Dear Sir:

    In the matter of the application for the enrollment of your minor child, John Boyd Combs, as a citizen of the Creek Nation, you are advised that the Commission desires further evidence as to the birth of said child.

    You will be allowed thirty days from date within which to appear before the Commission at its office in Muskogee, Indian Territory, along with your wife, Katie Combs, and two other witnesses who know the date of the birth of said child, for the purpose of being examined under oath.

                                        Respectfully,

                                                Chairman.

NC-165

                    Muskogee, Indian Territory, October 13, 1905.

M. L. Mott,
    Attorney for the Creek Nation,
        Muskogee, Indian Territory.

Applications for Enrollment of Creek Newborn
Act of 1905 Volume III

Sir:

There is herewith enclosed one copy of the decision of the Commissioner to the Five Civilized Tribes in the matter of the application for the enrollment of your minor child, you are advised that the Commission requires further evidence as to the birth of said child. of John Boyd Combs as a citizen by blood of the Creek Nation.

You are hereby notified that the Creek Nation will be allowed fifteen days from date within which to protest against said decision, and if, at the expiration of that time, no protest has been made, said John Boyd Combs will be regularly listed for enrollment as a citizen by blood of the Creek Nation.

Respectfully,

Commissioner.

JYM-13-5

File with Ba-473-B
--Lona Ethel Hughes;
this child is also known as
L.E.H.

DEPARTMENT OF THE INTERIOR,
COMMISSION TO THE FIVE CIVILIZED TRIBES.

Muskogee, Indian Territory, March 14, 1905.

In the matter of the application for the enrollment of Eveley Hughes as a citizen by blood of the Creek Nation.

Robert Hughes, being duly sworn, testified as follows:

EXAMINATION BY THE COMMISSION:
Q What is your name? A Robert Hughes.
Q What is your age? A I don't know; I am 28.
Q What is your postoffice address? A Checotah.

The witness is identified as Robert Hughes on Creek Indian card, field No. 482, and his name is contained in partial list of Creek citizens by blood, approved by the Secretary of the Interior March 13, 1902, Roll No. 1581.
Q Have you a child named Eveley Hughes? A Yes sir.
Q What is the name of the mother? A Lizzie.
Q When was Eveley born? A She was born in January, 1904--1903; she is just a little__two years old; going on two years.
Q She was born in January, 1903--she was two years old in January--is that right?
A (Yes) sir.
Q What is the name of the mother? A Lizzie Hughes.
Q You are married to Lizzie? A Yes sir.

Applications for Enrollment of Creek Newborn
Act of 1905   Volume III

Q Was this child born after your marriage? A Yes sir. There was two children oldest; one died, and then she left me and this child was born; we separated the first of August, in January the child was born. The date of its age I don't know exactly.
Q Did she leave you or you left her? A She left me.
Q Did you have any trouble with her previous to this separation? A No sir.
Q You have no doubt that this is your child? A No sir, I have no doubt.
Q Did you ever accuse her of going with other men? A No sir.
Q The child was born five months after you separated? A No (yes) sir.
Q Who is the child living with? A Her mother.
Q What is her postoffice address? A Checotah.

INDIAN TERRITORY, Western District.
    I, J. Y. Miller, a stenographer to the Commission to the Five Civilized Tribes, do hereby certify that the above and foregoing is a true and complete translation of my notes as same appear in my stenographic report of this case.

                        JY Miller

Sworn to and subscribed before me
   this the 24 day of April, 1905.   Zera E. Parrish
My Comm. expires April 11, 1909.   Notary Public.

                              Cr LF-164

DEPARTMENT OF THE INTERIOR, COMMISSION TO THE FIVE CIVILIZED TRIBES.

Muskogee, Indian Territory, May 24, 1905.

    In the matter of the application for the enrollment of Lena Ethel Hughes as a citizen by blood of the Creek Nation.

    Appearance: _____BURLINGAME, Attorney for the Applicant.

    Robert Hughes, being duly sworn, testified as follows:

EXAMINATION BY THE COMMISSION:
Q What is your name? A Robert Hughes.
Q What is your age? A I don't know; 27.
Q What is your postoffice? A Checotah.
Q Are you the same person that testified here on the 14th of March about a child of yours? A Yes sir.
Q Have you a child named Elsie Hughes? A They told me of Lena Ethel at first.
Q Have you two children, have you--one named Ethel? A Yes sir.
Q Elsie is dead? A Yes sir.
Q When did Elsie die? A About two years.
Q She had been dead two years? A Yes sir.

Applications for Enrollment of Creek Newborn
Act of 1905   Volume III

Q And your other child is named Lena Ethel? A Yes sir.
Q Have you a child named Evalie? A Well, that is the one chiled[sic] Lena Ethel.
Q Did you have a child named Evalie? A No sir.
Q In the testimony given March 14, 1905, the name was spelled Evalie Hughes; what child did you mean to testify about? A They told me (we are not living together, her name is Lena Ethel and when made application they put down the name different.
Q If you testified that the child was named Evalie, you were referring to Minnie Ethel, were you? A Yes sir.
Q When was Lena Ethel born? A Born in January, about the 10th of January, 1904.
Q Are you sure it was 1904? A Yes sir.
Q In the testimony that you gave in March you said it was in 1903; were you mistaken at that time? A Yes sir. I might have been mistaken.
Q You say you are not living with the child and its mother? A No sir
Q How old is this child now A It was a year old about the 10th of January.
Q It was born in January, 1904, is that right? A Yes sir.
Q And the correct name of that child is Lena Ethel Hughes? A Yes sir.
Q You have no child named Evalie Hughes? A No sir.
Q You are not living with your wife, are you? A No sir.
Q Were you living with her at the time the child was born? A No sir.
Q How long before it was born did you separate? A About six months.
Q You were married to her? A Yes sir.
Q You are certain that this child is your child? A I could not swear positively that it is mine[sic] child.
Q Have you reason to believe that she was going with any other men? A No sir.
Q You thought, like any other married man, that the child was yours? A Yes sir.

INDIAN TERRITORY, Western District.
    I, J. Y. Miller, a stenographer to the Commission to the Five Civilized Tribes, do hereby certify that the above and foregoing is a true and complete translation of my notes as same appear in my stenographic report of this case.

                                         JY Miller
Sworn to and subscribed before me
  this the 26 day of May, 1905.   Edw C Griesel
                                                  Notary Public.

DEPARTMENT OF THE INTERIOR.
COMMISSION TO THE FIVE CIVILIZED TRIBES.

    In the matter of the death of Elsie Hughes   a citizen of the Creek Nation, who formerly resided at or near Checotah   , Ind. Ter., and died on the 7th day of May , 1902.

Applications for Enrollment of Creek Newborn
Act of 1905 Volume III

AFFIDAVIT OF RELATIVE.

UNITED STATES OF AMERICA, Indian Territory, }
    Western   DISTRICT.

    I, Lizzie Hughes , on oath state that I am 26 years of age and a citizen by *(blank)* , of the United States Nation; that my postoffice address is Checotah , Ind. Ter.; that I am the mother of Elsie Hughes who was a citizen, by Blood , of the Creek Nation and that said Elsie Hughes died on the 7th day of May , 1902.

                              Lizzie Hughes

Witnesses To Mark:
{

    Subscribed and sworn to before me this 14th day of March, 1905.

My Commission Expires   J.B. Morrow
July 1st 1906   Notary Public.

AFFIDAVIT OF ACQUAINTANCE.

UNITED STATES OF AMERICA, Indian Territory, }
    Western   DISTRICT.

    I, J. J. Jackson , on oath state that I am 17 years of age, and a citizen by *(blank)* of the United States Nation; that my postoffice address is Checotah , Ind. Ter.; that I was personally acquainted with Elsie Hughes who was a citizen, by Blood, of the Creek Nation; and that said Elsie Hughes died on the 7th day of May , 1902

                              N. J. Jackson

Witnesses To Mark:
{

    Subscribed and sworn to before me this 14th day of March, 1905.

                              J.B. Morrow
                              Notary Public.

BIRTH AFFIDAVIT.

DEPARTMENT OF THE INTERIOR,
COMMISSION TO THE FIVE CIVILIZED TRIBES.

    IN RE Application for Enrollment, as a citizen of the Creek Nation, of Elsie Hughes, born on the 26 day of April , 1902

Applications for Enrollment of Creek Newborn
Act of 1905 Volume III

Name of Father: Robert Hughes   a citizen of the   Creek   Nation.
Name of Mother: Lizzie Hughes   a citizen of the United States Nation.

Postoffice   Checotah, Ind. Ter.

AFFIDAVIT OF MOTHER.

UNITED STATES OF AMERICA, Indian Territory,
Western   DISTRICT.

I, Lizzie Hughes , on oath state that I am 20 years of age and a citizen by *(blank)* , of the United States Nation; that I am the lawful wife of Robert Hughes , who is a citizen, by Blood of the Creek   Nation; that a Female   child was born to me on 26 day of April , 1902 , that said child has been named   Elsie Hughes , and is now ~~living~~.dead

Lizzie Hughes

Witnesses To Mark:
{

Subscribed and sworn to before me this 28 *day of* March, *1905*.

My Commission Expires   J.B. Morrow
July 1ˢᵗ 1906   Notary Public.

AFFIDAVIT OF ATTENDING PHYSICIAN OR MID-WIFE.

UNITED STATES OF AMERICA, Indian Territory,
Western   DISTRICT.

I, Flora Crabtree , a Midwife , on oath state that I attended on Mrs. Lizzie Hughes , wife of Robert Hughes on the 26ᵗʰ day of April , 1902 ; that there was born to her on said date a Female child; that said child is now ~~living~~ dead and is said to have been named Elsie Hughes.

Flora Crabtree

Witnesses To Mark:
{

Subscribed and sworn to before me this 14ᵗʰ *day of* March, *1905*.

J.B. Morrow
Notary Public.

Applications for Enrollment of Creek Newborn
Act of 1905   Volume III

NC 164   JLD
DEPARTMENT OF THE INTERIOR,
COMMISSIONER TO THE FIVE CIVILIZED TRIBES.
. . . .

In the matter of the application for the enrollment of Elsie Hughes, deceased, as a citizen by blood of the Creek Nation.
. . . .

STATEMENT AND ORDER.

The record in this case shows that on March 15, 1905, application was made, in affidavit form, supported by sworn testimony taken March 14, 1905, and by further testimony taken May 24, 1905, for the enrollment of Elsie Hughes, deceased, as a citizen by blood of the Creek Nation, under the provisions of the act of Congress approved March 3, 1905.

It appears from the affidavit filed in this matter that Elsie Hughes, deceased, was born April 26, 1902, and died May 7, 1902.

The act of Congress approved March 3, 1905, (33 Stats., 1048), provides:

"That the Commission to the Five Civilized Tribes is authorized for sixty days after the date of the approval of this act to receive and consider applications for enrollments of children <u>born subsequent to May twenty-fifth, nineteen hundred and one, and prior to March fourth, nineteen hundred and five, and living on said latter date, to ci</u>tizens of the Creek tribe of Indians whose enrollment has been approved by the Secretary of the Interior prior to the approval of this act; and to enroll and make allotments to such children."

It is, therefore, ordered that the application for the enrollment of said Elsie Hughes, deceased, as a citizen by blood of the Creek Nation, be, and the same is, hereby dismissed.

Tams Bixby   Commissioner.

Muskogee, Indian Territory.
JAN 15 1907

BIRTH AFFIDAVIT.
DEPARTMENT OF THE INTERIOR,
COMMISSION TO THE FIVE CIVILIZED TRIBES.

IN RE Application for Enrollment, as a citizen of the Creek Nation, of Lena Ethel Hughes, born on the 11th day of January , 1904

Name of Father: Robert Hughes   a citizen of the   Creek   Nation.
Name of Mother: Lizzie Hughes   a citizen of the United States Nation.

Postoffice   Checotah, I. T.

Applications for Enrollment of Creek Newborn
Act of 1905   Volume III

AFFIDAVIT OF MOTHER.

UNITED STATES OF AMERICA, Indian Territory,
    Western   DISTRICT.

I, Lizzie Hughes , on oath state that I am 20 years of age and a citizen by *(blank)* , of the United States Nation; that I am the lawful wife of Robert Hughes , who is a citizen, by Blood of the Creek Nation; that a Female child was born to me on 11th day of January , 1904 , that said child has been named Lena Ethel Hughes, and is now living.

                                              Lizzie Hughes

Witnesses To Mark:
{ A A Smith

Subscribed and sworn to before me this 11th *day of* March, *1905.*

My Commission Expires July 1, 1906.   JB Morrow
                                                          Notary Public.

AFFIDAVIT OF ATTENDING PHYSICIAN OR MID-WIFE.

UNITED STATES OF AMERICA, Indian Territory,
    Western   DISTRICT.

I, Flora Crabtree , a midwife , on oath state that I attended on Mrs. Lizzie Hughes , wife of Robert Hughes on the 11th day of January , 1904 ; that there was born to her on said date a Female child; that said child is now living and is said to have been named Lena Ethel Hughes.

                                              Flora Crabtree

Witnesses To Mark:
{ A A Smith

Subscribed and sworn to before me this 11th *day of* March, *1905.*

My Commission Expires July 1, 1906.   JB Morrow
                                                          Notary Public.

                                                           NC 164.

                              Muskogee, Indian Territory, May 19, 1905.

Robert Hughes,
    Checotah, Indian Territory.

Applications for Enrollment of Creek Newborn
Act of 1905   Volume III

Dear Sir:

In the matter of the application for the enrollment of your minor child, Lena Ethel Hughes, as a citizen of the Creek Nation, you are advised that the Commission requires further evidence as to the birth of said child.

You will be allowed thirty days from date within which to appear before the Commission at its office in Muskogee, Indian Territory, for the purpose of being examined under oath.

Respectfully,

Chairman.

NC 163.

Muskogee, Indian Territory, January 17, 1907.

Lizzie Hughes,
    c/o Robert Hughes,
        Checotah, Indian Territory.

Dear Madam:

There is herewith enclosed one copy of the Statement and Order of the Commissioner to the Five Civilized Tribes, dated January 15, 1907, dismissing the application made by you for the enrollment of your minor child Elsie Hughes, deceased, as a citizen by blood of the Creek Nation.

Respectfully,

Commissioner.

LM-73.

BIRTH AFFIDAVIT.

DEPARTMENT OF THE INTERIOR.
COMMISSION TO THE FIVE CIVILIZED TRIBES.

IN RE APPLICATION FOR ENROLLMENT, as a citizen of the CREEK Nation, of Edith Louise McIntosh, born on the 29 day of Nov , 1904

Name of Father:	Freeland B. McIntosh	a citizen of the Creek	Nation.
Name of Mother:	Kate "	a citizen of the U.S.	Nation.

Postoffice   Checotah

Applications for Enrollment of Creek Newborn
Act of 1905   Volume III

(child present)

AFFIDAVIT OF MOTHER.

UNITED STATES OF AMERICA, Indian Territory,
WESTERN   DISTRICT.

   I, Kate McIntosh, on oath state that I am 26 years of age and a citizen by ----- , of the U.S. Nation; that I am the lawful wife of Freeland B. McIntosh, who is a citizen, by blood of the Creek Nation; that a female child was born to me on 29 day of Nov, 1904, that said child has been named Edith Louise McIntosh, and is now living.

Kate McIntosh

Witnesses To Mark:
{

   Subscribed and sworn to before me this 13 day of March, 1905.

Edw C Griesel
Notary Public.

father

AFFIDAVIT OF ~~ATTENDING PHYSICIAN OR MID-WIFE~~.

UNITED STATES OF AMERICA, Indian Territory,
Western   DISTRICT.

husband
   I, Freeland B. McIntosh, a m , ~~on oath state that I attended on Mrs.   , wife~~ of Kate McIntosh on the 29 day of Nov, 1904; that there was born to her on said date a female child; that said child is now living and is said to have been named Edith Louise McIntosh.

Freeland B. McIntosh

Witnesses To Mark:
{

   Subscribed and sworn to before me this 13 day of March, 1905.

Edw C Griesel
Notary Public.

BA-63.

DEPARTMENT OF THE INTERIOR,
COMMISSION TO THE FIVE CIVILIZED TRIBES.

Muskogee, Indian Territory, March 13, 1905.

Applications for Enrollment of Creek Newborn
Act of 1905   Volume III

In the matter of the application for the enrollment of Jesse Martain as a Creek.

T. M. Martain, being duly sworn, testified as follows:

EXAMINATION BY THE COMMISSION:
Q What is your name? A T. M. Martain.
Q Are you a citizen of the Creek Nation? A No sir.
Q What is your age? A 37.
Q What is your postoffice? A Okfuskee.
Q Have you a child named Jesse Martin? A Yes sir.
Q When was Jesse born? A I can't tell you. You will have to go by that; at the time it says.
Q Don't you know what time? A No sir. It is three or four years old.
Q Was he born since the 25th day of May, 1901? A Yes sir.
Q There is an affidavit filed, by your wife I suppose--Anna Martin, is she your wife? A Yes sir.
Q It says born the 5th of October, 1901? A If it says on that it is correct.
Q Is that child living? A Yes sir.
Q What is the name of its mother? A Anna Martin.
Q Is she enrolled? A Yes sir.

Anna Martin, the mother of said child, is identified on Creek Indian card, field No. 50, and her name is contained in partial last[sic] of Creek citizens by blood approved by the Secretary of the Interior March 13, 1902, Roll No. 180.

INDIAN TERRITORY,)
Western District.   )   I, J. Y. Miller, a stenographer to the Commission
)   to the Five Civilized Tribes, do hereby certify
)   that the above and foregoing is a true and complete translation of my notes as same appear in my stenographic report of this case.

JY Miller

Sworn to and subscribed before me
  this the 19 day of April, 1905.
My Com. expires April 11, 1909.   Zera E Parrish
                                                               Notary Public.

NC 166.

Muskogee, Indian Territory, May 19, 1905.

Thomas Martin,
    Okfusky, Indian Territory.

Dear Sir:

Applications for Enrollment of Creek Newborn
Act of 1905   Volume III

In the matter of the application for the enrollment of your minor child, Leona Martin, as a citizen of the Creek Nation, you are advised that the Commission requires the affidavits of the mother and midwife or physician in attendance at the birth of said child.

There is herewith enclosed a blank form of birth affidavit, and in executing same care should be exercised to see that all blanks are properly filled, all names written in full and in the event that the person signing the affidavit is unable to write, signature by mark must be attested by two witnesses. Each affidavit must be executed before a Notary Public and the notarial seal and signature of the officer must be attached to each separate affidavit.

Respectfully,

BC.   Chairman.

N. C. 166   COPY

Okfuskee Ind. Ty.

May 23- 1905

The Commission to the Five Civilized Tribes
   Muskogee, Ind. Ty.

Gentlemen:

Your letter of the 19th enclosing it application blank for enrollment of Leona Martin is at hand.

Find enclosed the blank filled out and sworn to. The only difference in this one and the one I sent you on the 30th is the difference in spelling the name.

The Notary Public understood our name to be "Martain" instead of "Martin". If any thing else is necessary please let me know

Yours Truly
(Signed) Anna Martin

BIRTH AFFIDAVIT.
DEPARTMENT OF THE INTERIOR.
COMMISSION TO THE FIVE CIVILIZED TRIBES.

IN RE APPLICATION FOR ENROLLMENT, as a citizen of the CREEK Nation, of Leona Martin , born on the 23 day of Jan , 1903

| Name of Father: | Thomas Martin | a citizen of the | U. S. | Nation. |
| Name of Mother: | Anna   " | a citizen of the | Creek | Nation. |

Applications for Enrollment of Creek Newborn
Act of 1905   Volume III

Postoffice   Okfusky I.T.

AFFIDAVIT OF MOTHER.

UNITED STATES OF AMERICA, Indian Territory, ⎫
    WESTERN   DISTRICT. ⎭

    I, Thomas Martin , on oath state that I am 37 years of age and a citizen by ----- , of the U.S. Nation; that I am the lawful ~~wife~~ hus of Anna Martin , who is a citizen, by blood   of the Creek   Nation; that a female   child was born to me on 23 day of Jan. , 1903 , that said child has been named Leona Martin , and is now living.

                          His
                      Thomas x Martin
Witnesses To Mark: Mark
  ⎧ JY Miller
  ⎩ EC Griesel

    Subscribed and sworn to before me this 13 day of March, 1905.

                      Edw C Griesel
                          Notary Public.

BIRTH AFFIDAVIT.
DEPARTMENT OF THE INTERIOR.
COMMISSION TO THE FIVE CIVILIZED TRIBES.

    IN RE APPLICATION FOR ENROLLMENT, as a citizen of the Creek Nation, of Leona Martian, born on the 23rd day of January , 1903

| Name of Father: | Tom Martian | a citizen of the | Creek | Nation. |
| Name of Mother: | Anna Martian | a citizen of the | Creek | Nation. |

                Postoffice   Okfuskee, Ind. Ty.

AFFIDAVIT OF MOTHER.

UNITED STATES OF AMERICA, Indian Territory, ⎫
    Western   DISTRICT. ⎭

    I, Anna Martian , on oath state that I am twenty five years of age and a citizen by blood   , of the   Creek   Nation; that I am the lawful wife of Tom Martian , who is a citizen, by marriage of the Creek   Nation; that a female   child was born to me on the

Applications for Enrollment of Creek Newborn
Act of 1905   Volume III

23rd day of January, 1903, that said child has been named Leona Martian, and was living March 4, 1905.

Anna Martian

Witnesses To Mark:
{

Subscribed and sworn to before me this the 30th day of March, 1905.

My commission expires Nov. 18, 1908.   Cassius L. Pratt
                                                    Notary Public.

AFFIDAVIT OF ATTENDING PHYSICIAN OR MID-WIFE.

UNITED STATES OF AMERICA, Indian Territory, ⎤
    Western   DISTRICT.   ⎦

I, Mary D. Shannon, a mid-wife, on oath state that I attended on Mrs. Anna Martian, wife of Tom Martian on the 23rd day of January, 1903; that there was born to her on said date a female child; that said child was living March 4, 1905; and is said to have been named Leona Martian

Mary D. Shannon

Witnesses To Mark:
{

Subscribed and sworn to before me this the 30th day of March, 1905.

My commission expires Nov. 18, 1908.   Cassius L. Pratt
                                                    Notary Public.

BIRTH AFFIDAVIT.

DEPARTMENT OF THE INTERIOR.
COMMISSION TO THE FIVE CIVILIZED TRIBES.

IN RE APPLICATION FOR ENROLLMENT, as a citizen of the Creek or Muskogee Nation, of Leona Martian, born on the 23rd day of January, 1903

Name of Father: Tom Martin   a citizen of the   Creek   Nation.
Name of Mother: Anna Martin   a citizen of the   Creek   Nation.

Postoffice   Okfuskee, Ind. Ty.

Applications for Enrollment of Creek Newborn
Act of 1905 Volume III

AFFIDAVIT OF MOTHER.

UNITED STATES OF AMERICA, Indian Territory,
Western DISTRICT.

I, Anna Martin, on oath state that I am twenty five years of age and a citizen by blood, of the Creek or Muskogee Nation; that I am the lawful wife of Thomas Martin, who is a citizen, by marriage of the Creek Nation; that a female child was born to me on the 23rd day of January, 1903, that said child has been named Leona Martin, and was living March 4, 1905.

Anna Martin

Witnesses To Mark:
{

Subscribed and sworn to before me this the 23rd day of May, 1905.

My commission expires Nov. 18, 1908.   Cassius L. Pratt
Notary Public.

AFFIDAVIT OF ATTENDING PHYSICIAN OR MID-WIFE.

UNITED STATES OF AMERICA, Indian Territory,
Western DISTRICT.

I, Mary D. Shannon, a mid-wife, on oath state that I attended on Mrs. Anna Martin, wife of Thomas Martin on the 23rd day of January, 1903; that there was born to her on said date a female child; that said child was living March 4, 1905; and is said to have been named Leona Martin

Mary D. Shannon

Witnesses To Mark:
{

Subscribed and sworn to before me this the 23rd day of May, 1905.

My commission expires Nov. 18, 1908.   Cassius L. Pratt
Notary Public.

BIRTH AFFIDAVIT.

DEPARTMENT OF THE INTERIOR,
COMMISSION TO THE FIVE CIVILIZED TRIBES.

IN RE Application for Enrollment, as a citizen of the Creek Nation, of Jesse Martin, born on the 5 day of October, 1901

Name of Father:	Thomas Martin	a non citizen of the Creek Nation.
Name of Mother:	Anna Martin	a citizen of the Creek Nation.

Applications for Enrollment of Creek Newborn
Act of 1905   Volume III

Postoffice   Morse, I.T.

AFFIDAVIT OF MOTHER.

UNITED STATES OF AMERICA, Indian Territory,
    Northern   DISTRICT.

I, Anna Martin , on oath state that I am 21 years of age and a citizen by blood , of the Creek   Nation; that I am the lawful wife of Thomas Martin   , who is a non citizen, by *(blank)* of the Creek   Nation; that a male   child was born to me on 5 day of October , 1901 , that said child has been named Jesse Martin   , and is now living.

Anna Martin

Witnesses To Mark:
{

Subscribed and sworn to before me this 6" *day of* January, *1902*

William T Martin
Notary Public.

AFFIDAVIT OF ATTENDING PHYSICIAN OR MID-WIFE.

UNITED STATES OF AMERICA, Indian Territory,
    Northern   DISTRICT.

I, Mrs. Kate Colter , a mid wife , on oath state that I attended on Mrs. Anna Martin , wife of Thomas Martin on the 5 day of October , 1901 ; that there was born to her on said date a Male child; that said child is now living and is said to have been named Jesse Martin

Mrs. Kate Colter

Witnesses To Mark:
{

Subscribed and sworn to before me this 20 *day of* Jan., *1902*

Geo D. Harrison
Notary Public.

Applications for Enrollment of Creek Newborn
Act of 1905 Volume III

BIRTH AFFIDAVIT.

DEPARTMENT OF THE INTERIOR.
COMMISSION TO THE FIVE CIVILIZED TRIBES.

IN RE APPLICATION FOR ENROLLMENT, as a citizen of the CREEK Nation, of Robert Meagher Atkins, born on the 21 day of Nov., 1904

| Name of Father: | James P. Atkins | a citizen of the | U.S. | Nation. |
| Name of Mother: | Isabelle Atkins | a citizen of the | Creek | Nation. |

Postoffice   Wetumka

(Child present)

AFFIDAVIT OF MOTHER.

UNITED STATES OF AMERICA, Indian Territory,
WESTERN   DISTRICT.

I, Isabelle Atkins, on oath state that I am 24 years of age and a citizen by blood, of the Creek Nation; that I am the lawful wife of James P. Atkins, who is a citizen, by ----- of the U.S. Nation; that a male child was born to me on 21 day of Nov., 1904, that said child has been named Robert Meagher Atkins, and was living March 4, 1905.

Isabelle M. Atkins

Witnesses To Mark:

Subscribed and sworn to before me this 13 day of March, 1905.

Edw C Griesel
Notary Public.

BIRTH AFFIDAVIT.

DEPARTMENT OF THE INTERIOR.
COMMISSION TO THE FIVE CIVILIZED TRIBES.

IN RE APPLICATION FOR ENROLLMENT, as a citizen of the Creek Nation, of Robert Meagher Atkins, born on the 21st day of November, 1904

| Name of Father: | James P. Atkins | a citizen of the | U.S. | Nation. |
| Name of Mother: | Isabelle   " | a citizen of the | Creek | Nation. |

Postoffice   Wetumka I.T.

Applications for Enrollment of Creek Newborn
Act of 1905 Volume III

AFFIDAVIT OF ~~MOTHER~~. father

UNITED STATES OF AMERICA, Indian Territory, }
    Western   DISTRICT.

    I, James P. Atkins, on oath state that I am 31 years of age and a citizen ~~by~~ *(blank)*, of the United States ~~Nation~~; that I am the lawful ~~wife~~ husband of Isabelle Atkins, who is a citizen, by blood of the Creek Nation; that a male child was born to me on 21st day of November, 1904, that said child has been named Robert Meagher Atkins, and is now living.

                                  James P. Atkins

Witnesses To Mark:
{

    Subscribed and sworn to before me this 16th day of March, 1905.

    My Com. Exp July 1-1906   A.V. Skeleere
                                               Notary Public.

AFFIDAVIT OF ATTENDING PHYSICIAN OR MID-WIFE.

UNITED STATES OF AMERICA, Indian Territory, }
    Western   DISTRICT.

    I, V. Berry, a physician, on oath state that I attended on Mrs. Isabelle Atkins, wife of James P. Atkins on the 21st day of November, 1904; that there was born to her on said date a male child; that said child is now living and is said to have been named Robert Meagher Atkins

                                  Virgil Berry

Witnesses To Mark:
{

    Subscribed and sworn to before me this 16th day of March, 1905.

    My Com. Exp July 1-1906   A.V. Skeleere
                                               Notary Public.

Applications for Enrollment of Creek Newborn
Act of 1905   Volume III

BA- 51.

DEPARTMENT OF THE INTERIOR,
COMMISSION TO THE FIVE CIVILIZED TRIBES.
MUSKOGEE, INDIAN TERRITORY, March 13, 1905.

-ooOoo-

In the matter of the application for the enrollment of Ethel Kerr, as a citizen by blood of the Creek Nation.

ARSYNOS KERR, being duly sworn, testified as follows:

EXAMINATION BY COMMISSION:
Q What is your name? A Arsynos Kerr. I was enrolled as Arsynos McIntosh.
Q What is your age? A 23.
Q What is your postoffice address? A Wier.
Q Have you a child named Ethel Kerr? A Yes, sir.
Q What is its father's name? A Henry Kerr.
Q Is he a citizen of the Creek Nation? A No, sir.
Q Are you a citizen of the Creek Nation? A Yes, sir.

Witness is identified as Arsynos McIntosh on Creek Indian Card, Field Number 787, and her[sic] name is contained in the partial list of citizens by blood of the Creek Nation, approved by the Secretary of the Interior March 13, 1902, Roll No. 2548.

Q Is Ethel Kerr living? A Yes, sir.
Q When was she born? A August 23, 1901.
Q How old is she now? A Three--four---three, that is it.
Q Will it be three years or four this coming August? A Four--it is three now.
Q Who was present at Ethel's birth? A My grandmother.
Q What is her name? A Susan McIntosh.
Q Have you any other children A Yes, sir.
Q Are they enrolled? A Yes, sir. We put our little child, Commodore on the roll this evening.

The child, Ethel, is present and appears to be about the age indicated.

SUSAN B. McINTOSH, being duly sworn, testified as follows:

EXAMINATION BY COMMISSION:
Q What is your name? A Susan B. McIntosh.
Q What is your age? A 70.
Q What is your postoffice address? A Tullahassee.
Q Do you know Ethel Kerr? A Yes, sir.
Q Are you related to her? A She is my granddaughter.
Q Were you present when she was born? A Yes, sir.

Applications for Enrollment of Creek Newborn
Act of 1905 Volume III

Q Do you remember when she was born? A Yes, but I do not know the year---it is on the papers there somewhere.
Q But I want to see if you know it---do you know the month? A I am so forgetful--I do not know.
Q Was it in the Spring or Summer that she was born? A (No answer.
Q Do you know the time of the year that the darkies have their big picnic? A Yes, sir.
Q Was Ethel born near the time f one of those picnics? A I am so forgetful--I do not remember anything much now.
Q You made out an affidavit one time in which you stated that Ethel was born August 23, 1901, is that correct? A Yes, sir, and at that time I remembered something.

Zera Ellen Parrish, being sworn on her oath states that as a stenographer to the Commission to the Five Civilized Tribes she reported the above case and that this is a full, true and correct transcript of her stenographic notes in same.

Zera Ellen Parrish

Subscribed and sworn to before me this 17 day of March, 1905.

Edw C Griesel
Notary Public.

BIRTH AFFIDAVIT.

DEPARTMENT OF THE INTERIOR.
COMMISSION TO THE FIVE CIVILIZED TRIBES.

IN RE APPLICATION FOR ENROLLMENT, as a citizen of the CREEK Nation, of Commodore Kerr Jr. , born on the 30 day of ~~Jan~~. Aug. , 1904

Name of Father:	Henry Kerr	a citizen of the	U. S.	Nation.
Name of Mother:	Arsyno Kerr	a citizen of the	Creek	Nation.

Postoffice   Weer

(child present) HGH

AFFIDAVIT OF MOTHER.

UNITED STATES OF AMERICA, Indian Territory,⎫
 WESTERN   DISTRICT.   ⎬
                                        ⎭

I, Arsyno Kerr , on oath state that I am 23 years of age and a citizen by blood , of the Creek Nation; that I am the lawful wife of Henry Kerr , who is a citizen, by ----- of the U. S. Nation; that a male child was born to me on 30 day of Aug. , 1904 , that said child has been named Commodore Kerr Jr. , and was living March 4, 1905.

Arcenoe[sic] M. Kerr

Applications for Enrollment of Creek Newborn
Act of 1905   Volume III

Witnesses To Mark:

Subscribed and sworn to before me this 13 day of March , 1905.

Edw C Griesel
Notary Public.

AFFIDAVIT OF ATTENDING PHYSICIAN OR MID-WIFE.

UNITED STATES OF AMERICA, Indian Territory,
Western   DISTRICT.

I, Susan D McIntosh , a midwife , on oath state that I attended on Mrs. Arsyno Kerr , wife of Henry Kerr on the 30 day of Aug , 1904 ; that there was born to her on said date a male child; that said child was living March 4, 1905, and is said to have been named Commodore Kerr

Her
Susan D. x McIntosh
mark

Witnesses To Mark:
 JY Miller
 EC Griesel

Subscribed and sworn to before me this 13 day of March, 1905.

Edw C Griesel
Notary Public.

BIRTH AFFIDAVIT.

DEPARTMENT OF THE INTERIOR,
COMMISSION TO THE FIVE CIVILIZED TRIBES.

IN RE Application for Enrollment, as a citizen of the Creek Nation, of Ethel Kerr, born on the 23rd day of August , 1901

Name of Father:	Henry Kerr	a citizen of the United States	Nation.
Name of Mother:	Arsynos Kerr	a citizen of the Creek	Nation.

Postoffice   Wier, Ind. Ter.

Applications for Enrollment of Creek Newborn
Act of 1905   Volume III

AFFIDAVIT OF MOTHER.

UNITED STATES OF AMERICA, Indian Territory,
    Northern   DISTRICT.

    I, Arsynos Kerr , on oath state that I am 19 years of age and a citizen by blood , of the Creek Nation; that I am the lawful wife of Henry Kerr , who is a citizen, ~~by~~ of U.S. ~~of the~~ (blank) ~~Nation~~; that a female child was born to me on 23rd day of August , 1901 , that said child has been named Ethel Kerr , and is now living.

                                  Arcenoe Kerr

Witnesses To Mark:
{

Subscribed and sworn to before me this 26th *day of* September, *1901*.

                                  John G. Lieber
                                  Notary Public.

AFFIDAVIT OF ATTENDING PHYSICIAN OR MID-WIFE.

UNITED STATES OF AMERICA, Indian Territory,
    Northern   DISTRICT.

    I, Susan D. McIntosh , a midwife , on oath state that I attended on Mrs. Arsynos Kerr , wife of Henry Kerr on the 23rd day of August , 1901 ; that there was born to her on said date a female child; that said child is now living and is said to have been named Ethel Kerr

                                    Her
                            Susan x D McIntosh
                                  mark

Witnesses To Mark:
{ *(Name Illegible)*
  R. B. Eisenberg

Subscribed and sworn to before me this 26th *day of* September, *1901*

                                  John G. Lieber
                                  Notary Public.

Applications for Enrollment of Creek Newborn
Act of 1905 Volume III

(Correcting af. of 3-13-05 in which mothers name appears in body of af. as Arsyno)

BIRTH AFFIDAVIT.

DEPARTMENT OF THE INTERIOR.
COMMISSION TO THE FIVE CIVILIZED TRIBES.

IN RE APPLICATION FOR ENROLLMENT, as a citizen of the CREEK Nation, of Commodore Kerr Jr. , born on the 30 day of Aug. , 1904

Name of Father:	Henry Kerr	a citizen of the	U. S.	Nation.
Name of Mother:	Arcenoe M. Kerr	a citizen of the	Creek	Nation.

Postoffice   Weer I.T.

AFFIDAVIT OF MOTHER.

UNITED STATES OF AMERICA, Indian Territory, }
    WESTERN   DISTRICT.

I, Arcenoe M. Kerr , on oath state that I am 23 years of age and a citizen by blood , of the Creek Nation; that I am the lawful wife of Henry Kerr , who is a citizen, by ----- of the U. S. Nation; that a male child was born to me on 30 day of August, 1904 , that said child has been named Commodore Kerr Jr. , and was living March 4, 1905.

                    Arcenoe M. Kerr

Witnesses To Mark:
{

Subscribed and sworn to before me this 10 day of June , 1905.

                    Henry G. Hains
                    Notary Public.

NEW BORN   COPY.

BIRTH AFFIDAVIT.

DEPARTMENT OF THE INTERIOR.
COMMISSION TO THE FIVE CIVILIZED TRIBES.

IN RE APPLICATION FOR ENROLLMENT, as a citizen of the Creek Nation, of Ethel Kerr , born on the 23 day of August , 1901

Name of Father:	Henry Kerr	a citizen of the	U. S.	Nation.
Name of Mother:	Arcenoe Kerr	a citizen of the	Creek	Nation.

Applications for Enrollment of Creek Newborn
Act of 1905   Volume III

Postoffice   Wier, I.T.

AFFIDAVIT OF MOTHER.

UNITED STATES OF AMERICA, Indian Territory,
Western   DISTRICT.

I, Arcenoe Kerr, on oath state that I am 23 years of age and a citizen by blood, of the Creek Nation; that I am the lawful wife of Henry Kerr, who is a citizen, by *(blank)* of the United States ~~Nation~~; that a female child was born to me on 23 day of August, 1901, that said child has been named Ethel Kerr, and was living March 4, 1905.

Arcenoe Kerr

Witnesses To Mark:
{

Subscribed and sworn to before me this 21st day of October, 1905.

Orlando U. Holdeman
My Commission Expires July 20th 1909   Notary Public.

NC-168

Muskogee, Indian Territory, May 29, 1905.

Arcenoe M. Kerr,
    Weer, Indian Territory.

Dear Madam:

There is on file with the Commission an affidavit executed by you in the matter of the enrollment of your minor child, Commodore Kerr, Jr., as a citizen of the Creek Nation. Your name appears in the body of said affidavit as Arsyno M. Kerr, while the signature to same is spelled Arcenoe M. Kerr.

There is herewith enclosed a blank form of birth affidavit. In executing same care should be taken to see that all blanks are properly filled, all names written in full and in the event that the person signing the affidavit is unable to write, signature by mark must be attested by two witnesses. Care must also be taken to see that the signature of the affiant must be spelled the same as it is in the body of the affidavit.

This matter should receive your prompt attention.

Respectfully,

Chairman.

Applications for Enrollment of Creek Newborn
Act of 1905   Volume III

BA-268-268-1/2-B

DEPARTMENT OF THE INTERIOR,
COMMISSION TO THE FIVE CIVILIZED TRIBES.

Muskogee, Indian Territory, March 13, 1905.

In the matter of the application for the enrollment of Eugene Miller as a citizen by blood of the Creek Nation.

Nora F. Miller, being duly sworn, testified as follows:

EXAMINATION BY THE COMMISSION:
Q State your name, age and postoffice address? A Nora F. Miller; 31; postoffice Sasakwa.
Q You have a child named Eugene Miller? A Yes sir.
Q When was Eugene born? A Born October 7, 1904.
Q Are you a citizen of the Creek Nation? A Citizen of the Seminole Nation.
Q Is the father of Eugene a citizen of the Creek Nation? A Yes sir.
Q Is this child living? A Yes sir.
Q If Eugene had any rights in both the Creek and Seminole Nations, in which Nation do you elect to have him enrolled and receive an allotment of land? A In the Creek Nation.

Samuel H Miller, being duly sworn, testified as follows:

EXAMINATION BY THE COMMISSION:
Q What is your name? A Samuel H. Miller.
Q What is your age? A 35; will be 36 in April.
Q What is your postoffice? A Sasakwa.
Q You have a child named Eugene Miller? A Yes sir.
Q You are a citizen of the Creek Nation? A Yes sir.
Q What is the name of the mother of Eugene Miller? A Nora.
Q Is she a citizen of any Nation? A Seminole.
Q If your child had rights in both the Creek and Seminole Nations, in which do you elect to have him enrolled? A Creek.

INDIAN TERRITORY, Western District.
    I, J. Y. Miller, a stenographer to the Commission to the Five Civilized Tribes, do hereby certify upon oath that the above and foregoing is a true and complete translation of my notes as same appear in my stenographic report of this case.

                                        JY Miller

Sworn to and subscribed before me
    this the 24 day of April, 1905.   Zera E Parrish
My Comm expires April 11, 1909.   Notary Public.

Applications for Enrollment of Creek Newborn
Act of 1905   Volume III

BIRTH AFFIDAVIT.

DEPARTMENT OF THE INTERIOR.
COMMISSION TO THE FIVE CIVILIZED TRIBES.

IN RE APPLICATION FOR ENROLLMENT, as a citizen of the Creek Nation, of Eugene Miller, born on the 7 day of October , 1904

Name of Father:	Samuel H. Miller	a citizen of the	Creek	Nation.
Name of Mother:	Nora F. Miller	a citizen of the	Seminole	Nation.

Postoffice   Sasakwa

Child Present - Donovan

AFFIDAVIT OF MOTHER.

UNITED STATES OF AMERICA, Indian Territory,
    Western   DISTRICT.

I, Nora F. Miller, on oath state that I am 31 years of age and a citizen by blood, of the Seminole Nation; that I am the lawful wife of Samuel H. Miller , who is a citizen, by blood of the Creek Nation; that a male child was born to me on 7 day of October , 1904 , that said child has been named Eugene Miller , and is now living.

Nora F. Miller

Witnesses To Mark:
{

Subscribed and sworn to before me this 13 day of March , 1905.

Edw C Griesel
Notary Public.

AFFIDAVIT OF ATTENDING PHYSICIAN OR MID-WIFE.

UNITED STATES OF AMERICA, Indian Territory,
    Western   DISTRICT.

I, Lillie Miller , a midwife , on oath state that I attended on Mrs. Nora F. Miller, wife of Sam'l H. Miller on the 7th day of October , 1904 ; that there was born to her on said date a male child; that said child is now living and is said to have been named Eugene Miller

Lillie Miller

Witnesses To Mark:
{

Applications for Enrollment of Creek Newborn
Act of 1905   Volume III

Subscribed and sworn to before me this 14th day of March, 1905.

            LMMiller
                Notary Public.
         My Com. ex. May 16th 1908

N.C. 169.

           Muskogee, Indian Territory, November 10, 1906.

Chief Clerk,
  Seminole Enrollment Division,
    General Office.

Dear Sir:

  You are hereby advised that the name of Eugene Miller, born October 7, 1904, to Samuel H. Miller, who is identified opposite Creek Indian Roll No. 5385, and Nora F. Miller, a citizen of the Seminole Nation, is contained in a schedule of citizens by blood of the Creek Nation, approved by the Secretary of the Interior July 28, 1905, opposite Roll No. 112.

           Respectfully,

                Commissioner.

BIRTH AFFIDAVIT.

DEPARTMENT OF THE INTERIOR.
COMMISSION TO THE FIVE CIVILIZED TRIBES.

IN RE APPLICATION FOR ENROLLMENT, as a citizen of the CREEK Nation, of Tine Winburn Campbell, born on the 11 day of Nov., 1903

Name of Father: Tom Campbell a citizen of the U.S. Nation.
Name of Mother: Jessie " a citizen of the Creek Nation.

        Postoffice Muskogee

(baby present)

       AFFIDAVIT OF MOTHER.

UNITED STATES OF AMERICA, Indian Territory,
  WESTERN   DISTRICT.

  I, Jessie Campbell, on oath state that I am 18 years of age and a citizen by blood, of the Creek Nation; that I am the lawful wife of Tom Campbell, who is a

Applications for Enrollment of Creek Newborn
Act of 1905   Volume III

citizen, by ~~bloo~~ of the U.S. ~~Nation~~; that a male child was born to me on 11 day of Nov., 1903, that said child has been named Tine Winburn Campbell, and was living March 4, 1905.

Jessie Campbell

Witnesses To Mark:
{

Subscribed and sworn to before me this 13 day of March, 1905.

Edw C Griesel
Notary Public.

AFFIDAVIT OF ATTENDING PHYSICIAN OR MID-WIFE.

UNITED STATES OF AMERICA, Indian Territory, }
      Western   DISTRICT.

I, Mattie Campbell, a midwife, on oath state that I attended on Mrs. Jessie Campbell, wife of Tom Campbell on the 11 day of Nov, 1903; that there was born to her on said date a male child; that said child was living March 4, 1905, and is said to have been named Tine Winburn Campbell

Mattie Campbell

Witnesses To Mark:
{

Subscribed and sworn to before me this 13 day of March, 1905.

Edw C Griesel
Notary Public.

Geo. W. McGuire, M. D.
OFFICE OVER M. D. KNISELEY & CO.'S DRUG STORE.
TELEPHONE 138.

Checotah, Ind. Ter., _____ 190__

It is hereby certified that there was born to Choney & Ida Minton on Oct. 27, 1903 a girl baby afterward named Ada Ethel the child is yet alive

Geo. W. McGuire MD

It is hereby certified that there was born to Clarence & Lea Reynolds on Sept 21, 1904 a boy baby subsequently named *(Name Illegible)* & that he is still living.

Geo W McGuire MD

Applications for Enrollment of Creek Newborn
Act of 1905   Volume III

Indian Territory }
Western District }

Subscribed and sworn to before me this 9th day of March 1905.

JB Morrow

My Commission Expires July 1, 1906.   **Notary Public**

BIRTH AFFIDAVIT.

DEPARTMENT OF THE INTERIOR.
COMMISSION TO THE FIVE CIVILIZED TRIBES.

IN RE APPLICATION FOR ENROLLMENT, as a citizen of the CREEK Nation, of Ada Minton, born on the 27 day of October, 1903

Name of Father:	Chanie Minton	a citizen of the	U.S.	Nation.
Name of Mother:	Annie Minton	a citizen of the	Creek	Nation.

Postoffice   Checotah

Child is present J.D.

AFFIDAVIT OF MOTHER.

UNITED STATES OF AMERICA, Indian Territory, }
  WESTERN   DISTRICT. }

melia

I, ~~Annie~~ Minton, on oath state that I am 30 years of age and a citizen by blood, of the Creek Nation; that I am the lawful wife of Chanie Minton, who is a citizen, by ----- of the U. S. Nation; that a female child was born to me on 27 day of October, 1903, that said child has been named Ada Minton, and is now living.

Amelia Minton

Witnesses To Mark:
{

Subscribed and sworn to before me this day of , 1905.
My Commission
Expires July 25" 1907   J. McDermott
                                Notary Public.

Applications for Enrollment of Creek Newborn
Act of 1905 Volume III

NC 172.

Muskogee, Indian Territory, May 19, 1905.

Frank B. Aultman,
    Hanna, Indian Territory.

Dear Sir:

    In the matter of the application for the enrollment of your minor children, Claude L. and Franklin C. Aultman, as citizens of the Creek Nation, you are advised that the Commission requires the affidavit of the midwife or physician in attendance at the birth of said children.

    There are herewith enclosed two blank forms of birth affidavits, and in executing same care should be exercised to see that all blanks are properly filled, all names written in full and in the event that the persons signing the affidavits are unable to write, signature by mark must be attested by two witnesses. Each affidavit must be executed before a Notary Public and the notarial seal and signature of the officer must be attached to each separate affidavit.

                    Respectfully,

BC.   Chairman.

BIRTH AFFIDAVIT.

DEPARTMENT OF THE INTERIOR.
COMMISSION TO THE FIVE CIVILIZED TRIBES.

    IN RE APPLICATION FOR ENROLLMENT, as a citizen of the Creek Nation, of Fraklin[sic] Clyde Aultman , born on the 24 day of September , 1904

Name of Father:	Franklin B. Aultman	a citizen of the Creek Nation.
Name of Mother:	Millie W. Aultman	a citizen of the (non citizen) Nation.

                    Postoffice   Hanna, Indian Territory

AFFIDAVIT OF MOTHER.

UNITED STATES OF AMERICA, Indian Territory, ⎫
    Western   DISTRICT.   ⎭

    I, Millie W. Aultman , on oath state that I am 22 years of age and a citizen by (non citizen) , of the *(blank)* Nation; that I am the lawful wife of Franklin B. Aultman, who is a citizen, by blood of the Creek Nation; that a male child was born

Applications for Enrollment of Creek Newborn
Act of 1905   Volume III

to me on 24 day of September, 1904, that said child has been named Franklin Clyde Aultman, and was living March 4, 1905.

Millie W. Aultman

Witnesses To Mark:
{

Subscribed and sworn to before me this 17 day of June, 1905.

W.R. Allen
Notary Public.

My Commission Expires Feby. 10, 1901

AFFIDAVIT OF ATTENDING PHYSICIAN OR MID-WIFE.

UNITED STATES OF AMERICA, Indian Territory, ⎱
    Western   DISTRICT.   ⎰

I, Sarah F Young, a Mid-Wife, on oath state that I attended on Mrs. Millie W. Aultman, wife of Franklin B. Aultman on the 24 day of September, 1904; that there was born to her on said date a male child; that said child was living March 4, 1905, and is said to have been named *(blank)*

sarah f young[sic]

Witnesses To Mark:
{

Subscribed and sworn to before me this 17 day of June, 1905.

W.R. Allen
Notary Public.

My Commission Expires Feby. 10, 1901

BIRTH AFFIDAVIT.

DEPARTMENT OF THE INTERIOR.
COMMISSION TO THE FIVE CIVILIZED TRIBES.

    IN RE APPLICATION FOR ENROLLMENT, as a citizen of the CREEK Nation, of Claud L. Aultman, born on the 18 day of Jan, 1903

Name of Father:	Frank B. Aultman	a citizen of the	Creek	Nation.
Name of Mother:	Millie "	a citizen of the	U. S.	Nation.

Postoffice   Hanna, I.T.

Applications for Enrollment of Creek Newborn
Act of 1905   Volume III

(child present)

AFFIDAVIT OF MOTHER.

UNITED STATES OF AMERICA, Indian Territory, }
　　WESTERN　　　　DISTRICT.

　　I, Millie Aultman , on oath state that I am 22 years of age and a citizen by ----- , of the U. S. Nation; that I am the lawful wife of ~~Millie~~ Frank B. Aultman , who is a citizen, by blood of the Creek Nation; that a male child was born to me on 18 day of Jan , 1903 , that said child has been named Claud L. Aultman , and is now living.

　　　　　　　　　　　　　　　　Millie Aultman

Witnesses To Mark:
{

　　Subscribed and sworn to before me this 13 day of March , 1905.

　　　　　　　　　　　　　　　　Edw C Griesel
　　　　　　　　　　　　　　　　　Notary Public.

AFFIDAVIT OF ATTENDING PHYSICIAN OR MID-WIFE.

UNITED STATES OF AMERICA, Indian Territory, }
　　Western　　　　DISTRICT.

　　　　　　　　　　　　　　　　　　　　　　　husband
　　I, Frank B Aultman , a m , ~~on oath state that I~~ attended on Mrs. , ~~wife~~ of Millie Aultman on the 18 day of Jan , 1903 ; that there was born to her on said date a male child; that said child is now living and is said to have been named Claud L. Aultman

　　　　　　　　　　　　　　　　Frank B Aultman

Witnesses To Mark:
{

　　Subscribed and sworn to before me this 13 day of March, 1905.

　　　　　　　　　　　　　　　　Edw C Griesel
　　　　　　　　　　　　　　　　　Notary Public.

Applications for Enrollment of Creek Newborn
Act of 1905 Volume III

BIRTH AFFIDAVIT.

DEPARTMENT OF THE INTERIOR.
COMMISSION TO THE FIVE CIVILIZED TRIBES.

IN RE APPLICATION FOR ENROLLMENT, as a citizen of the Creek Nation, of Claude Leon Aultman , born on the 18 day of January , 1903

Name of Father: Franklin B. Aultman   a citizen of the   Creek   Nation.
Name of Mother: Millie W. Aultman   a citizen of the (non citizen) Nation.

Postoffice   Hanna, Indian Territory

AFFIDAVIT OF MOTHER.

UNITED STATES OF AMERICA, Indian Territory, }
    Western   DISTRICT.

I, Millie W. Aultman , on oath state that I am 22 years of age and a citizen by (non citizen) , of the *(blank)* Nation; that I am the lawful wife of Franklin B. Aultman, who is a citizen, by blood of the Creek Nation; that a male child was born to me on 18 day of January , 1903 , that said child has been named Claude Leone Aultman , and was living March 4, 1905.

Millie W. Aultman

Witnesses To Mark:
{

Subscribed and sworn to before me this 17th. day of June , 1905.

W.R. Allen
Notary Public.

My Commission Expires Feby. 10, 1901

AFFIDAVIT OF ATTENDING PHYSICIAN OR MID-WIFE.

UNITED STATES OF AMERICA, Indian Territory, }
    Western   DISTRICT.

I, Mrs. Malvina L. Taylor , a Mid-Wife , on oath state that I attended on Mrs. Millie W. Aultman , wife of Franklin B. Aultman on the 18 day of January , 1903 ; that there was born to her on said date a male child; that said child was living March 4, 1905, and is said to have been named Claude Leon Aultman

Malvina Taylor

Witnesses To Mark:
{

Applications for Enrollment of Creek Newborn
Act of 1905 Volume III

Subscribed and sworn to before me this 17 day of June, 1905.

            W.R. Allen
              Notary Public.
My Commission Expires Feby. 10, 1901

BIRTH AFFIDAVIT.

DEPARTMENT OF THE INTERIOR.
COMMISSION TO THE FIVE CIVILIZED TRIBES.

IN RE APPLICATION FOR ENROLLMENT, as a citizen of the CREEK Nation, of Franklin C. Aultman, born on the 24 day of Sept., 1904

Name of Father:	Frank B. Aultman	a citizen of the	Creek	Nation.
Name of Mother:	Millie "	a citizen of the	U. S.	Nation.

        Postoffice Hanna, I.T.

(child present)

AFFIDAVIT OF MOTHER.

UNITED STATES OF AMERICA, Indian Territory,
  WESTERN   DISTRICT.

  I, Millie Aultman, on oath state that I am 22 years of age and a citizen by -----, of the U.S. Nation; that I am the lawful wife of ~~Millie~~ Frank B. Aultman, who is a citizen, by blood of the Creek Nation; that a male child was born to me on 24 day of Sept., 1904, that said child has been named Franklin C. Aultman, and is now living.

            Millie Aultman

Witnesses To Mark:

  Subscribed and sworn to before me this 13 day of March, 1905.

            Edw C Griesel
              Notary Public.

AFFIDAVIT OF ATTENDING PHYSICIAN OR MID-WIFE.

UNITED STATES OF AMERICA, Indian Territory,
  (blank)   DISTRICT.

        husband   of
  I, Frank B Aultman, a m, ~~on oath state that I attended on~~ Mrs. Millie Aultman, ~~wife of (blank)~~ on the 24 day of Sept., 1904; that there was born to her on said

Applications for Enrollment of Creek Newborn
Act of 1905   Volume III

date a male child; that said child is now living and is said to have been named Franklin C. Aultman

Frank B Aultman

Witnesses To Mark:
{

    Subscribed and sworn to before me this 13 day of March, 1905.

Edw C Griesel
Notary Public.

NC. 173.

Muskogee, Indian Territory, August 16, 1905.

Jackson Yahola,
    Yeager, Indian Territory.

Dear Sir:

    Receipt is acknowledged of your letter of August 14, 1905, relative to the enrollment of your children, names not given. It is presumed that you refer to your children, Roman Yahola, born February 28, 1902, and Houston Yahola, born March 22, 1904.

    You are again advised that this office requires the affidavit of the midwife or physician in attendance at the birth of said children, and if there was no midwife or physician present, the affidavits of two disinterested witnesses as to the birth of both children should be supplied at once.

    There are herewith enclosed two blank forms of birth affidavits, and in executing same care should be exercised to see that all blanks are properly filled, all names written in full and in the event that the persons signing the affidavits are unable to write, signature by mark must be attested by two witnesses. Each affidavit must be executed before a Notary Public and the notarial seal and signature of the officer must be attached to each separate affidavit.

Respectfully,

2 BA.   Acting Commissioner.

Applications for Enrollment of Creek Newborn
Act of 1905   Volume III

COMMISSIONERS:
TAMS BIXBY,
THOMAS B. NEEDLES,
C.R. BRECKINBRIDGE.

WM. O. BEALL
Secretary

DEPARTMENT OF THE INTERIOR,
COMMISSIONER TO THE FIVE CIVILIZED TRIBES.

HGH

REFER IN REPLY TO THE FOLLOWING:

NC 173.

ADDRESS ONLY THE
COMMISSION TO THE FIVE CIVILIZED TRIBES.

Celia   Muskogee, Indian Territory, May 19, 1905.
Jackson Yahola,
   Holdenville, Indian Territory.

Dear Sir:

   In the matter of the application for the enrollment of your minor children, Roman and Houston Yahola, as citizens of the Creek Nation, you are advised that the Commission requires the affidavit of the midwife or physician in attendance at the birth of said children.

   There is herewith enclosed two blank forms of birth affidavit, and in executing same care should be exercised to see that all blanks are properly filled, all names written in full and in the event that the person signing the affidavits is unable to write, signature by mark must be attested by two witnesses. Each affidavit must be executed before a Notary Public and the notarial seal and signature of the officer must be attached to each separate affidavit.

   Respectfully,

BC.   Tams Bixby   Chairman.

COMMISSIONERS:
TAMS BIXBY,
THOMAS B. NEEDLES,
C.R. BRECKINBRIDGE.

WM. O. BEALL
Secretary

DEPARTMENT OF THE INTERIOR,
COMMISSIONER TO THE FIVE CIVILIZED TRIBES.

HGH

REFER IN REPLY TO THE FOLLOWING:

NC 173.

ADDRESS ONLY THE
COMMISSION TO THE FIVE CIVILIZED TRIBES.

   Muskogee, Indian Territory, June 22, 1905.

Celia Yahola,
   Holdenville, Indian Territory.

Dear Madam:

   In the matter of the application for the enrollment of your minor children, Roman and Houston Yahola, as citizens of the Creek Nation, you are advised that the Commission requires the affidavit of the midwife or physician in attendance at the birth of said children.

Applications for Enrollment of Creek Newborn
Act of 1905   Volume III

There are herewith enclosed two blank forms of birth affidavit, and in executing same care should be exercised to see that all blanks are properly filled, all names written in full and in the event that either of the persons signing the affidavits is unable to write, signature by mark must be attested by two witnesses. Each affidavit must be executed before a Notary Public and the notarial seal and signature of the officer must be attached to each separate affidavit.

          Respectfully,

          Tams Bixby   Chairman.

BIRTH AFFIDAVIT.

DEPARTMENT OF THE INTERIOR.
COMMISSION TO THE FIVE CIVILIZED TRIBES.

IN RE APPLICATION FOR ENROLLMENT, as a citizen of the CREEK Nation, of Houston Yahola, born on the 22 day of March, 1904

Name of Father:	Jackson Yahola	a citizen of the	Creek	Nation.
Name of Mother:	Celia "	a citizen of the	"	Nation.

          Postoffice   Holdenville

(child present)

AFFIDAVIT OF MOTHER.

UNITED STATES OF AMERICA, Indian Territory,
    WESTERN   DISTRICT.

    I, Celia Yahola, on oath state that I am 35 years of age and a citizen by blood, of the Creek Nation; that I am the lawful wife of Jackson Yahola, who is a citizen, by blood of the Creek Nation; that a male child was born to me on 22 day of March, 1904, that said child has been named Houston Yahola, and is now living.

          Her
          Celia x Yahola
Witnesses To Mark: mark
  { J. McDermott
    EC Griesel

Subscribed and sworn to before me this 13 day of March, 1905.

          Edw C Griesel
              Notary Public.

Applications for Enrollment of Creek Newborn
Act of 1905 Volume III

father
AFFIDAVIT OF ~~ATTENDING PHYSICIAN OR MID-WIFE~~.

UNITED STATES OF AMERICA, Indian Territory,
Western DISTRICT.

I, Jackson Yahola , a m , ~~on oath state that I attended on Mrs~~. husband , ~~wife~~ of Celia Yahola on the 22 day of March , 1904 ; that there was born to her on said date a male child; that said child is now living and is said to have been named Houston Yahola.

Jackson Yahola

Witnesses To Mark:
{

Subscribed and sworn to before me this 13 day of March, 1905.

Edw C Griesel
Notary Public.

BIRTH AFFIDAVIT.

DEPARTMENT OF THE INTERIOR.
COMMISSION TO THE FIVE CIVILIZED TRIBES.

IN RE APPLICATION FOR ENROLLMENT, as a citizen of the Creek Nation, of Roman Yahola , born on the 28 day of Feb , 1902

Name of Father:	Jackson Yahola	a citizen of the	Creek	Nation.
Name of Mother:	Celia Yahola	a citizen of the	Creek	Nation.

Postoffice YEAGER, I.T.

AFFIDAVIT OF MOTHER.

UNITED STATES OF AMERICA, Indian Territory,
Western DISTRICT. Don't know about
24

I, Celia Yahola, on oath state that I am ~~24~~ years of age and a citizen by blood , of the Creek Nation; that I am the lawful wife of Jackson Yahola , who is a citizen, by blood of the Creek Nation; that a male child was born to me on 28 day of February , 1902 , that said child has been named Roman Yahola , and was living March 4, 1905.

her
Celia Yahola x
mark

Witnesses To Mark:
{ WR Clawson
  (Name Illegible)

Applications for Enrollment of Creek Newborn
Act of 1905   Volume III

Subscribed and sworn to before me this 19 day of Aug, 1905.

                          W.R. Clawson

My Commission Expires June 13, 1908.   Notary Public.

AFFIDAVIT OF ATTENDING PHYSICIAN OR MID-WIFE.

UNITED STATES OF AMERICA, Indian Territory,
    Western   DISTRICT.

We, I, Wisey Derre & Haina Yorgee, a Midwives, on oath state that I we attended on Mrs. Celia Yahola, wife of Jackson Yahola on the 28 day of Feb, 1902; that there was born to her on said date a male child; that said child was living March 4, 1905, and is said to have been named Roman Yahola

                                      her
                              Wisey x Deere
                                  mark

Witnesses To Mark: her
  { WR Clawson   Haina x Yorgee
   (Name Illegible)   mark

Subscribed and sworn to before me this 19 day of Aug, 1905.

                          W.R. Clawson

My Commission Expires June 13, 1908.   Notary Public.

BIRTH AFFIDAVIT.

DEPARTMENT OF THE INTERIOR.
COMMISSION TO THE FIVE CIVILIZED TRIBES.

IN RE APPLICATION FOR ENROLLMENT, as a citizen of the CREEK Nation, of Roman Yahola, born on the 28 day of Feb, 1902

Name of Father:	Jackson Yahola	a citizen of the	Creek	Nation.
Name of Mother:	Celia "	a citizen of the	"	Nation.

                          Postoffice   Holdenville

Applications for Enrollment of Creek Newborn
Act of 1905   Volume III

(child present)

AFFIDAVIT OF ~~MOTHER~~. father

UNITED STATES OF AMERICA, Indian Territory, ⎱
    WESTERN   DISTRICT. ⎰

I, Jackson Yahola , on oath state that I am 40 years of age and a citizen by blood, of the Creek Nation; that I am the lawful ~~wife~~ hus of Celia Yahola , who is a citizen, by blood of the Creek Nation; that a male child was born to me on 28 day of Feb , 1902 , that said child has been named Roman Yahola , and is now living.

                            Jackson Yahola

Witnesses To Mark:
{

Subscribed and sworn to before me this 13 day of March, 1905.

                            Edw C Griesel
                              Notary Public.

---

                  mother
AFFIDAVIT OF ~~ATTENDING PHYSICIAN OR MID-WIFE~~.

UNITED STATES OF AMERICA, Indian Territory, ⎱
    Western   DISTRICT. ⎰

I, Celia Yahola , ~~a   , on oath state that~~ I ~~attended on Mrs.~~ am , wife of Jackson Yahola on the 28 day of Feb , 1902 ; that there was born to ~~her~~ me on said date a male child; that said child is now living and is said to have been named Roman Yahola

                            Her
                        Celia x Yahola

Witnesses To Mark: mark
{ J. McDermott
  EC Griesel

Subscribed and sworn to before me this 13 day of March, 1905.

                            Edw C Griesel
                              Notary Public.

Applications for Enrollment of Creek Newborn
Act of 1905 Volume III

BIRTH AFFIDAVIT.

DEPARTMENT OF THE INTERIOR.
COMMISSION TO THE FIVE CIVILIZED TRIBES.

IN RE APPLICATION FOR ENROLLMENT, as a citizen of the Creek Nation, of Houston Yahola, born on the 22 day of March, 1904

Name of Father:	Jackson Yahola	a citizen of the	Creek	Nation.
Name of Mother:	Celia Yahola	a citizen of the	Creek	Nation.

Postoffice   YEAGER, I.T.

AFFIDAVIT OF MOTHER.

UNITED STATES OF AMERICA, Indian Territory,
Western   DISTRICT.

about

I, Celia Yahola, on oath state that I am 24 years of age and a citizen by blood, of the Creek Nation; that I am the lawful wife of Jackson Yahola, who is a citizen, by blood of the Creek Nation; that a male child was born to me on 22 day of March, 1904, that said child has been named Houston Yahola, and was living March 4, 1905.

　　　　　　　　　　　　　　　　her
　　　　　　　　　　　Celia Yahola x
Witnesses To Mark:　　　　　　　　mark
  { WR Clawson
  { (Name Illegible)
Subscribed and sworn to before me this 19 day of Aug, 1905.

　　　　　　　　　　　　　　W.R. Clawson
My Commission Expires June 13, 1908.　　　Notary Public.

AFFIDAVIT OF ATTENDING PHYSICIAN OR MID-WIFE.

UNITED STATES OF AMERICA, Indian Territory,
Western   DISTRICT.

We, I, Wisey Derre & Haina Yorgee, a Midwives, on oath state that I we attended on Mrs. Celia Yahola, wife of Jackson Yahola on the 22 day of March, 1904; that there was born to her on said date a male child; that said child was living March 4, 1905, and is said to have been named Houston Yahola

　　　　　　　　　　　　her
　　　　　　　Wisey x Deere
　　　　　　　　　mark

Applications for Enrollment of Creek Newborn
Act of 1905   Volume III

Witnesses To Mark:
{ *(Name Illegible)*

her
Haina x Yorgee
mark

Subscribed and sworn to before me this 19 day of Aug , 1905.

My Commission Expires June 13, 1908.

W.R. Clawson
Notary Public.

BIRTH AFFIDAVIT.

DEPARTMENT OF THE INTERIOR.
COMMISSION TO THE FIVE CIVILIZED TRIBES.

IN RE APPLICATION FOR ENROLLMENT, as a citizen of the CREEK Nation, of Ora Pearl Hopwood , born on the 28 day of July , 1903

Name of Father: Kellen F. Hopwood   a citizen of the   Creek   Nation.
Name of Mother: Mollie   "   a citizen of the   U. S.   Nation.

Postoffice   Morse, I.T.

AFFIDAVIT OF MOTHER.

UNITED STATES OF AMERICA, Indian Territory, ⎱
        WESTERN   DISTRICT. ⎰

I, Kellen F. Hopwood, on oath state that I am 33 years of age and a citizen by blood , of the Creek Nation; that I am the lawful ~~wife~~ hus of Mollie Hopwood , who is a citizen, by ----- of the U. S. Nation; that a female child was born to me on 28 day of July , 1903, that said child has been named Ora Pearl Hopwood , and is now living.

K. F. Hopwood

Witnesses To Mark:
{

Subscribed and sworn to before me this 13 day of March, 1905.

My Commission
   of July 25" 1907

J. McDermott
Notary Public.

Applications for Enrollment of Creek Newborn
Act of 1905 Volume III

BIRTH AFFIDAVIT.

DEPARTMENT OF THE INTERIOR.
COMMISSION TO THE FIVE CIVILIZED TRIBES.

IN RE APPLICATION FOR ENROLLMENT, as a citizen of the Muskogee Nation, of Ora Pearle Hopwood, born on the 28 day of July, 1903

Name of Father: Kellen F. Hopwood   a citizen of the Muskogee Nation.
Name of Mother: Mollie Hopwood   a citizen of the U. S.   Nation.

Postoffice   Morse, I.T.

AFFIDAVIT OF MOTHER.

UNITED STATES OF AMERICA, Indian Territory,
Western DISTRICT.

I, Mollie Hopwood, on oath state that I am 31 years of age and a citizen by *(blank)*, of the U. S. Nation; that I am the lawful wife of Kellen F. Hopwood, who is a citizen, by blood of the Muskogee Nation; that a female child was born to me on 28 day of July, 1903, that said child has been named Ora Pearle Hopwood, and is now living.

Mollie Hopwood

Witnesses To Mark:
{

Subscribed and sworn to before me this 11 day of March, 1905.

C. C. Eskridge
My Commission Expires March 5th, 1908.   Notary Public.

AFFIDAVIT OF ATTENDING PHYSICIAN OR MID-WIFE.

UNITED STATES OF AMERICA, Indian Territory,
Western DISTRICT.

I, Bettie Mounds, a mid-wife, on oath state that I attended on Mrs. Mollie Hopwood, wife of Kellen F. Hopwood on the 28 day of July, 1903; that there was born to her on said date a female child; that said child is now living and is said to have been named Ora Pearle Hopwood

her
Bettie x Mounds
mark

Witnesses To Mark:
{ SM Wilson
  Edgar Wisdom

Applications for Enrollment of Creek Newborn
Act of 1905   Volume III

Subscribed and sworn to before me this 11 day of March, 1905.

C. C. Eskridge

My Commission Expires March 5th, 1908.   Notary Public.

DEPARTMENT OF THE INTERIOR,
COMMISSIONER TO THE FIVE CIVILIZED TRIBES.
Muskogee, Indian Territory, August 8, 1905.

In the matter of the application for the enrollment of Lee Charley Anderson as a citizen by blood of the Creek Nation.

Martha Anderson, being duly sworn, testified as follows:

Through Jesse McDermott Official Interpreter.

By Commissioner.

Q What is your name? Martha Anderson
Q How old are you? A About forty
Q What is your post office address? A Holdenville.
Q Are you a citizen of the Creek Nation? A Yes, sir
Q What is the name of your father? A Thomas Anderson, he is dead
Q What is the name of your mother? A I didn't know her. She died when I was a small child.
Q To what Indian town do you belong? A Eufaula Deep Fork.
Q What is the name of your boy here? A Lee Charley, his name is Charley but they nickname him Lee Charley therefore I call him that.
Q What is the correct name of the child? A Charley is the right name.
Q You don't want Lee in there? A No, sir
Q When was Charley born? A The 29th of January. The child is over three years old.
Q What is the name of the father of this child? A Newman Jacobs is his name, but he doesn't claim him.
Q You know him to be the father? but he won't admit it, is that right? A Yes, sir
Q You were never married were you? A No, sir.
Q Was he a citizen of the Creek Nation? A Yes, sir
Q In an affidavit made out before the Commission here you swore that this child was the child of Thomas Anderson? A I Don't recollect making that affidavit, Thomas Anderson is my brother He was my brother but he died a short time ago
Q So that was a mistake? A Yes, sir.
Q And when you stated that you were the lawful wife of Thomas Anderson that was a mistake and you are not the lawful wife of the father of this child or any one? A Yes, sir that was a mistake

Applications for Enrollment of Creek Newborn
Act of 1905   Volume III

Q Afterwards you sent in an affidavit in which you stated the child was Newman Jacob's and that you were not the lawful wife of Newman Jacobs, that is correct is it? A Yes, sir.
Q What was the name of the midwife? A Sissie Coser. she was present when the child was born. She signed the affidavit and we sent it in.
Q The name of the father according to her is Jacobs, is the childs[sic] name Anderson? A I don't know.
Q You gave the name Anderson, is that the correct name? A Yes, sir

Katie Long, being duly sworn, testified as follows:

Q What is your name? A Katie Long.
Q What is your age? A 23
Q What is your post office address? A Holdenville.
Q Are you a citizen of the Creek Nation? A No, a Seminole.
Q Do you know Martha Anderson? A Yes, sir
Q Do you know her child Charley? A Yes, sir
Q Do you know who was the father? A Yes, sir
Q Who? A Newman Jacob
Q You know that do you? A Yes, sir
Q How do you know, have you any other way only that she told you? A No, sir.
Q Have you ever seen them together? A Yes, sir.
Q And you think he is the father? A Yes, sir
Q There wasn't anybody else that you think might be the father? A No, sir

---

Anna Garrigues on oath states that the above and foregoing is a true and correct copy of her stenographic notes taken in said cause on said date.

Anna Garrigues

Subscribed and sworn to before me
this 9th day of September 1905.   Henry G. Haines
                                          Notary Public.

BIRTH AFFIDAVIT.
DEPARTMENT OF THE INTERIOR.
COMMISSION TO THE FIVE CIVILIZED TRIBES.

IN RE APPLICATION FOR ENROLLMENT, as a citizen of the CREEK Nation, of Lee Charley Anderson , born on the 29 day of Jan , 1902

Name of Father:	Thomas Anderson	a citizen of the	Creek	Nation.
Name of Mother:	Martha "	a citizen of the	"	Nation.

Applications for Enrollment of Creek Newborn
Act of 1905 Volume III

Postoffice ~~Okmulgee~~ Holdenville

(child present)

AFFIDAVIT OF MOTHER.

UNITED STATES OF AMERICA, Indian Territory,
WESTERN DISTRICT.

I, Martha Anderson, on oath state that I am 30+ years of age and a citizen by blood, of the Creek Nation; that I am the lawful wife of Thomas Anderson, who is a citizen, by blood of the Creek Nation; that a male child was born to me on 29 day of Jan., 1902, that said child has been named Lee Charley Anderson, and is now living.

                                          her
                                 Martha x Anderson
Witnesses To Mark: mark
  { H G Hains
    J McDermott

Subscribed and sworn to before me this 13 day of March, 1905.

My Commission   J. McDermott
Expires July 25" 1907   Notary Public.

BIRTH AFFIDAVIT.

DEPARTMENT OF THE INTERIOR.
COMMISSION TO THE FIVE CIVILIZED TRIBES.

IN RE APPLICATION FOR ENROLLMENT, as a citizen of the Creek Nation, of Charley Anderson, born on the 29 day of January, 1902

Name of Father:	Newman Jacobs	a citizen of the	Creek	Nation.
Name of Mother:	Martha Anderson	a citizen of the	Creek	Nation.

                               Postoffice   Holdenville, Ind. Terry

AFFIDAVIT OF MOTHER.

UNITED STATES OF AMERICA, Indian Territory,
Western DISTRICT.

I, Martha Anderson, on oath state that I am 36 years of age and a citizen by birth, of the Creek Nation; that I am the lawful wife of have none, who is a citizen, by --- -- of the ----- Nation; that a male child was born to me on 29 day of January, 1902, that said child has been named Charley Anderson, and was living March 4, 1905.

Applications for Enrollment of Creek Newborn
Act of 1905 Volume III

her
Martha Anderson x
mark

Witnesses To Mark:
{ Wardley Goat
{ Chas Rider

Subscribed and sworn to before me this 29th day of July, 1905.

Chas Rider
Notary Public.

AFFIDAVIT OF ATTENDING PHYSICIAN OR MID-WIFE.

UNITED STATES OF AMERICA, Indian Territory, }
    Western   DISTRICT.

I, Sissie Cosar, a midwife, on oath state that I attended on Mrs. Martha Anderson, wife of *(blank)* on the 29th day of January, 1902; that there was born to her on said date a male child; that said child was living March 4, 1905, and is said to have been named Charley Anderson

her
Sissie Cosar x
mark

Witnesses To Mark:
{ Wardley Goat
{ Chas Rider

Subscribed and sworn to before me this 29th day of July, 1905.

Chas Rider
Notary Public.

NC 175.

Muskogee, Indian Territory, May 19, 1905.

Thomas Anderson,
    Holdenville, Indian Territory.

Dear Sir:

    In the matter of the application for the enrollment of your minor child, Lee Charley Anderson, as a citizen of the Creek Nation, you are advised that the Commission requires the affidavit of the midwife or physician in attendance at the birth of said child.

    There is herewith enclosed a blank form of birth affidavit, and in executing same care should be exercised to see that all blanks are properly filled, all names written in full

Applications for Enrollment of Creek Newborn
Act of 1905   Volume III

and in the event that the person signing the affidavit is unable to write, signature by mark must be attested by two witnesses. Each affidavit must be executed before a Notary Public and the notarial seal and signature of the officer must be attached to each separate affidavit.

Respectfully,

BC.   Chairman.

NC 175.

Muskogee, Indian Territory, June 30, 1905.

Martha Anderson,
    Holdenville, Indian Territory.

Dear Sir[sic]:

    In the matter of the application for the enrollment of your minor child, Lee Charley Anderson, as a citizen of the Creek Nation, you are advised that the Commission requires the affidavit of the midwife or physician in attendance at the birth of said child.

    There is herewith enclosed a blank form of birth affidavit, and in executing same care should be exercised to see that all blanks are properly filled, all names written in full and in the event that the person signing the affidavit is unable to write, signature by mark must be attested by two witnesses. Each affidavit must be executed before a Notary Public and the notarial seal and signature of the officer must be attached to each separate affidavit.

Respectfully,

BC.   Chairman.

NC-175

Muskogee, Indian Territory, July 27, 1905.

Martha Anderson,
    Holdenville, Indian Territory.

Dear Sir[sic]:

    In the matter of the application for the enrollment of your minor child, Lee Charley Anderson, as a citizen of the Creek Nation, you are advised that the Commission requires the affidavit of the midwife or physician in attendance at the birth of said child.

Applications for Enrollment of Creek Newborn
Act of 1905 Volume III

There is herewith enclosed a blank form of birth affidavit, and in executing same care should be exercised to see that all blanks are properly filled, all names written in full and in the event that the person signing the affidavit is unable to write, signature by mark must be attested by two witnesses. Each affidavit must be executed before a Notary Public and the notarial seal and signature of the officer must be attached to each separate affidavit.

Respectfully,

BC.   Chairman.

N.C. 175.

Muskogee, Indian Territory, Augu *(Page torn)*

Martha Anderson,
    Holdenville, Indian Territory.

Dear Madam:

In the matter of the application for the en *(page torn)* minor child, Lee Charley Anderson, as a citizen by blood *(page torn)* Nation, you are advised that you will be allowed fifteen days from date within which to appear at the office of the Commissioner to the Five Civilized Tribes, in Muskogee, Indian Territory, for the purpose of being examined under oath.

Respectfully,

Commissioner.

DCS.

BIRTH AFFIDAVIT.

DEPARTMENT OF THE INTERIOR.
COMMISSION TO THE FIVE CIVILIZED TRIBES.

IN RE APPLICATION FOR ENROLLMENT, as a citizen of the Creek Nation, of Jennie Murrell Miles, born on the 19th day of Sept., 1901

Name of Father:	Wm S Miles	a citizen of the	Cherokee Nation.
Name of Mother:	Rosalee Miles	a citizen of the	Creek Nation.

Postoffice   Big Spring, Texas

Applications for Enrollment of Creek Newborn
Act of 1905   Volume III

AFFIDAVIT OF MOTHER.

UNITED STATES OF AMERICA, Indian Territory,
Western   DISTRICT.

    I, Rosalee Miles , on oath state that I am 36 years of age and a citizen by blood , of the Creek   Nation; that I am the lawful wife of Wm S. Miles   , who is a citizen, by marriage of the Cherokee   Nation; that a female   child was born to me on 19th day of September , 1901 , that said child has been named Jennie Murrell Miles   , and was living March 4, 1905.

                                                    Rosalee Miles

Witnesses To Mark:

    Subscribed and sworn to before me this 24th day of May , 1905.

                                              S H. Morrison
                                                   Notary Public.
                                                 Howard Co, Texas

---

AFFIDAVIT OF ATTENDING PHYSICIAN OR MID-WIFE.

UNITED STATES OF AMERICA, Indian Territory,
Western   DISTRICT.

    I, J. G. Wright   , a Physician , on oath state that I attended on Mrs. Rosalee Miles , wife of Wm S Miles on the 19 day of Sept , 1901 ; that there was born to her on said date a female child; that said child was living March 4, 1905, and is said to have been named Jennie Murrell Miles

                                              J. G. Wright M.D.

Witnesses To Mark:

    Subscribed and sworn to before me this 24th day of May, 1905.

                                              S. H. Morrison
                                                  Notary Public.
                                                 Howard Co, Texas

Applications for Enrollment of Creek Newborn
Act of 1905   Volume III

BIRTH AFFIDAVIT.

DEPARTMENT OF THE INTERIOR.
COMMISSION TO THE FIVE CIVILIZED TRIBES.

IN RE APPLICATION FOR ENROLLMENT, as a citizen of the Creek Nation, of Jennie Murrell Miles, born on the 19 day of Sept., 1901

Name of Father:	W S Miles	a citizen of the	I M.Cher	Nation.
Name of Mother:	Rosalee "	a citizen of the	Creek	Nation.

Postoffice   Big Spring, Texas

AFFIDAVIT OF MOTHER.

UNITED STATES OF AMERICA, Indian Territory, }
Western   DISTRICT.

I, W S Miles, on oath state that I am 50 years of age and a citizen by marriage, of the Cherokee Nation; that I am the lawful ~~wife~~ hus of Rosalie Miles, who is a citizen, by blood of the Creek Nation; that a female child was born to me on 19 day of Sept, 1901, that said child has been named Jennie Murrell Miles, and was living March 4, 1905.

W.S. Miles

Witnesses To Mark:
{

Subscribed and sworn to before me this 13 day of March, 1905.

Edw C Griesel
Notary Public.

BIRTH AFFIDAVIT.

DEPARTMENT OF THE INTERIOR.
COMMISSION TO THE FIVE CIVILIZED TRIBES.

IN RE APPLICATION FOR ENROLLMENT, as a citizen of the Creek Nation, of Vivian Miles, born on the 25 day of October, 1903

Name of Father:	William S. Miles	a citizen of the	Cherokee	Nation.
Name of Mother:	Rosalie Miles	a citizen of the	Creek	Nation.

Postoffice   Big Springs, Texas.

Applications for Enrollment of Creek Newborn
Act of 1905 Volume III

AFFIDAVIT OF MOTHER.

UNITED STATES OF AMERICA, Indian Territory,
    (blank)   DISTRICT.

    I, Rosalie Miles, on oath state that I am 36 years of age and a citizen by blood, of the Creek Nation; that I am the lawful wife of William S. Miles, who is a citizen, by marriage of the Cherokee Nation; that a female child was born to me on 25th day of October, 1903, that said child has been named Vivian Miles, and is now living.

                                       Rosalie Miles

Witnesses To Mark:
{

    Subscribed and sworn to before me this 4th day of April, 1905.

                                       S. H. Morrison
                                               Notary Public.
                                             Howard Co, Texas

---

AFFIDAVIT OF ATTENDING PHYSICIAN OR MID-WIFE.

UNITED STATES OF AMERICA, Indian Territory,
    Western   DISTRICT.

    I, Chas Heitzmon, a Physician, on oath state that I attended on Mrs. Rosalie Miles, wife of William S. Miles on the 25th day of October, 1903; that there was born to her on said date a female child; and that said child is now living as I verily believe and is said to have been named Vivian Miles

                                   Chas W Heitzmon M D

Witnesses To Mark:
{

    Subscribed and sworn to before me this 14th day of March, 1905.

                                       E. R. Jones
                                           Notary Public.

Applications for Enrollment of Creek Newborn
Act of 1905   Volume III

BIRTH AFFIDAVIT.

DEPARTMENT OF THE INTERIOR.
COMMISSION TO THE FIVE CIVILIZED TRIBES.

IN RE APPLICATION FOR ENROLLMENT, as a citizen of the Creek Nation, of Vivian Miles, born on the 25 day of Oct. , 1903

Name of Father: W S Miles   a citizen of the I.M.Cherokee Nation.
Name of Mother: Rosalee "   a citizen of the   Creek   Nation.

Postoffice   Big Spring, Texas

AFFIDAVIT OF ~~MOTHER~~.
father

UNITED STATES OF AMERICA, Indian Territory,
Western   DISTRICT.

I, W. S. Miles , on oath state that I am 50 years of age and a citizen by marriage, of the Cherokee   Nation; that I am the lawful ~~wife~~ husband of Rosalie Miles , who is a citizen, by blood of the Creek Nation; that a female child was born to me on 25 day of Oct   , 1903 , that said child has been named   Vivian Miles , and was living March 4, 1905.

W.S. Miles

Witnesses To Mark:
{

Subscribed and sworn to before me this 13 day of March, 1905.

Edw C Griesel
Notary Public.

DEPARTMENT OF THE INTERIOR.
COMMISSION TO THE FIVE CIVILIZED TRIBES.

In the matter of the death of Vivian Miles   a citizen of the Creek Nation, who formerly resided at or near Muskogee   , Ind. Ter., and died on the 28 day of April, 1905

Applications for Enrollment of Creek Newborn
Act of 1905   Volume III

AFFIDAVIT OF RELATIVE.

UNITED STATES OF AMERICA, Indian Territory, }
    (blank)   DISTRICT.

    I, Rosalie Miles , on oath state that I am 36 years of age and a citizen by Blood , of the Creek Nation; that my postoffice address is Big Springs, Tex. , Ind. Ter.; that I am the Mother of Vivian Miles who was a citizen, by Blood , of the Creek Nation and that said Vivian Miles died on the 28 day of April, 1905

                                      Rosalie Miles

Witnesses To Mark:
  {

    Subscribed and sworn to before me this 8th day of June, 1905.

                                    S. H. Morrison
                                        Notary Public.
                                      Howard Co, Texas

AFFIDAVIT OF ACQUAINTANCE.

UNITED STATES OF AMERICA, Indian Territory, }
    (blank)   DISTRICT.

    I, SH Morrison , on oath state that I am 46 years of age, and a citizen by birth of the State of Texas ~~Nation~~; that my postoffice address is Big Springs in Howard Co. Texas , ~~Ind. Ter.~~; that I was personally acquainted with Vivian Miles who was a citizen, by birth , of the Creek Nation; and that said Vivian Miles died on the 28 day of April , 1905

                                      S H Morrison

Witnesses To Mark:
  {

    Subscribed and sworn to before me this 8th day of June, 1905.

                                        R B Canon
                                        Notary Public.
                                        Howard Co. Texas

Applications for Enrollment of Creek Newborn
Act of 1905   Volume III

NC 176,

Muskogee, Indian Territory, May 19, 1905.

W. J[sic]. Miles
    Big Springs, Texas.

Dear Sir:

    In the matter of the application for the enrollment of your minor child, Jennie Murrell Miles, as a citizen of the Creek Nation, you are advised that the Commission requires the affidavits of the mother of said child and of the midwife or physician in attendance at the birth of said child.

    There is herewith enclosed a blank form of birth affidavit, and in executing same care should be exercised to see that all blanks are properly filled, all names written in full and in the event that the person signing the affidavit is unable to write, signatures by mark must be attested by two witnesses. Each affidavit must be executed before a Notary Public and the notarial seal and signature of the officer must be attached to each separate affidavit.

                          Respectfully,

BC.   Chairman.

NC 176.

Muskogee, Indian Territory, June 3, 1905.

Rosalie Miles,
    Big Springs, Texas.

Dear Madam:

    The Commission has been informed that your minor child Vivian Miles is dead.

    There is herewith enclosed blank form of death affidavit which you are requested to have filled out and properly executed before an officer authorized to administer oaths, and return it to the Commission in the enclosed envelope.

                          Respectfully,

1 DA.   Commissioner in Charge.

;

Applications for Enrollment of Creek Newborn
Act of 1905   Volume III

Cr NC-176

Muskogee, Indian Territory, June 12, 1905.

Rosalie Miles,
    Big Springs, Texas.

Dear Madam:

    In the matter of the application for the enrollment of your minor child, Vivian Miles (deceased), as a citizen of the Creek Nation, you are hereby advised that you will be allowed fifteen days from date hereof within which to appear before the Commission at its office in Muskogee, Indian Territory, with two disinterested witnesses, for the purpose of testifying relative to the birth and death of said child.

Respectfully,

Chairman.

NC-176

Muskogee, Indian Territory, October 31, 1905.

The Honorable,
    The Secretary of the Interior.

Sir:

    October 19, 1905, (I.T.D. 3802-1904), the Department callod[sic] attention to the fact that the Commission to the Five Civilized Tribes denied the right to enrollment of Rosalie Miles and Louisa Miles as citizens by blood of the Cherokee Nation, and held that Jennie Murrell Miles, minor child of Rosalie Miles, should be enrolled as a citizen of said Nation; that the Department, in its letter of May 14, 1904 (I.T.D. 3802,2618), affirmed the Commission's decision as to Rosalie Miles and Louisa Miles, and reversed its decision as to Jennie Murrell Miles, and directed the Commission not to enroll her as a citizen of the Cherokee Nation; that it appears that Jennie Murrell Miles was born September 19, 1901, and that the name of her mother, Rosalie Miles, appears upon the approved roll of citizens of the Creek Nation. The Department quotes from the act of March 3, 1905, and says that "The case is hereby reopened in so far as it affects Jennie Murrell Miles and it is desired that you re-adjudicate the case in so far as is affects said applicant, and accord her any rights to which she may be entitled under the act above referred to."

    Reporting in the matter, I have the honor to advise the Department that the name of said Jennie Murrell Miles is contained in the schedule of new-born Creeks by blood approved by the Department July 28, 1905, opposite Roll No. 116.

Applications for Enrollment of Creek Newborn
Act of 1905   Volume III

                              Respectfully,

                                                            Commissioner.
    Through the
Commissioner of Indian Affairs.

—————

NC 176.

                              Muskogee, Indian Territory, November 12, 1906.

Chief Clerk,
       Cherokee Enrollment Division,
              General Office.

Dear Sir:

   You are hereby advised that the names of Jennie Murrell and Vivian Miles, children of W. S. Miles, an alleged intermarried Cherokee, and Rosalie Miles, a citizen of the Creek Nation, are contained in a schedule of New Born citizens by blood of the Creek Nation, approved by the Secretary of the Interior, July 28, 1905, opposite Nos. 116 and 117.

                              Respectfully,

                                                            Commissioner.

BIRTH AFFIDAVIT.

DEPARTMENT OF THE INTERIOR.
COMMISSION TO THE FIVE CIVILIZED TRIBES.

—————

   IN RE APPLICATION FOR ENROLLMENT, as a citizen of the Creek Nation, of Zelma Fay Applegeet, born on the 14th day of Oct. , 1902

| Name of Father: | W. F. Applegeet | a citizen of the | U.S. | Nation. |
| Name of Mother: | Cora F.   " | a citizen of the | Creek | Nation. |

                    Postoffice   Bixby, Ind. Ter.

Applications for Enrollment of Creek Newborn
Act of 1905   Volume III

AFFIDAVIT OF ~~MOTHER~~. Father

UNITED STATES OF AMERICA, Indian Territory, }
    Western   DISTRICT.

    I, W.F. Applegeet , on oath state that I am 37 years of age and a citizen by birth , of the U.S. Nation; that I am the lawful ~~wife~~ husband of Cora F. Applegeet , who is a citizen, by blood of the Creek Nation; that a female child was born to me on 14th day of October , 1902 , that said child has been named Zelma Fay Applegeet , and is now living.

                                      W. F. Applegeet

Witnesses To Mark:
{

    Subscribed and sworn to before me this 16th day of March, 1905.

                              Allen Henry
    My Commission expires Oct. 19, 1907   Notary Public.

AFFIDAVIT OF ATTENDING ~~PHYSICIAN~~ OR MID-WIFE.

UNITED STATES OF AMERICA, Indian Territory, }
    Western   DISTRICT.

    I, Sarah Berryhill , a mid-wife , on oath state that I attended on Mrs. Cora F. Applegeet , wife of W. F. Applegeet on the 14th day of October , 1902 ; that there was born to her on said date a female child; that said child is now living and is said to have been named Zelma Fay Applegeet

                                      Sarah Berryhill

Witnesses To Mark:
{

    Subscribed and sworn to before me this 16th day of March, 1905.

                              Allen Henry
    My Commission expires Oct. 19, 1907   Notary Public.

Applications for Enrollment of Creek Newborn
Act of 1905 Volume III

BIRTH AFFIDAVIT.

DEPARTMENT OF THE INTERIOR.
COMMISSION TO THE FIVE CIVILIZED TRIBES.

IN RE APPLICATION FOR ENROLLMENT, as a citizen of the CREEK Nation, of Zelma Fay Applegeet, born on the 14th day of Oct. , 1902

Name of Father: W. F. Applegeet   a citizen of the   U.S.   Nation.
Name of Mother: Cora F.   "   a citizen of the   Creek   Nation.

Postoffice   Bixby, Ind. Ter.

(Child present)

AFFIDAVIT OF MOTHER.

UNITED STATES OF AMERICA, Indian Territory,
    WESTERN   DISTRICT.

I, Cora F. Applegeet , on oath state that I am 20 years of age and a citizen by blood , of the Creek Nation; that I am the lawful wife of W.F. Applegeet , who is a citizen, by ----- of the U.S. Nation; that a female child was born to me on 14 day of Oct , 190 , that said child has been named Zelma Fay Applegeet , and was living March 4, 1905.

                              Cora F Applegeet

Witnesses To Mark:

Subscribed and sworn to before me this 13 day of March , 1905.

                              Edw C Griesel
                              Notary Public.

Indian Territory
               ss.
Western District

Charles Bailey being first duly sworn on oath says that he is a duly enrolled citizen of the Creek Nation, that he is well-acquainted with the within named Eugene Willie Maxey and has known him all his live, that he was not present at its birth, that said child was born on or about September 25, 1904, and is now living in good health, that said child is the child of the within named Eugene Maxey, who is a citizen of the United States, but not a citizen of the Creek Nation, and the within named Neosho P. Maxey whose maiden name was Neosho P. Brown a duly enrolled citizen of the Creek Nation.

                              Charles Bailey

Applications for Enrollment of Creek Newborn
Act of 1905   Volume III

Subscribed and sworn to before me March 14, 1905.

Francis R. Brennan
Notary Public.

Indian Territory ⎱
⎰ ss.
Western District ⎰

    Simeon C. Maxey being first duly sworn on oath says that he is the grandfather of the within named Eugene Willie Maxey and has known him all his life, that he was at its mother's home the day it was born in September, 1904, that it is still living, that he is the child of the within named Eugen[sic] Maxey, who is a citizen of the United Stated, but not a citizen of the Creek Nation, that its mother is the within named Neosho P. Maxey whose maiden name was Neosho P. Brown and who is a duly enrolled citizen of the Creek Nation.

Simeon C Maxey

Subscribed and sworn to before me March 14, 1905.

Francis R. Brennan
Notary Public.

BIRTH AFFIDAVIT.

DEPARTMENT OF THE INTERIOR,
COMMISSION TO THE FIVE CIVILIZED TRIBES.

    IN RE Application for Enrollment, as a citizen of the Creek Nation, of Eugene Willie Maxey, born on the 25th day of September, 1904

Name of Father: Eugene Maxey   not a citizen of the CreekNationNation.
Name of Mother: Neosho P. Maxey (nee Brown) a citizen of the   Creek   Nation.

                              Postoffice   Wealaka[sic], Ind. Ter.

AFFIDAVIT OF MOTHER.

UNITED STATES OF AMERICA, Indian Territory, ⎱
    Western   DISTRICT. ⎰

    I, Neosho P. Maxey, on oath state that I am twenty-three years of age and a citizen by blood, of the Creek Nation; that I am the lawful wife of Eugene Maxey, who is not a citizen, by *(blank)* of the Creek Nation; that a male child was born to me on 25th day of September, 1904, that said child has been named Eugene Willie Maxey, and is now living and that my maiden name was Neosho P. Brown by which

Applications for Enrollment of Creek Newborn
Act of 1905 Volume III

name I am on the Creek roll and that my enrollment has been approved by the Secretary of the Interior prior to March 3, 1905.

Neosha P. Maxey

Witnesses To Mark:
- Charlie Bailey Wealaka I.T.
- Simeon C Maxey Sr. Wealaka I.T.

Subscribed and sworn to before me this 14th *day of* March, *1905*.

Francis R. Brennan
Notary Public.

AFFIDAVIT OF ATTENDING PHYSICIAN OR MID-WIFE.

UNITED STATES OF AMERICA, Indian Territory,
Western DISTRICT.

I, Charles E. Coppedge , a Physician , on oath state that I attended on Mrs. Neosho P. Maxey , wife of Eugene Maxey on the 25th day of September , 1904 ; that there was born to her on said date a male child; that said child is now living and is said to have been named Eugene Willie Maxey

Charles E. Coppedge

Witnesses To Mark:
- Charles M. Best Bixby I.T.
- James Hart Bixby I.T.

Subscribed and sworn to before me this 14th *day of* March, *1905*.

Francis R. Brennan
Notary Public.

Indian Territory
Western District } ss.

Charles Bailey being first duly sworn on oath says that he is a duly enrolled citizen of the Creek Nation, that he is well acquainted with the within named Simeon C. Maxey and has known him all his life, that he was present at its birth, that said child was born on January 16, 1903, and is now living in good health, that said child is the child of the within named Eugene Maxey, who is a citizen of the United States, but not a citizen of the Creek Nation, and the within named Neosho P. Maxey whose maiden name was Neosho P. Brown a duly enrolled citizen of the Creek Nation.

Charles Bailey

Applications for Enrollment of Creek Newborn
Act of 1905   Volume III

Subscribed and sworn to before me March 14, 1905.

                         Francis P. Brennan,
                         Notary Public.

BIRTH AFFIDAVIT.

DEPARTMENT OF THE INTERIOR,
COMMISSION TO THE FIVE CIVILIZED TRIBES.

IN RE Application for Enrollment, as a citizen of the Creek Nation, of Simeon C. Maxey, born on the 16th day of January, 1903

Name of Father: Eugene Maxey   not a citizen of the   Creek   Nation.
Name of Mother: Neosho P. Maxey (nee Brown) a citizen of the   Creek   Nation.

                     Postoffice   Wealaka[sic], Ind. Ter.

AFFIDAVIT OF MOTHER.

UNITED STATES OF AMERICA, Indian Territory,
     Western   DISTRICT.

I, Neosho P. Maxey, on oath state that I am twenty-three years of age and a citizen by blood, of the Creek Nation; that I am the lawful wife of Eugene Maxey, who is not a citizen, by *(blank)* of the Creek Nation; that a male child was born to me on 16th day of January, 1903, that said child has been named Simeon C. Maxey, and is now living and that my maiden name was Neosho P. Brown by which name I am on the Creek roll and that my enrollment has been approved by the Secretary of the Interior prior to March 3, 1905.

                         Neosho P. Maxey
Witnesses To Mark:
     { Charles Bailey   Wealaka I.T.
       Simeon C. Maxey Sr. Wealaka I T

Subscribed and sworn to before me this 14th *day of* March, *19*05.

                         Francis R. Brennan
                         Notary Public.

Applications for Enrollment of Creek Newborn
Act of 1905 Volume III

AFFIDAVIT OF ATTENDING PHYSICIAN OR MID-WIFE.

UNITED STATES OF AMERICA, Indian Territory,
    Western   DISTRICT.

    I, Charles E. Coppedge , a Physician , on oath state that I attended on Mrs. Neosho P. Maxey , wife of Eugene Maxey on the 16th day of January , 1903 ; that there was born to her on said date a male child; that said child is now living and is said to have been named Simeon C. Maxey

                              Charles E. Coppedge

Witnesses To Mark:
- Charles M Best   Bixby I.T.
- James Hart   Bixby I.T.

Subscribed and sworn to before me this 14th *day of* March, *1905.*

                              Francis R. Brennan
                              Notary Public.

BIRTH AFFIDAVIT.

DEPARTMENT OF THE INTERIOR.
COMMISSION TO THE FIVE CIVILIZED TRIBES.

IN RE APPLICATION FOR ENROLLMENT, as a citizen of the CREEK Nation, of Adeline Belle Robison , born on the 7 day of April , 1902

Name of Father:	Joe S. Robison	a citizen of the	Creek	Nation.
Name of Mother:	Mattie Robison	a citizen of the	Creek	Nation.

                        Postoffice   Wetumka, Indian Territory.

AFFIDAVIT OF MOTHER.

UNITED STATES OF AMERICA, Indian Territory,
    WESTERN   DISTRICT.

    I, Mattie Robison , on oath state that I am thirty years of age and a citizen by blood , of the Creek Nation; that I am the lawful wife of Joe S. Robison , who is a citizen, by blood of the Creek Nation; that a female child was born to me on 7 day of April , 1902 , that said child has been named Adeline Belle Robison , and is now living.

                              Mattie Robison

Witnesses To Mark:

Applications for Enrollment of Creek Newborn
Act of 1905 Volume III

Subscribed and sworn to before me this day of , 1905.

                                      Jas. P. Atkins
My Com. Exp. June 13- 1908   Notary Public.

AFFIDAVIT OF ATTENDING PHYSICIAN OR MID-WIFE.

UNITED STATES OF AMERICA, Indian Territory, ⎫
    WESTERN   DISTRICT. ⎭

I, Nancy Alexander , a Mid Wife , on oath state that I attended on Mrs. Mattie Robison , wife of Joe S. Robison on the 7 day of April , 1902 ; that there was born to her on said date a female child; that said child is now living and is said to have been named Adeline Belle Robison   her
                                    Nancy x Alexander
Witnesses To Mark: mark
   ⎧ W.D. Atkins Wetumka I.T.
   ⎩ C. P. Hicks Wetumka I.T.

Subscribed and sworn to before me this 10 day of March, 1905.

                                    Jas. P. Atkins
My Com. Exp. June 13- 1908   Notary Public.

BIRTH AFFIDAVIT.

DEPARTMENT OF THE INTERIOR.
COMMISSION TO THE FIVE CIVILIZED TRIBES.

    IN RE APPLICATION FOR ENROLLMENT, as a citizen of the CREEK Nation, of Newman Joseph Robison , born on the 1st day of October , 1903

Name of Father: Joe S. Robison   a citizen of the   Creek   Nation.
Name of Mother: Mattie Robison   a citizen of the   Creek   Nation.

                        Postoffice   Wetumka, Indian Territory.

AFFIDAVIT OF MOTHER.

UNITED STATES OF AMERICA, Indian Territory, ⎫
    WESTERN   DISTRICT. ⎭

    I, Mattie Robison , on oath state that I am thirty years of age and a citizen by blood , of the Creek Nation; that I am the lawful wife of Joe S. Robison , who is a citizen, by blood of the Creek Nation; that a male child was born to me on 1st day

Applications for Enrollment of Creek Newborn
Act of 1905   Volume III

of October, 1903, that said child has been named Newman Joseph Robison, and is now living.

Mattie Robison

Witnesses To Mark:
{

Subscribed and sworn to before me this 10th. day of March, 1905.

Jas. P. Atkins

My Com. Exp. June 13- 1908   Notary Public.

AFFIDAVIT OF ATTENDING PHYSICIAN OR MID-WIFE.

UNITED STATES OF AMERICA, Indian Territory, }
    WESTERN   DISTRICT.

I, Nancy Alexander, a Mid Wife, on oath state that I attended on Mrs. Mattie Robison, wife of Joe S. Robison on the 1st day of October, 1903; that there was born to her on said date a male child; that said child is now living and is said to have been named Newman Joseph Robison

her
Nancy x Alexander
mark

Witnesses To Mark:
{ W.D. Atkins Wetumka I.T.
{ C. P. Hicks Wetumka I.T.

Subscribed and sworn to before me this 10 day of March, 1905.

Jas. P. Atkins

My Com. Exp. June 13- 1908   Notary Public.

BIRTH AFFIDAVIT.

DEPARTMENT OF THE INTERIOR.
COMMISSION TO THE FIVE CIVILIZED TRIBES.

IN RE APPLICATION FOR ENROLLMENT, as a citizen of the Creek or Muskogee Nation, of Lewis Mikey, born on the 23 day of April, 1903

Name of Father:	Josiah Mikey	a Chickasaw Freedman	Nation.
Name of Mother:	Lizzie Mikey	a citizen of the Creek	Nation.

Postoffice   Bristow Ind Tey

Applications for Enrollment of Creek Newborn
Act of 1905   Volume III

AFFIDAVIT OF MOTHER.

UNITED STATES OF AMERICA, Indian Territory,   ⎫
  Western Judicial   DISTRICT. ⎭

 I, Lizzie Mikey , on oath state that I am 29 years of age and a citizen by birth , of the Creek or Muskogee   Nation; that I am the lawful wife of Josiah Mikey , who is a ~~citizen, by~~ a Chickasaw Freedman   ~~of the (blank)   Nation~~; that a   male child was born to me on 23   day of April , 1903 , that said child has been named Lewis Mikey , and was living March 4, 1905.

Lizzie Mikey

Witnesses To Mark:
 {

 Subscribed and sworn to before me this 15 day of March , 1905.

E.W. Sims
Notary Public.

AFFIDAVIT OF ATTENDING PHYSICIAN OR MID-WIFE.

UNITED STATES OF AMERICA, Indian Territory,   ⎫
  Western Judicial   DISTRICT. ⎭

 I, Rhoda Freeman , a Midwife , on oath state that I attended on Mrs. Lizzie Mikey , wife of Josiah Mikey on the 23 day of April , 1903 ; that there was born to her on said date a male child; that said child was living March 4, 1905, and is said to have been named Lewis Mikey

her
Rhoda x Freeman
mark

Witnesses To Mark:
 { N E Wiggins
   (Name Illegible)

 Subscribed and sworn to before me this 15 day of March, 1905.

E.W. Sims
Notary Public.

N.C. 181

Muskogee, Indian Territory, November 10, 1906.

Chief Clerk,
  Choctaw-Chickasaw Enrollment division[sic],
    General Office,

Applications for Enrollment of Creek Newborn
Act of 1905   Volume III

Dear Sir:

You are hereby advised that the name of Lewis Mikey, born April 23, 1903, to Josiah Mikey, an alleged Choctaw Freedman, and Lizzie Mikey, a citizen of the Creek Nation, is contained in the schedule of New Born Creeks by blood, approved by the Secretary of the Interior July 28, 1905, opposite Roll No. 123.

Respectfully,

Commissioner.

NC 182.

DEPARTMENT OF THE INTERIOR,
COMMISSION TO THE FIVE CIVILIZED TRIBES.
MUSKOGEE, I.T. May 30, 1905.

In the matter of the application for the enrollment of Eva Doyle , as a citizen by blood of the Creek Nation.

Burris Doyle, being duly sworn, testified as follows:

Examination by the Commission
Q What is your name? A Burris Doyle.
Q What is your age? A 22.
Q What is your post office address? A Okmulgee.
Q Are you a citizen of the Creek Nation? A Yes sir.
Q To what town do you belong? A Broken Arrow.
Q You have two new born children have you for whom you wish to make application? A Yes sir.
Q Who is the mother of these children? A Ada Doyle.
Q Is she a citizen of the Creek Nation? A No sir.
Q What are the names of these children? A Eva and Walter Doyle.
Q When was Eva born? A December 24, 1902.
Q That child is living now is it? A Yes sir.
Q When was Walter born? A November 28, 1904.
Q Both of these children are present here with you? A yes sir.
Q You made out some affidavits concerning these children at Okmulgee did you? A Yes sir.
Q What date did you give for the birth of Eva? A December 28, 1903.
Q You now admit you were mistaken when you gave that date? A Yes sir.
Q How did you happen to make this mistake? A I just thought it was born in 1903.
Q Did you make a record of the birth of these children? In a Bible or other book? A No sir.
Q You are now positive that this child was born December 24, 1902? A Yes sir.

Applications for Enrollment of Creek Newborn
Act of 1905   Volume III

Ada Doyle, being duly sworn, testified as follows:

Q What is your name? A Ada Doyle.
Q What is your age? A 19.
Q What is your post office? A Okmulgee.
Q You are the lawful wife or[sic] Burris Doyle, are you? A Yes sir.
Q You are not a citizen of the Creek Nation are you? A No sir.
Q You are the mother of Eva and Walter Doyle, are you? A Yes sir.
Q When was Eva born? A December 24, 1902.
Q And when was Walter born? A November 28, 1904.
Q You are positive of these dates are you? A Yes sir.
Q Who was present at the birth of these children A My mother and Dr. Mitchner. Dr. Mitchner was present at the birth of Eva and My mother and Dr. Mitchner both were present at the birth of Walter.
Q Your mother has already made out an affidavit as the midwife in each case, has she? A Yes sir, at Okmulgee.

E. C. Griesel, being duly sworn, on his oath, states that the above and foregoing is a true and correct transcript of his stenographic notes as taken in said cause on said date.

Edw C Griesel

Subscribed and sworn to before me this 31st day of May, 1905.

Zera E Parrish
Notary Public.

BIRTH AFFIDAVIT.

DEPARTMENT OF THE INTERIOR.
COMMISSION TO THE FIVE CIVILIZED TRIBES.

IN RE APPLICATION FOR ENROLLMENT, as a citizen of the CREEK Nation, of Walter Doyle , born on the 28 day of November , 1904

| Name of Father: | Burris Doyle | a citizen of the | Creek | Nation. |
| Name of Mother: | Ada Doyle | a citizen of the | U.S. | Nation. |

Postoffice   Okmulgee, Ind. Ter.

Applications for Enrollment of Creek Newborn
Act of 1905   Volume III

AFFIDAVIT OF MOTHER.

UNITED STATES OF AMERICA, Indian Territory, }
WESTERN DISTRICT.

I, Ada Doyle , on oath state that I am 19 years of age and a citizen ~~by (blank)~~ , of the United States ~~Nation~~; that I am the lawful wife of Burris Doyle , who is a citizen, by blood of the Creek Nation; that a male child was born to me on 28 day of November , 1904 , that said child has been named Walter Doyle , and was living March 4, 1905.

Ada Doyle

Witnesses To Mark:
{

Subscribed and sworn to before me this 13 day of March , 1905.

Edward Merrick
Notary Public.

AFFIDAVIT OF ATTENDING PHYSICIAN OR MID-WIFE.

UNITED STATES OF AMERICA, Indian Territory, }
WESTERN DISTRICT.

I, Burris Doyle ~~, a (blank)~~ , on oath state that I attended on Mrs. Ada Doyle, who is my wife ~~of~~ on the 28 day of November , 1904 ; that there was born to her on said date a male child; that said child was living March 4, 1905, and is said to have been named Walter Doyle

Burris Doyle

Witnesses To Mark:
{

Subscribed and sworn to before me this 13 day of March , 1905.

Edward Merrick
Notary Public.

Applications for Enrollment of Creek Newborn
Act of 1905 Volume III

BIRTH AFFIDAVIT.

DEPARTMENT OF THE INTERIOR.
COMMISSION TO THE FIVE CIVILIZED TRIBES.

IN RE APPLICATION FOR ENROLLMENT, as a citizen of the Creek Nation, of Walter Doyle , born on the 28th. day of November , 1904

Name of Father: Burris Doyle   a citizen of the   Creek   Nation.
Name of Mother: Ada Doyle   a citizen of the United States Nation.

Postoffice   Okmulgee, I.T.

AFFIDAVIT OF MOTHER.

UNITED STATES OF AMERICA, Indian Territory,
Western Judicial   DISTRICT.

I, Ada Doyle , on oath state that I am 19 years of age and a citizen ~~by~~ *(blank)* , of the United States ~~Nation~~; that I am the lawful wife of Burris Doyle , who is a citizen, by Birth of the Creek Nation; that a Male child was born to me on 28th. day of November , 1904 , that said child has been named Walter Doyle , and was living March 4, 1905.

                            Ada Doyle
Witnesses To Mark:

{

Subscribed and sworn to before me this 22nd. day of May , 1905.

My Com Exp July 24 1907   N D Boyd
                                 Notary Public.

AFFIDAVIT OF ATTENDING PHYSICIAN OR MID-WIFE.

UNITED STATES OF AMERICA, Indian Territory,
Western Judicial   DISTRICT.

I, Mary Phegley , a Mid-wife , on oath state that I attended on Mrs. Ada Doyle , wife of Burris Doyle on the 28th. day of November , 1904 ; that there was born to her on said date a Male child; that said child was living March 4, 1905, and is said to have been named Walter Doyle

                            Mary Phegley
Witnesses To Mark:

{

Subscribed and sworn to before me this 22nd. day of May, 1905.

Applications for Enrollment of Creek Newborn
Act of 1905 Volume III

                         N D Boyd
                         Notary Public.
My Com Exp July 24 1907

BIRTH AFFIDAVIT.

DEPARTMENT OF THE INTERIOR.
COMMISSION TO THE FIVE CIVILIZED TRIBES.

IN RE APPLICATION FOR ENROLLMENT, as a citizen of the Creek Nation[sic] Nation, of Eva Doyle , born on the 28th. day of December , 1903

Name of Father:	Burris Doyle	a citizen of the	Creek Nation.
Name of Mother:	Ada Doyle	a citizen of the United States Nation.	

                   Postoffice   Okmulgee, I.T.

AFFIDAVIT OF MOTHER.

UNITED STATES OF AMERICA, Indian Territory,
    Western Judicial   DISTRICT.

     I, Ada Doyle , on oath state that I am 19 years of age and a citizen by Birth , of the United States Nation; that I am the lawful wife of Burris Doyle , who is a citizen, by Blood of the Creek Nation; that a Female child was born to me on 28th. day of December , 1903 , that said child has been named Eva Doyle , and was living March 4, 1905.

                        Ada Doyle

Witnesses To Mark:

     Subscribed and sworn to before me this 22nd. day of May , 1905.

My Com Exp July 24 1907   N D Boyd
                              Notary Public.

AFFIDAVIT OF ATTENDING PHYSICIAN OR MID-WIFE.

UNITED STATES OF AMERICA, Indian Territory,
    Western Judicial   DISTRICT.

     I, Mary Phegley , a Mid-wife , on oath state that I attended on Mrs. Ada Doyle , wife of Burris Doyle on the 28th. day of December , 1903 ; that there was born to her on said date a Female child; that said child was living March 4, 1905, and is said to have been named Eva Doyle

Applications for Enrollment of Creek Newborn
Act of 1905   Volume III

Mary Phegley

Witnesses To Mark:
{

Subscribed and sworn to before me this 22nd. day of May, 1905.

N D Boyd

My Com Exp July 24 1907   Notary Public.

BIRTH AFFIDAVIT.

DEPARTMENT OF THE INTERIOR.
COMMISSION TO THE FIVE CIVILIZED TRIBES.

IN RE APPLICATION FOR ENROLLMENT, as a citizen of the Creek Nation, of Eva Doyle, born on the 24 day of Dec , 1902

Name of Father:	Burris Doyle	a citizen of the	Creek	Nation.
Broken Arrow				
Name of Mother:	Ada Doyle	a citizen of the	U. S.	Nation.

Postoffice   Okmulgee

AFFIDAVIT OF ~~MOTHER~~. Father

Child Present

UNITED STATES OF AMERICA, Indian Territory, ⎫
  Western   DISTRICT.   ⎭

I, Burris Doyle , on oath state that I am 22 years of age and a citizen by blood , of the Creek Nation; that I am the lawful ~~wife~~ Hus of Ada Doyle , who is a citizen, by ----- of the U.S. Nation; that a female child was born to me on 24 day of Dec. , 1902 , that said child has been named Eva Doyle , and was living March 4, 1905.

Burris Doyle

Witnesses To Mark:
{
  Subscribed and sworn to before me this 30 day of May, 1905.

Edw C Griesel
Notary Public.

Applications for Enrollment of Creek Newborn
Act of 1905 Volume III

BIRTH AFFIDAVIT.

DEPARTMENT OF THE INTERIOR.
COMMISSION TO THE FIVE CIVILIZED TRIBES.

IN RE APPLICATION FOR ENROLLMENT, as a citizen of the CREEK Nation, of Eva Doyle, born on the 24 day of December , 1902

Name of Father:	Burris Doyle	a citizen of the	Creek	Nation.
Name of Mother:	Ada Doyle	a citizen of the	U.S.	Nation.

Postoffice Okmulgee, Ind. Ter.

AFFIDAVIT OF MOTHER.

UNITED STATES OF AMERICA, Indian Territory, }
WESTERN   DISTRICT.

I, Ada Doyle , on oath state that I am 19 years of age and a citizen ~~by (blank)~~ , of the United States ~~Nation~~; that I am the lawful wife of Burris Doyle , who is a citizen, by blood of the Creek Nation; that a female   child was born to me on 24" day of December , 1902 , that said child has been named Eva Doyle , and was living March 4, 1905.

Ada Doyle

Witnesses To Mark:
{

Subscribed and sworn to before me this 13th day of March , 1905.

Edward Merrick
Notary Public.

AFFIDAVIT OF ATTENDING PHYSICIAN OR MID-WIFE.

UNITED STATES OF AMERICA, Indian Territory, }
WESTERN   DISTRICT.

I, Burris Doyle   ~~, a (blank)~~ , on oath state that I attended on Mrs. Ada Doyle, who is my wife ~~of~~ on the   24" day of December , 1904 ; that there was born to her on said date a female child; that said child was living March 4, 1905, and is said to have been named   Eva Doyle

Burris Doyle

Witnesses To Mark:
{

Applications for Enrollment of Creek Newborn
Act of 1905   Volume III

Subscribed and sworn to before me this 13" day of March , 1905.

Edward Merrick
Notary Public.

NC 182.

Muskogee, Indian Territory, May 19, 1905.

Burris Doyle,
    Okmulgee, Indian Territory.

Dear Sir:

    In the matter of the application for the enrollment of your minor children, Eva and Walter Doyle, as citizens of the Creek Nation, you are advised that the Commission requires the affidavit of the midwife or physician in attendance at the birth of said child.

    There is herewith enclosed a blank form of birth affidavit, and in executing same care should be exercised to see that all blanks are properly filled, all names written in full and in the event that the person signing the affidavit is unable to write, signature by mark must be attested by two witnesses. Each affidavit must be executed before a Notary Public and the notarial seal and signature of the officer must be attached to each separate affidavit.

Respectfully,

BC.   Chairman.

NC 182

Muskogee, Indian Territory, May 25, 1905.

Ada Doyle,
    Okmulgee, Indian Territory.

Dear Madam:

    There are on file with the Commission affidavits relative to the birth of your minor child, Eva Doyle which contains conflicting dates.

    You are required to appear before the Commission at its office at Muskogee, Indian Territory, for the purpose of being examined under oath.

Respectfully,

Chairman.

Applications for Enrollment of Creek Newborn
Act of 1905   Volume III

N.C. 182   COPY

Okmulgee, I. T., May 27, 1905.

Commission to the Five Civilized Tribes,
    Muskogee, I. T.

Gentlemen:

Referring to your communication of the 25th, inst, NC 182 addressed to Ada Doyle we note that there has been some error in the affidavit relative to the birth of the minor child of Ada Doyle, and you advise her in the letter to appear at your office in Muskogee for the purpose of being examined under oath in regard to the matter.

Ada Doyle advises us that the affidavit reads date of birth Dec. 28, 1903, when it should read Dec. 24, 1902. She further advises us that she is financially unable to make the trip to Muskogee unless it is absolutely necessary for her to com, and requests us to ask you if the matter can not be arranged from here by affidavit or other proper proof.

We you please advise us in the matter. Thanking you very kindly we beg to remain.

Yours very truly,

(Signed) Moore & Noble-

NC 183.

Muskogee, Indian Territory, May 19, 1905.

Chapley Yarholar,
    Wetumka, Indian Territory.

Dear Sir:

In the matter of the application for the enrollment of your minor child, Clarence Yarholar, as a citizen of the Creek Nation, you are advised that the Commission requires the affidavit of the midwife or physician in attendance at the birth of said child.

There is herewith enclosed a blank form of birth affidavit, and in executing same care should be exercised to see that all blanks are properly filled, all names written in full and in the event that the person signing the affidavit is unable to write, signature by mark must be attested by two witnesses. Each affidavit must be executed before a Notary

Applications for Enrollment of Creek Newborn
Act of 1905   Volume III

Public and the notarial seal and signature of the officer must be attached to each separate affidavit.

Respectfully,

BC.   Chairman.

BIRTH AFFIDAVIT.

DEPARTMENT OF THE INTERIOR.
COMMISSION TO THE FIVE CIVILIZED TRIBES.

IN RE APPLICATION FOR ENROLLMENT, as a citizen of the CREEK Nation, of Clarence Yarholar, born on the 5 day of Feby, 1903

Name of Father:	Chapley Yarholar	a citizen of the Creek	Nation.
Name of Mother:	Wisey Yarholar	a citizen of the Creek	Nation.

Postoffice   Wetumka, I.T.

AFFIDAVIT OF MOTHER.

UNITED STATES OF AMERICA, Indian Territory,
    WESTERN   DISTRICT.

    I, Wisey Yarholar, on oath state that I am 38 years of age and a citizen by blood, of the Creek Nation; that I am the lawful wife of Chapley Yarholar, who is a citizen, by blood of the Creek Nation; that a male child was born to me on 5" day of Feb'y, 1903, that said child has been named Clarence Yarholar, and was living March 4, 1905.

Wisey Yarholar

Witnesses To Mark:
{

    Subscribed and sworn to before me this 13" day of March, 1905.

Edward Merrick
Notary Public.

AFFIDAVIT OF ATTENDING PHYSICIAN OR MID-WIFE.

UNITED STATES OF AMERICA, Indian Territory,
    WESTERN   DISTRICT.

    I, Chapley Yarholar ~~, a~~, on oath state that I attended on Mrs. Wisey Yarholar, who is my, wife ~~of~~ on the 5" day of February, 1903; that there was born to her

Applications for Enrollment of Creek Newborn
Act of 1905   Volume III

on said date a male child; that said child was living March 4, 1905, and is said to have been named   Clarence Yarholar

                                        Chapley Yarholar

Witnesses To Mark:
{

    Subscribed and sworn to before me this 13" day of March, 1905.

                                        Edward Merrick
                                        Notary Public.

                                                          N C 183

BIRTH AFFIDAVIT.
                    DEPARTMENT OF THE INTERIOR.
             COMMISSION TO THE FIVE CIVILIZED TRIBES.

    IN RE APPLICATION FOR ENROLLMENT, as a citizen of the Creek Nation, of Clarence Yahola, born on the 5" day of Feby, 1903

Name of Father: Chapley Yahola   a citizen of the   Creek   Nation.
Name of Mother: Wisey   "   a citizen of the   Creek   Nation.

                            Postoffice   Wetumka, IT

                                  Witnesses
                       AFFIDAVIT OF MOTHER.

UNITED STATES OF AMERICA, Indian Territory, ⎫
    Western   DISTRICT. ⎭

                                                             we are
        We I, J.T. Canard and Isaac McGirt, on oath state that I am   years of age and a citizens by   blood, of the   Creek   Nation; that I am the we are personally acquainted with Wisey Yarhola lawful wife of   Chapley Yahola, who is a citizen, by   blood of the Creek   Nation; that a male   child was born to me her on or about the 5"   day of Feb., 1903, that said child has been named Clarence Yahola, and is now living.

                                      J.T. Canard
                                          his
Witnesses To Mark: Isaac x McGirt
  { Henry G. Hains   mark
    Jesse McDermott

Applications for Enrollment of Creek Newborn
Act of 1905   Volume III

Subscribed and sworn to before me this 18" day of Sept., 1905.

                    J. McDermott
My Com. Ex   Notary Public.
July 25" 1907

BIRTH AFFIDAVIT.

DEPARTMENT OF THE INTERIOR.
COMMISSION TO THE FIVE CIVILIZED TRIBES.

IN RE APPLICATION FOR ENROLLMENT, as a citizen of the Creek Nation, of Clarence Yarholar, born on the ~~fifth~~ 5th day of Feby, 1903

Name of Father: Chapley Yarholar   a citizen of the   Creek   Nation.
Name of Mother: Wisey Yarholar   a citizen of the   Creek   Nation.

                  Postoffice   Wetumka, I.T.

AFFIDAVIT OF MOTHER.

UNITED STATES OF AMERICA, Indian Territory,
    Western   DISTRICT.

    I, Wisey Yarholar, on oath state that I am 38 years of age and a citizen by blood, of the Creek Nation; that I am the lawful wife of Chapley Yarholar, who is a citizen, by blood of the Creek Nation; that a Male child was born to me on 5th day of Feby, 1903, that said child has been named Clarence Yarholar, and was living March 4, 1905.

                              Wisey Yarholar
Witnesses To Mark:

{

Subscribed and sworn to before me this 29th day of May, 1905.

                              Jeff T. Canard
                              Notary Public.
    Com. Ex. Aug 2-1906

AFFIDAVIT OF ATTENDING PHYSICIAN OR MID-WIFE.

UNITED STATES OF AMERICA, Indian Territory,
    Western   DISTRICT.

    I, Chapley Yarholar, a midwife, on oath state that I attended on Mrs. Wisey Yarholar, wife of Chapley Yarholar on the 5th day of Feby, 1903; that there was

Applications for Enrollment of Creek Newborn
Act of 1905   Volume III

born to her on said date a Male child; that said child was living March 4, 1905, and is said to have been named   Clarence Yarholar

Chapley Yarholar

Witnesses To Mark:

{

Subscribed and sworn to before me this 29th day of May , 1905.

Jeff T. Canard
Notary Public.

Com. Ex. Aug 2-1906

NC 184.

Muskogee, Indian Territory, May 19, 1905.

Gilbert R. Gregory,
    Inola, Indian Territory.

Dear Sir:

    In the matter of the application for the enrollment of your minor child, Rose Ida Gregory, as a citizen of the Creek Nation, you are advised that the Commission requires the affidavit of the midwife or physician in attendance at the birth of said child.

    There is herewith enclosed a blank form of birth affidavit, and in executing same care should be exercised to see that all blanks are properly filled, all names written in full and in the event that the person signing the affidavit is unable to write, signature by mark must be attested by two witnesses. Each affidavit must be executed before a Notary Public and the notarial seal and signature of the officer must be attached to each separate affidavit.

Respectfully,

BC.   Chairman.

Applications for Enrollment of Creek Newborn
Act of 1905   Volume III

BIRTH AFFIDAVIT.

DEPARTMENT OF THE INTERIOR.
COMMISSION TO THE FIVE CIVILIZED TRIBES.

IN RE APPLICATION FOR ENROLLMENT, as a citizen of the CREEK Nation, of Rose Ida Gregory, born on the 17" day of January , 1904

Name of Father:	Gilbert R. Gregory	a citizen of the	Creek Nation.
Name of Mother:	Ina Gregory	a citizen of the United States	Nation.

Postoffice   Inola, Ind Ter

AFFIDAVIT OF MOTHER.

UNITED STATES OF AMERICA, Indian Territory,
    WESTERN   DISTRICT.

I, Ina Gregory , on oath state that I am 18 years of age and a citizen by ----- , of the United States ~~Nation~~; that I am the lawful wife of Gilbert R. Gregory , who is a citizen, by blood of the Creek Nation; that a female child was born to me on 17th day of January , 1904 , that said child has been named Rose Ida Gregory   , and was living March 4, 1905.

                                    her
Witnesses To Mark: Ina x Gregory
   { Edward Merrick   mark
    Irwin Donovan

Subscribed and sworn to before me this 13" day of March , 1905.

                                  Edward Merrick
                                  Notary Public.

AFFIDAVIT OF ATTENDING PHYSICIAN OR MID-WIFE.

UNITED STATES OF AMERICA, Indian Territory,
    WESTERN   DISTRICT.

I, Gilbert R. Gregory ~~, a ,~~ on oath state that I attended on Mrs. Ina Gregory, who is my wife ~~of~~ on the 17" day of January , 1904 ; that there was born to her on said date a female child; that said child was living March 4, 1905, and is said to have been named   Rose Ida Gregory

                                  Gilbert R.Gregory

Witnesses To Mark:

{

Applications for Enrollment of Creek Newborn
Act of 1905   Volume III

Subscribed and sworn to before me this 13" day of March, 1905.

                                            Edward Merrick
                                            Notary Public.

BIRTH AFFIDAVIT.

DEPARTMENT OF THE INTERIOR.
COMMISSION TO THE FIVE CIVILIZED TRIBES.

IN RE APPLICATION FOR ENROLLMENT, as a citizen of the Creek Nation, of Rose Ida Gregory, born on the 17th day of January, 1904

Name of Father:	Gilbert R. Gregory	a citizen of the	Creek	Nation.
Name of Mother:	Ina Gregory	a citizen of	no	Nation.

                              Postoffice   Inola, I. T.

AFFIDAVIT OF MOTHER.

UNITED STATES OF AMERICA, Indian Territory, ⎫
      Western   **DISTRICT.** ⎭

    I, Ina Gregory, on oath state that I am 18 years of age and a citizen by Birth , of the United States ~~Nation~~; that I am the lawful wife of Gilbert R. Gregory , who is a citizen, by Blood of the Creek Nation; that a Female child was born to me on 17th day of January , 1904 , that said child has been named Rose Ida Gregory , and was living March 4, 1905.

                                        ina gregory
Witnesses To Mark: Ina Gregory
{

Subscribed and sworn to before me this 22nd day of May , 1905.

       Com expires Sept 6-08   T Rice
                                                  Notary Public.

AFFIDAVIT OF ATTENDING PHYSICIAN OR MID-WIFE.

UNITED STATES OF AMERICA, Indian Territory, ⎫
      Western   **DISTRICT.** ⎭

    I, Susan P. Blackwell , a mid wife , on oath state that I attended on Mrs. Ina Gregory , wife of Gilbert R. Gregory on the 17th day of January , 1904 ; that there

Applications for Enrollment of Creek Newborn
Act of 1905 Volume III

was born to her on said date a female child; that said child was living March 4, 1905, and is said to have been named *(blank)*

Witnesses To Mark:
{

Susan B Blackill
Susan P Blackwell

Subscribed and sworn to before me this 22nd day of May , 1905.

Com expires Sept 6-08   T Rice
                                            Notary Public.

BIRTH AFFIDAVIT.

DEPARTMENT OF THE INTERIOR.
COMMISSION TO THE FIVE CIVILIZED TRIBES.

IN RE APPLICATION FOR ENROLLMENT, as a citizen of the Creek Nation, of Dessie Lee Dawson, born on the 22^d day of October , 1902

Name of Father: Cooper Dawson   a citizen of the United States Nation.
Name of Mother: Martha Wells   a citizen of the   Creek   Nation.

Postoffice   Checotah Ind. Ter.

AFFIDAVIT OF MOTHER.

UNITED STATES OF AMERICA, Indian Territory,
     Western   DISTRICT.

I, Martha Wells , on oath state that I am 24 years of age and a citizen by Blood , of the Creek Nation; that I am ~~the lawful wife of~~ Unmarried , who is a citizen, by *(blank)* of the *(blank)* Nation; that a Female child was born to me on 22^d day of October , 1902 , that said child has been named Dessie Lee Dawson , and was living March 4, 1905.

                                            Martha Wells
Witnesses To Mark:
{ J W Combs
  JB Morrow

Subscribed and sworn to before me this 13th day of March , 1905.

                                            JB Morrow
My Commission Expires July 1, 1906.   Notary Public.

Applications for Enrollment of Creek Newborn
Act of 1905 Volume III

AFFIDAVIT OF ATTENDING PHYSICIAN OR MID-WIFE.

UNITED STATES OF AMERICA, Indian Territory, ⎫
    Western   DISTRICT.   ⎬

I, Lydia Wells , a Midwife , on oath state that I attended on ~~Mrs.~~ Martha Wells, ~~wife of~~ Unmarried on the 22^d day of October , 1902 ; that there was born to her on said date a Female child; that said child was living March 4, 1905, and is said to have been named Dessie Lee Dawson

her
Lydia x Wells
mark

Witnesses To Mark:
{ J W Combs
{ JB Morrow

Subscribed and sworn to before me this 13th day of March , 1905.

JB Morrow
Notary Public.

My Commission Expires July 1, 1906.

BA-3

DEPARTMENT OF THE INTERIOR,
COMMISSION TO THE FIVE CIVILIZED TRIBES.

Muskogee, Indian Territory, March 14, 1905.

In the matter of the application for the enrollment of Iola Arnett as a citizen by blood of the Creek Nation.

Albert Arnett, being duly sworn, testified as follows:

EXAMINATION BY THE COMMISSION:
Q What is your name? A Albert Arnett.
Q What is your age? A 34.
Q What is your postoffice? A Checotah.
Q Are you a citizen of the Creek Nation? A No sir.
Q What is the name of your wife? A Maggie.
Q Is she a citizen of the Creek Nation? A Yes sir.
Q Enrolled under what name? A Yes sir. Her name if Maggie Smith and enrolled as Maggie Arnett.
Q Is she the mother of your child? A Yes sir.
Q Is Iola living? A Yes sir.
Q How old is she now? A This coming July will be four years old; born in 1901.

Applications for Enrollment of Creek Newborn
Act of 1905   Volume III

The mother of the child is identified as Maggie Arnett on Creek Indian card, field No. 805, and her name is contained in partial list of Creek citizens by blood approved by the Secretary of the Interior March 13, 1902, Roll No. 2609.

The witness is notified that it will be necessary to send in the affidavit of the mother that this child is now living and was living March 4, 1905 on the 4th day of March 1905.

INDIAN TERRITORY,)
Western District.)
)   I, J. Y. Miller, a stenographer to the Commission
)   to the Five Civilized Tribes, do hereby certify
            that the above and foregoing is a true and complete translation of my notes as same appear in my stenographic report of this case.

JY Miller

Sworn to and subscribed before me
this the 24 day of April, 1905.

My Comm. expires April 11, 1909.

Zera E Parrish
Notary Public.

BIRTH AFFIDAVIT.
DEPARTMENT OF THE INTERIOR,
COMMISSION TO THE FIVE CIVILIZED TRIBES.

IN RE Application for Enrollment, as a citizen of the Creek Nation, of Iola Arnett, born on the 20th day of July, 1901

Name of Father:	A. W. Arnett	a citizen of the	Creek	Nation.
Name of Mother:	Maggie Arnett	a citizen of the	Creek	Nation.

Postoffice   Checotah I.T.

AFFIDAVIT OF MOTHER.

UNITED STATES OF AMERICA, Indian Territory,
Northern   DISTRICT.

I, Maggie Arnett, on oath state that I am 22 years of age and a citizen by Blood, of the Creek Nation; that I am the lawful wife of A. W. Arnett, who is a citizen, by marriage of the Creek Nation; that a Female child was born to me on 20th day of July, 1901, that said child has been named Iola Arnett, and is now living.

her
Maggie Arnett x
mark

Applications for Enrollment of Creek Newborn
Act of 1905   Volume III

Witnesses To MarWitnesses[sic]:
{   Cora Roberts
    JB Morrow

Subscribed and sworn to before me this 2^d *day of* August, *190*1.
My Commission Expires
September 9, 1902   JB Morrow
                                            Notary Public.

AFFIDAVIT OF ATTENDING PHYSICIAN OR MID-WIFE.

UNITED STATES OF AMERICA, Indian Territory,
    Northern   DISTRICT.

I, J. M. Vanderpool , a Physician , on oath state that I attended on Mrs. Maggie Arnett , wife of A. W. Arnett on the 20th day of July , 1901 ; that there was born to her on said date a Female child; that said child is now living and is said to have been named Iola Arnett

                                J. M. Vanderpool M.D.

Witnesses To Mark:
{

Subscribed and sworn to before me this 2^d *day of* August, *190*1.
My Commission Expires
September 9, 1902   JB Morrow
                                            Notary Public.

SUPPLEMENTAL PROOF.
DEPARTMENT OF THE INTERIOR,
COMMISSION TO THE FIVE CIVILIZED TRIBES.

IN RE Application for Enrollment, as a citizen of the Creek (or Muskogee) Nation, of Iola Arnett , born on the 20 day of July , 1901

Name of Father: AW Arnett   a citizen of the United States ~~Nation~~.
Name of Mother: Maggie Arnett   a citizen of the   Creek   Nation.

                        Postoffice   Checotah I.T.

Applications for Enrollment of Creek Newborn
Act of 1905   Volume III

AFFIDAVIT OF PARENT.
(To be made if child is now living)

UNITED STATES OF AMERICA,
    Indian Territory,
(blank)   DISTRICT.

I, Albert W Arnett , on oath state that I am 31 years of age and a citizen by *(blank)* , of the ~~Creek (or Muskogee) Nation~~ United States; that I am the Father of Iola Arnett a female child who was born on the 20 day of July , 1901, that said child is now living.

Albert W Arnett

Witnesses To Mark:

Subscribed and sworn to before me this 4 day of November, 1902.

W.A. (Illegible)
Notary Public.

My Commission expires Sept. 4, 1906.

BIRTH AFFIDAVIT.

DEPARTMENT OF THE INTERIOR,
COMMISSION TO THE FIVE CIVILIZED TRIBES.

IN RE Application for Enrollment, as a citizen of the Creek Nation, of Iola Arnett , born on the 20th day of July, 1901

Name of Father: A.W. Arnett   a citizen of the United States Nation.
Name of Mother: Maggie Arnett   a citizen of the   Creek   Nation.

Post-Office: Checotah I.T.

AFFIDAVIT OF MOTHER.

UNITED STATES OF AMERICA,
    Indian Territory,
  Western   District.

I, Maggie Arnett , on oath state that I am 28 years of age and a citizen by Blood , of the Creek Nation; that I am the lawful wife of A. W. Arnett , who is a citizen, by *(blank)* of the United States Nation; that a Female child was born to me on 20th day of July , 1901 , that said child has been named Iola Arnett , and is now living.

Maggie Arnett

Applications for Enrollment of Creek Newborn
Act of 1905   Volume III

WITNESSES TO MARK:
{

Subscribed and sworn to before me this 15th *day of* March, 1905.

My Commission Expires July 1, 1906.   JB Morrow
                                                              Notary Public.

BIRTH AFFIDAVIT.

DEPARTMENT OF THE INTERIOR.
COMMISSION TO THE FIVE CIVILIZED TRIBES.

IN RE APPLICATION FOR ENROLLMENT, as a citizen of the Creek Nation, of Iola Arnett, born on the 20th day of July, 1901

Name of Father:	Albert W Arnett	a citizen of the United States Nation.
Name of Mother:	Maggie Arnett	a citizen of the Creek Nation.

Postoffice   Checotah I.T.

AFFIDAVIT OF MOTHER.

UNITED STATES OF AMERICA, Indian Territory, }
    Western   DISTRICT.

I, Maggie Arnett, on oath state that I am 29 years of age and a citizen by blood, of the Creek Nation; that I am the lawful wife of Albert W. Arnett, who is a citizen, by *(blank)* of the United States ~~Nation~~; that a Female child was born to me on 20th day of July, 1901, that said child has been named Iola, and was living March 4, 1905.

                                                              Maggie Arnett

Witnesses To Mark:
{

Subscribed and sworn to before me this 20th day of May, 1905.

                                                    (Name Illegible)
My Commission Expires May 16, 1909.   Notary Public.

Applications for Enrollment of Creek Newborn
Act of 1905 Volume III

AFFIDAVIT OF ATTENDING PHYSICIAN OR MID-WIFE.

UNITED STATES OF AMERICA, Indian Territory,
Central DISTRICT.

I, J. M. Vanderpool , a Physician , on oath state that I attended on Mrs. Maggie Arnett , wife of Albert W. Arnett on the 20th day of July , 1901 ; that there was born to her on said date a Female child; that said child was living March 4, 1905, and is said to have been named Iola

J. M. Vanderpool M.d[sic].

Witnesses To Mark:

Subscribed and sworn to before me this 24th day of May, 1905.

WA Foyil
Notary Public.

My commission expires Feb. 28-1907

NC 186.

Muskogee, Indian Territory, May 19, 1905.

A. W. Arnett,
Checotah, Indian Territory.

Dear Sir:

In the matter of the application for the enrollment of your minor child, Iola Arntt, as a citizen of the Creek Nation, you are advised that the Commission requires the affidavit of the midwife or physician in attendance at the birth of said child.

There is herewith enclosed a blank form of birth affidavit, and in executing same care should be exercised to see that all blanks are properly filled, all names written in full and in the event that the person signing the affidavit is unable to write, signature by mark must be attested by two witnesses. Each affidavit must be executed before a Notary Public and the notarial seal and signature of the officer must be attached to each separate affidavit.

Respectfully,

BC. Chairman.

Applications for Enrollment of Creek Newborn
Act of 1905 Volume III

BIRTH AFFIDAVIT.

DEPARTMENT OF THE INTERIOR.
COMMISSION TO THE FIVE CIVILIZED TRIBES.

IN RE APPLICATION FOR ENROLLMENT, as a citizen of the CREEK Nation, of Oscar Reynolds, born on the 21 day of September, 1904

Name of Father: Clarence *(no other name given)* a citizen of the U.S. Nation.
Name of Mother: Leila Reynolds a citizen of the Creek Nation.

Postoffice Checotah

AFFIDAVIT OF MOTHER.

UNITED STATES OF AMERICA, Indian Territory,
WESTERN DISTRICT.

I, Annie Minton, on oath state that I am 30 years of age and a citizen by blood, of the Creek Nation; that I am the lawful ~~wife~~ sister of Mrs. Leila Reynolds, who is a citizen, by blood of the Creek Nation; that a male child was born to ~~me~~ her on 21 day of September, 1904, that said child has been named Oscar Reynolds, and is now living.

Amelia Minton

Witnesses To Mark:
{

Subscribed and sworn to before me this 11th day of Mar., 1905.

My Commission J. McDermott
Expires July 25" 1907 Notary Public.

BIRTH AFFIDAVIT.

DEPARTMENT OF THE INTERIOR.
COMMISSION TO THE FIVE CIVILIZED TRIBES.

IN RE APPLICATION FOR ENROLLMENT, as a citizen of the Creek Nation, of Oscar Lee Reynolds, born on the 21st day of September, 1904

Name of Father: Clarence Reynolds a citizen of the United States Nation.
Name of Mother: Leila Reynolds (nee Price) a citizen of the Creek Nation.

Postoffice Checotah I.T.

Applications for Enrollment of Creek Newborn
Act of 1905   Volume III

AFFIDAVIT OF MOTHER.

UNITED STATES OF AMERICA, Indian Territory,
Western DISTRICT.

   I, Leila Reynolds (nee Price), on oath state that I am 26 years of age and a citizen by Blood, of the Creek Nation; that I am the lawful wife of Clarence Reynolds, who is a citizen, by *(blank)* of the United States Nation; that a male child was born to me on 21st day of September, 1904, that said child has been named Oscar Lee Reynolds, and was living March 4, 1905.

Leila Reynolds (nee Price)

Witnesses To Mark:

   Subscribed and sworn to before me this 23^d day of May, 1905.

   My Commission Expires July 1, 1906.   JB Morrow
                                                                     Notary Public.

AFFIDAVIT OF ATTENDING PHYSICIAN OR MID-WIFE.

UNITED STATES OF AMERICA, Indian Territory,
Western DISTRICT.

   I, George W. McGuire, a Physician, on oath state that I attended on Mrs. Leila Reynolds, wife of Clarence Reynolds on the 21st day of September, 1904; that there was born to her on said date a male child; that said child was living March 4, 1905, and is said to have been named Oscar Lee Reynolds

Geo W. McGuire MD

Witnesses To Mark:

   Subscribed and sworn to before me this 23^d day of May, 1905.

   My Commission Expires July 1, 1906.   JB Morrow
                                                                     Notary Public.

NC 187.

Muskogee, Indian Territory, May 20, 1905.

Leila Reynolds,
   Checotah, Indian Territory.

Dear Madam:

Applications for Enrollment of Creek Newborn
Act of 1905 Volume III

There is on file with the Commission an affidavit executed by Annie Minton, relative to the birth of your minor child, Oscar Lee Reynolds, you are advised that the Commission requires your affidavit and the affidavit of the midwife or physician in attendance at the birth of said child.

There is herewith enclosed a blank form of birth affidavit, and in executing same care should be exercised to see that all blanks are properly filled, all names written in full and in the event that the person signing the affidavit is unable to write, signature by mark must be attested by two witnesses. Each affidavit must be executed before a Notary Public and the notarial seal and signature of the officer must be attached to each separate affidavit.

Respectfully,

BC.   Chairman.

BIRTH AFFIDAVIT.

DEPARTMENT OF THE INTERIOR.
COMMISSION TO THE FIVE CIVILIZED TRIBES.

IN RE APPLICATION FOR ENROLLMENT, as a citizen of the Creek Nation, of Joseph Pressgrove, born on the 20th day of May, 1903

Name of Father: Aaron Pressgrove   a citizen of the United States Nation.
Name of Mother: Lizzie Pressgrove (nee Wells) a citizen of the   Creek   Nation.

Postoffice   Checotah Ind. Ter.

AFFIDAVIT OF MOTHER.

UNITED STATES OF AMERICA, Indian Territory, ⎱
    Western   DISTRICT.   ⎰

I, Lizzie Pressgrove (nee Wells), on oath state that I am 20 years of age and a citizen by Blood, of the Creek Nation; that I am the lawful wife of Aaron Pressgrove, who is a citizen, by ----- of the United States Nation; that a male child was born to me on 20th day of May, 1903, that said child has been named Joseph Pressgrove, and was living March 4, 1905.   (nee Wells)
                                       Lizzie Pressgrove

Witnesses To Mark:
{

Subscribed and sworn to before me this 13th day of March, 1905.

Applications for Enrollment of Creek Newborn
Act of 1905   Volume III

My Commission Expires July 1, 1906.   JB Morrow
                                            Notary Public.

AFFIDAVIT OF ATTENDING PHYSICIAN OR MID-WIFE.

UNITED STATES OF AMERICA, Indian Territory,
Western   DISTRICT.

I, Lydia Wells , a Midwife , on oath state that I attended on Mrs. Lizzie Pressgrove , wife of Aaron Pressgrove on the 20th day of May , 1903 ; that there was born to her on said date a male child; that said child was living March 4, 1905, and is said to have been named   Joseph Pressgrove   her
                                                        Lydia x Wells
Witnesses To Mark: mark
{ JB Morrow
{ ARSmith

Subscribed and sworn to before me this 13th day of March, 1905.

My Commission Expires July 1, 1906.   JB Morrow
                                            Notary Public.

NC-189.

Muskogee, Indian Territory, July 25, 1905.

Sarah E. Hackett,
    Wagoner, Indian Territory.

Dear Madam:

In the matter of the application for the enrollment of your minor child, Henryetta Williams, as a citizen of the Creek Nation, you are requested to fill out and execute and to have the physician in attendance at the birth of the child fill out and execute the enclosed affidavits, and return same to this office in the enclosed envelope.

In having the affidavits executed, care should be taken to see that all blanks are properly filled, all names written in full, and in the event that either of you sign by mark, the same must be attested by two witnesses.

Respectfully,

Commissioner.

JYM-25-1

Applications for Enrollment of Creek Newborn
Act of 1905 Volume III

BIRTH AFFIDAVIT.

DEPARTMENT OF THE INTERIOR.
COMMISSION TO THE FIVE CIVILIZED TRIBES.

IN RE APPLICATION FOR ENROLLMENT, as a citizen of the Creek Nation, of Henryetta Williams, born on the 17th day of August, 1904

Name of Father: John H. Williams   a citizen of the United States Nation.
Name of Mother: Sarah E. Hackett Nee Williams   a citizen of the Creek Nation.

Postoffice   Wagoner I.T.

AFFIDAVIT OF MOTHER.

UNITED STATES OF AMERICA, Indian Territory,
Western Judicial   DISTRICT.

I, Sarah E. Hackett Nee Williams, on oath state that I am 22 years of age and a citizen by Blood, of the Creek Nation; that I am the lawful wife of F.J. Hackett, who is a citizen, by *(blank)* of the United States ~~Nation~~; that a Female child was born to me on 17th day of August, 1904, that said child has been named Henryetta Williams, and was living March 4, 1905.

                               Sarah E Hackett

Witnesses To Mark:
{

Subscribed and sworn to before me this 14 day of March, 1905.

                               H R Bonnet
                               Notary Public.

AFFIDAVIT OF ATTENDING PHYSICIAN OR MID-WIFE.

UNITED STATES OF AMERICA, Indian Territory,
Western Judicial   DISTRICT.

I, C.F. McGuire, a Physician, on oath state that I attended on Mrs. Sarah E Hackett, wife of F J Hackett on the 17th day of August, 1*(blank)*; that there was born to her on said date a Female child; that said child was living March 4, 1905, and is said to have been named Henryetta Williams

                               C.F. McGuire M.D.

Witnesses To Mark:
{

Applications for Enrollment of Creek Newborn
Act of 1905 Volume III

Subscribed and sworn to before me this 14 day of March, 1905.

                                                        H R Bonnet
                                                        Notary Public.

My Com Ex July 1st 1906

BIRTH AFFIDAVIT.

DEPARTMENT OF THE INTERIOR.
COMMISSION TO THE FIVE CIVILIZED TRIBES.

      IN RE APPLICATION FOR ENROLLMENT, as a citizen of the Creek Nation, of John F. Williams, born on the 15th day of June, 1902

Name of Father: John H. Williams   a citizen of the   *(blank)*   Nation.
Name of Mother: Sarah E Hackett nee Williams   a citizen of the   Creek   Nation.

                              Postoffice   Wagoner I.T.

AFFIDAVIT OF MOTHER.

UNITED STATES OF AMERICA, Indian Territory, ⎫
    Western Judicial   DISTRICT. ⎭

      I, Sarah E. Hackett Nee Williams, on oath state that I am 22 years of age and a citizen by Blood, of the Creek Nation; that I am the lawful wife of F.J. Hackett, who is a citizen, by *(blank)* of the United States ~~Nation~~; that a male child was born to me on 15th day of June, 1902, that said child has been named John F. Williams, and was living March 4, 1905.

                                            Sarah E. Hackett
Witnesses To Mark:
    {

      Subscribed and sworn to before me this 14 day of March, 1905.

                                            H R Bonnet
                                            Notary Public.

AFFIDAVIT OF ATTENDING PHYSICIAN OR MID-WIFE.

UNITED STATES OF AMERICA, Indian Territory, ⎫
    Western Judicial   DISTRICT. ⎭

      I, Mary L Posey, a Mid Wife, on oath state that I attended on Mrs. Sarah E. Williams, wife of F.J. Hackett on the 15th day of June, 1902; that there was born to

Applications for Enrollment of Creek Newborn
Act of 1905   Volume III

her on said date a male child; that said child was living March 4, 1905, and is said to have been named   John F. Williams

Mary L. Posey

Witnesses To Mark:
{

Subscribed and sworn to before me this 14 day of March, 1905.

H R Bonnet
Notary Public.

My Com Ex July 1st 1906

BIRTH AFFIDAVIT.   N.C. #189.
DEPARTMENT OF THE INTERIOR.
COMMISSION TO THE FIVE CIVILIZED TRIBES.

IN RE APPLICATION FOR ENROLLMENT, as a citizen of the Creek Nation, of Henryetta Williams, born on the 17th day of August, 1904

Name of Father: John H. Williams   a citizen of the United States ~~Nation~~.
                                  (formerly Williams)
Name of Mother: Sarah E. Hackett   a citizen of the   Creek   Nation.

Postoffice   Wagoner, I.T.

AFFIDAVIT OF MOTHER.

UNITED STATES OF AMERICA, Indian Territory, }
    Western   DISTRICT.

I, Sarah E. Hackett , on oath state that I am 22 years of age and a citizen by blood , of the Creek   Nation; that I ~~am~~ was the lawful wife of John H. Williams , who is a citizen, by *(blank)* of the United States ~~Nation~~; that a female child was born to me on 17th day of August , 1904 , that said child has been named Henryetta Williams , and was living March 4, 1905.

Sarah E Hackett

Witnesses To Mark:
{

Subscribed and sworn to before me this 26 day of July , 1905.

H R Bonnet
Notary Public.

Applications for Enrollment of Creek Newborn
Act of 1905 Volume III

AFFIDAVIT OF ATTENDING PHYSICIAN OR MID-WIFE.

UNITED STATES OF AMERICA, Indian Territory,
Western DISTRICT.

I, C. F. McGuire , a physician , on oath state that I attended on Mrs. Sarah E Hackett (formerly Williams), ~~wife of~~ *(blank)* on the 17th day of August , 1904 ; that there was born to her on said date a female child; that said child was living March 4, 1905, and is said to have been named Henryetta Williams

C.F. McGuire

Witnesses To Mark:

{ Subscribed and sworn to before me this 26 day of July, 1905.

H R Bonnet
Notary Public.

My Com Ex July 1st 1906

Western Judicial District
Indian Territory.

I the undersigned Sam'l C Davis being of lawful age and a Citizen of the "Creek Nation" do certify that I am personally acquainted with Meeser Naharkey and his wife Martha Naharkey and knew that there was born to them on the 13" day June 1904, a female child which was named Millie Naharkey, and is now living, Meeser Naharkey is a Creek Physician and there was no one present at the birth of the child except himself and wife.

Samuel C. Davis

Subscribed and acknowledged to before me this the 13" day of March 1905.

My commission Expires July 3" 1906   Robert E Lynch
Notary Public.

BIRTH AFFIDAVIT.

DEPARTMENT OF THE INTERIOR.
COMMISSION TO THE FIVE CIVILIZED TRIBES.

IN RE APPLICATION FOR ENROLLMENT, as a citizen of the Creek Nation[sic] Nation, of Millie Naharkey , born on the 13 day of June, 1904

Applications for Enrollment of Creek Newborn
Act of 1905 Volume III

Name of Father: Mosser Naharkey   a citizen of the Creek Nation.
Name of Mother: Martha Naharkey   a citizen of the Creek Nation.

       Postoffice Inesa Ind Ter

AFFIDAVIT OF MOTHER.

UNITED STATES OF AMERICA, Indian Territory, }
 Western   DISTRICT.

  I, Martha Naharkey, on oath state that I am 28 years of age and a citizen by Blood, of the Creek Nation; that I am the lawful wife of Mooser Naharkey, who is a citizen, by Blood of the Creek Nation; that a Female child was born to me on 13" day of June, 1904, that said child has been named Millie Naharkey, and was living March 4, 1905.

             Her
         Martha x Naharkey
Witnesses To Mark: mark
 { Sam'l. C. David

  Subscribed and sworn to before me this 13 day of March, 1905.

         Robert E Lynch
         Notary Public.

AFFIDAVIT OF ATTENDING PHYSICIAN OR MID-WIFE.

UNITED STATES OF AMERICA, Indian Territory, }
 Western   DISTRICT.

  I, Mooser Naharkey an Indian Physician, on oath state that I attended on Mrs. Martha Naharkey, wife of Myself on the 13 day of June, 1904 ; that there was born to her on said date a Female child; that said child was living March 4, 1905, and is said to have been named Millie Naharkey
There was no one else present   Mooser Naharkey

Witnesses To Mark:
 { Sam'l C Davis

  Subscribed and sworn to before me this 13" day of March, 1905.

         Robert E Lynch
         Notary Public.

Com Ex 7/3/1906

Applications for Enrollment of Creek Newborn
Act of 1905   Volume III

BIRTH AFFIDAVIT.

DEPARTMENT OF THE INTERIOR.
COMMISSION TO THE FIVE CIVILIZED TRIBES.

IN RE APPLICATION FOR ENROLLMENT, as a citizen of the Creek Nation, of Millie Narhahkay, born on the 13 day of June , 1904

Name of Father: Mose Narhahkay   citizen of the   Creek   Nation.
(Tulsa)   nee Red
Name of Mother: Martha Narhahkay   a citizen of the   Creek   Nation.
(Tuckabatchee[sic])
                                 Postoffice   Red Fork

AFFIDAVIT OF MOTHER.
Child Present

UNITED STATES OF AMERICA, Indian Territory,
    Western   DISTRICT.

I, Martha Narhahkay, on oath state that I am 28 years of age and a citizen by blood , of the Creek Nation; that I am the lawful wife of Moses Narhahkay , who is a citizen, by blood of the Creek Nation; that a female child was born to me on 13 day of June , 1904 , that said child has been named Millie Narhahkay , and was living March 4, 1905.

                                                Her
                                   Martha x Narhahkay
Witnesses To Mark: mark
   { David Shelby
     Jesse McDermott

Subscribed and sworn to before me this 28 day of April , 1905.

                                     Edw C Griesel
(Seal)   Notary Public.

AFFIDAVIT OF ATTENDING ~~PHYSICIAN OR MID-WIFE~~.
Father

UNITED STATES OF AMERICA, Indian Territory,
    Western   DISTRICT.

I, Moses Narhahkay , ~~a~~ (blank) , on oath state that I attended on Mrs. Martha Narhahkay ,my wife ~~of~~ on the 13 day of June , 1904 ; that there was born to her on said date a female child; that said child was living March 4, 1905, and is said to have been named Millie Narhahkay

                                     Moses Nahakey
Witnesses To Mark:
   {

Applications for Enrollment of Creek Newborn
Act of 1905   Volume III

Subscribed and sworn to before me this 28 day of April, 1905.

             Edw C Griesel
(Seal)   Notary Public.

BIRTH AFFIDAVIT.

DEPARTMENT OF THE INTERIOR.
COMMISSION TO THE FIVE CIVILIZED TRIBES.

IN RE APPLICATION FOR ENROLLMENT, as a citizen of the Creek Nation, of Annie Lila McIntosh, born on the 24 day of January, 1903

Name of Father:	D. N. McIntosh, Jr.	a citizen of the Creek	Nation.
Name of Mother:	Alice McIntosh	a citizen of the ~~Creek~~ U.S.	Nation.

        Postoffice Checotah, Ind. Ter.

AFFIDAVIT OF MOTHER.

UNITED STATES OF AMERICA, Indian Territory, ⎫
  Western   DISTRICT.   ⎬

  I, Alice McIntosh, on oath state that I am 26 years of age and a citizen by marriage , of the Creek Nation; that I am the lawful wife of D.N. McIntosh, Jr. , who is a citizen, by blood of the Creek Nation; that a female child was born to me on 24 day of January, 1903 , that said child has been named Annie Lila McIntosh , and is now living.

             Alice McIntosh

Witnesses To Mark:
{

Subscribed and sworn to before me this 10 day of March , 1905.

            Ben D. Gross
            Notary Public.

AFFIDAVIT OF ATTENDING PHYSICIAN OR MID-WIFE.

UNITED STATES OF AMERICA, Indian Territory, ⎫
  Western   DISTRICT.   ⎬

  I, Annie Ausborn , a midwife , on oath state that I attended on Mrs. Alice McIntosh , wife of D.N. McIntosh, Jr. on the 24 day of January , 1903 ; that there

Applications for Enrollment of Creek Newborn
Act of 1905   Volume III

was born to her on said date a female   child; that said child is now living and is said to have been named   Annie Lila McIntosh

(Name Illegible)

Witnesses To Mark: (Osborne)

{

Subscribed and sworn to before me this 10 day of March , 1905.

Ben D. Gross
Notary Public.

BIRTH AFFIDAVIT.

DEPARTMENT OF THE INTERIOR.
COMMISSION TO THE FIVE CIVILIZED TRIBES.

IN RE APPLICATION FOR ENROLLMENT, as a citizen of the Creek Nation, of Annie Lila McIntosh, born on the 24 day of Jan , 1903

Name of Father:	D. N. McIntosh, Jr.	a citizen of the Creek	Nation.
Name of Mother:	Alice McIntosh	a citizen of the U.S.	Nation.

Postoffice   Checotah

AFFIDAVIT OF ~~MOTHER~~. father

UNITED STATES OF AMERICA, Indian Territory, ⎫
    Western   DISTRICT.   ⎭

I, D.N. McIntosh, Jr. , on oath state that I am 42 years of age and a citizen by blood , of the Creek Nation; that I am the lawful ~~wife~~ Husband of Alice McIntosh , who is a citizen, by blood of the Creek Nation; that a Female child was born to me on 24 day of Jan , 1903 , that said child has been named Annie Lila McIntosh , and is now living.

D.N. McIntosh Jr

Witnesses To Mark:

{

Subscribed and sworn to before me this 13 day of March, 1905.

Edw C Griesel
Notary Public.

Applications for Enrollment of Creek Newborn
Act of 1905 Volume III

NC 191.

Muskogee, Indian Territory, May 19, 1905.

D.N. McIntosh, Jr.,
    Checotah, Indian Territory.

Dear Sir:

    In the matter of the application for the enrollment of your minor child, Annie Lila McIntosh, as a citizen of the Creek Nation, you are advised that the Commission requires the affidavits of the mother and midwife or physician in attendance at the birth of said child.

    There is herewith enclosed a blank form of birth affidavit, and in executing same care should be exercised to see that all blanks are properly filled, all names written in full and in the event that the person signing the affidavit is unable to write, signatures by mark must be attested by two witnesses. Each affidavit must be executed before a Notary Public and the notarial seal and signature of the officer must be attached to each separate affidavit.

    Respectfully,

BC.   Chairman.

NC 192.

Muskogee, Indian Territory, May 20, 1905.

Canuky Lowe,
    Holdenville, Indian Territory.

Dear Sir:

    In the matter of the application for the enrollment of your minor child, Joe Lowe, as a citizen of the Creek Nation, you are advised that the Commission requires the affidavit of the midwife or physician in attendance at the birth of said child.

    There is herewith enclosed a blank form of birth affidavit, and in executing same care should be exercised to see that all blanks are properly filled, all names written in full and in the event that the person signing the affidavit is unable to write, signature by mark must be attested by two witnesses. Each affidavit must be executed before a Notary Public and the notarial seal and signature of the officer must be attached to each separate affidavit.

Applications for Enrollment of Creek Newborn
Act of 1905 Volume III

Respectfully,

BC.   Chairman.

BIRTH AFFIDAVIT.

DEPARTMENT OF THE INTERIOR.
COMMISSION TO THE FIVE CIVILIZED TRIBES.

IN RE APPLICATION FOR ENROLLMENT, as a citizen of the Creek Nation, of Joe Lowe , born on the 15 day of Aug , 1903

Name of Father: Canuky Lowe   a citizen of the   Creek   Nation.
Tuckabatche[sic]
Name of Mother: Toche (nee Smith)   a citizen of the   "   Nation.
Tuckabatchee[sic]

Postoffice   Holdenville

AFFIDAVIT OF MOTHER.

UNITED STATES OF AMERICA, Indian Territory, ⎫
    Western   DISTRICT.   ⎭

I, Toche Lowe , on oath state that I am 28 years of age and a citizen by blood , of the Creek Nation; that I am the lawful wife of Canuky Lowe , who is a citizen, by blood of the Creek Nation; that a male child was born to me on 15 day of Aug , 1903 , that said child has been named Joe Lowe , and is now living.

                                                          Her
                                         Toche x Lowe
Witnesses To Mark: mark
  ⎧ J McDermott
  ⎩ EC Griesel

Subscribed and sworn to before me this 13 day of March , 1905.

                                           Edw C Griesel
                                                Notary Public.

AFFIDAVIT OF ATTENDING PHYSICIAN OR MID-WIFE.

UNITED STATES OF AMERICA, Indian Territory, ⎫
    Western   DISTRICT.   ⎭

                                                         are personally acquainted with We ~~I~~, the undersigned , a *(blank)* , on oath state that ~~I~~ we ^ ~~attended on~~ Mrs. Tocha Lowe, wife of Canuky Lowe ~~on the~~ *(blank)* ~~day of~~ *(blank)* , ~~I~~*(blank)* ; that

Applications for Enrollment of Creek Newborn
Act of 1905   Volume III

there was born to her on Aug. 15, 1903 ~~said date~~ a male child; that said child is now living and is said to have been named   Joe Lowe

                                           her
                                     Kizzie x Long
                                       mark

Witnesses To Mark: his
  { Alex Posey   Lawyer x Deere
    EC Griesel   mark

Subscribed and sworn to before me this 8 day of Aug, 1905.

                              Edw C Griesel
                                  Notary Public.

BIRTH AFFIDAVIT.

DEPARTMENT OF THE INTERIOR.
COMMISSION TO THE FIVE CIVILIZED TRIBES.

IN RE APPLICATION FOR ENROLLMENT, as a citizen of the CREEK Nation, of Joe Lowe, born on the 15 day of Aug , 1903

Name of Father: Canuky Lowe   a citizen of the   Creek   Nation.
Name of Mother: Toche   "   a citizen of the   "   Nation.

                        Postoffice   Holdenville

Child Present Gr.

                    AFFIDAVIT OF ~~MOTHER~~. father

UNITED STATES OF AMERICA, Indian Territory, ⎱
     WESTERN   DISTRICT. ⎰

    I, Canuky Lowe , on oath state that I am 29 years of age and a citizen by blood , of the Creek Nation; that I am the lawful ~~wife~~ husb of Toche Lowe , who is a citizen, by blood of the Creek Nation; that a male child was born to me on 15 day of Aug, 1903 , that said child has been named Joe Lowe , and is now living.

                                Canuky Lowe

Witnesses To Mark:
  {

Subscribed and sworn to before me this 13 day of March, 1905.

                              Edw C Griesel
                                  Notary Public.

Applications for Enrollment of Creek Newborn
Act of 1905 Volume III

BIRTH AFFIDAVIT.

DEPARTMENT OF THE INTERIOR.
COMMISSION TO THE FIVE CIVILIZED TRIBES.

IN RE APPLICATION FOR ENROLLMENT, as a citizen of the CREEK Nation, of Joe Lowe, born on the 15 day of Aug , 1903

Name of Father:	Canuky Lowe	a citizen of the	Creek	Nation.
Name of Mother:	Tuche Lowe	a citizen of the	Creek	Nation.

Postoffice   Meager I.T.

AFFIDAVIT OF MOTHER.

UNITED STATES OF AMERICA, Indian Territory,
Western   DISTRICT.

I, Tuche Lowe , on oath state that I am 22 years of age and a citizen by blood , of the Creek Nation; that I am the lawful wife of Canuky Lowe , who is a citizen, by blood of the Creek Nation; that a male child was born to me on 15 day of August , 1903 , that said child has been named Joe Lowe , and was living March 4, 1905.

Her
Tuche x Lowe
mark

Witnesses To Mark:
W R Clawson
D D Clawson

Subscribed and sworn to before me this 23 day of May , 1905.

W R Clawson
Notary Public.

AFFIDAVIT OF ATTENDING PHYSICIAN OR MID-WIFE.

UNITED STATES OF AMERICA, Indian Territory,
Western   DISTRICT.

I, Canuky Lowe , a Father , on oath state that I attended on Mrs. Tuchy Lowe , wife of My wife on the 15 day of August , 1903 ; that there was born to her on said date a male child; that said child was living March 4, 1905, and is said to have been named Joe Lowe
and that there was not[sic] other attendant

Canuky Lowe

Applications for Enrollment of Creek Newborn
Act of 1905 Volume III

Witnesses To Mark:
{ WR Clawson

Subscribed and sworn to before me this 23 day of May, 1905.

W R Clawson
Notary Public.

BA- 500-B.

DEPARTMENT OF THE INTERIOR,
COMMISSION TO THE FIVE CIVILIZED TRIBES.
MUSKOGEE, INDIAN TERRITORY, March 17, 1905.

-ooOoo-

In the matter of the application for the enrollment of Patrick Highland, Jr. , as a citizen by blood of the Creek Nation.

PATRICK HIGHLAND, being duly sworn, testified as follows:

EXAMINATION BY COMMISSION:
Q What is your name? A Pat---Patrick Highland.
Q How old are you? A 26.
Q What is your postoffice address? A Eufaula.
Q Are you the father of Patrick Highland, Jr.? A Yes, sir.
Q What is the name of Patrick Highland's mother? A[sic] Lula N. Highland.
Q Is she a citizen of the Creek Nation? A Yes, sir.
Q What was her name before it was Highland? A Lula N. McIntosh.

Lula N. Highland is identified as Lula N. McIntosh on Creek Indian Card, Field Number 549, and her name is contained in the partial list of Creek citizens by blood, approved by the Secretary of the Interior March 13, 1902, Roll Number 1775.

Q Are you a citizen of the Creek Nation? A No, sir.
Q Are you a citizen of any Nation in Indian Territory A Cherokee.
Q If it should be found that your child, Patrick Highland, Jr., has rights in both the Creek and Cherokee Nation, in which Nation do you elect to have him enrolled and receive his allotment of land? A In the Creek Nation.
Q When was Patrick Highland, Jr. born? A February 7, 1904.
Q Is he living? A Yes.
Q Have you ever made application to have him enrolled in the Cherokee Nation? A No.

Applications for Enrollment of Creek Newborn
Act of 1905   Volume III

Zera Ellen Parrish, being sworn on her oath states that as stenographer to the Commission to the Five Civilized Tribes she reported the above case and that this is a full, true and correct transcript of her stenographic [sic] in same.

Zera Ellen Parrish

Subscribed and sworn to before me this 22nd day of March, 1905.

Edw C Griesel.

Notary Public.

BIRTH AFFIDAVIT.

DEPARTMENT OF THE INTERIOR.
COMMISSION TO THE FIVE CIVILIZED TRIBES.

IN RE APPLICATION FOR ENROLLMENT, as a citizen of the CREEK Nation, of Patrick Highland, born on the 7 day of Feb. , 1904

Name of Father:	Pat Highland	a citizen of the	U.S.	Nation.
Name of Mother:	Lula N. Highland	a citizen of the	Creek	Nation.

Postoffice   Eufaula

AFFIDAVIT OF ~~MOTHER~~. Father

UNITED STATES OF AMERICA, Indian Territory,
WESTERN   DISTRICT.

I, Pat Highland , on oath state that I am 26 years of age and a citizen by ----- , of the U.S. Nation; that I am the lawful ~~wife~~ hus of Lula N. Highland , who is a citizen, by blood of the Creek Nation; that a male child was born to me on 7 day of Feb , 1904 , that said child has been named   Patrick Highland , and is now living.

Pat Highland

Witnesses To Mark:

Subscribed and sworn to before me this 18 day of March, 1905.

Edw C Griesel
Notary Public.

Applications for Enrollment of Creek Newborn
Act of 1905   Volume III

COMMISSION TO THE FIVE CIVILIZED TRIBES.

In Re Application of Patrick Highland, born February 7, 1904. Name of Father Patrick A. Highland, Name of Mother Lulu N. HIGHLAND, Nee Mc,Intosh[sic], a citizen by blood of the Creek Nation, Post Office Eufaula, Indian Territory., Indian Territory.

Affidavit of Mother.

United States of America
    Western District
    Indian Territory.

    Lulu N. Highland, being duly sworn, states that I 21 years old, citizen by blood of the Creek Nation; that I am the lawful wife of Patrick A. Highland; that on the 7 day of February 1904, there was born unto me a male child; that said child is now living and has been named Patrick Highland.

Lulu N Highland

Sworn to and subscribed to before me this the 13, day of March 1905.

E. J. O'Reilly
Notary Public.

My Commission expires July 2, 1906.

United States of America
    Western District
    Indian Territory.   Affidavit of attendant.

    Mrs. M.C. Franklin, being duly sworn on oath states that I attended on Mrs. Lulu N. Highland, wife of Patrick A. Highland on the 7, day of February 1904.; that there was born unto her on the said date a male child; that the said child is now living and has been named Patrick Highland.

M. C. Franklin

Sworn and subscribed to before me this the 13, day of February 1905.

E. J. O'Reilly
Notary Public.

My Commission expires July 2, 1906.

Applications for Enrollment of Creek Newborn
Act of 1905   Volume III

NC 193.

Muskogee, Indian Territory, November 12, 1906.

Chief Clerk,
    Cherokee Enrollment Division,
        General Office.

Dear Sir:

    You are hereby advised that the name of Patrick Highland Jr., born to Pat Highland, an alleged citizen of the Cherokee Nation, and Lula N. Highland, a citizen of the Creek Nation, February 7, 1904, is contained in a schedule of New Born Citizens of the Creek Nation, approved by the Secretary of the Interior July 28, 1905, opposite Roll No. 128.

Respectfully,

Commissioner.

AFFIDAVIT OF ATTENDING PHYSICIAN OR MID-WIFE.

UNITED STATES OF AMERICA, Indian Territory,
    Western   DISTRICT.

    I, Wm Cott , a Physician , on oath state that I attended on Mrs. Missouri Dilsaver , wife of Wm Dilsaver on the 21 day of Sept , 1904 ; that there was born to her on said date a male child; that said child is now living and is said to have been named Robert Lowe Dilsaver

Wm Cott M.D.

Witnesses To Mark:

    Subscribed and sworn to before me this 20th day of March, 1905.

J.C. Stone
Notary Public.

Applications for Enrollment of Creek Newborn
Act of 1905 Volume III

BIRTH AFFIDAVIT.

DEPARTMENT OF THE INTERIOR.
COMMISSION TO THE FIVE CIVILIZED TRIBES.

IN RE APPLICATION FOR ENROLLMENT, as a citizen of the CREEK Nation, of Robert Lowe Dillsaver, born on the 21 day of September, 1904

Name of Father:	Mode Dillsaver	a citizen of the	U.S.	Nation.
Name of Mother:	Missouri Dillsaver	a citizen of the	Creek	Nation.

Postoffice   Okmulgee

Child present J.D.

AFFIDAVIT OF MOTHER.

UNITED STATES OF AMERICA, Indian Territory,
WESTERN   DISTRICT.

I, Missouri Dillsaver, on oath state that I am 21 years of age and a citizen by blood, of the Creek Nation; that I am the lawful wife of Mode Dillsaver, who is a citizen, by ----- of the U. S. Nation; that a male child was born to me on 21 day of September, 1904, that said child has been named Robert Lowe Dillsaver, and is now living.

Misouri[sic] Dillsaver

Witnesses To Mark:
{

Subscribed and sworn to before me this 17" day of Mar., 1905.

J. McDermott
Notary Public.

AFFIDAVIT OF ATTENDING PHYSICIAN OR MID-WIFE.

UNITED STATES OF AMERICA, Indian Territory,
Western   DISTRICT.

I, Wm Cott, a Physician, on oath state that I attended on Mrs. Missouri Dalsaver[sic], wife of Wm Dalsaver on the 17 day of June, 1902; that there was born to her on said date a male child; that said child is now living and is said to have been named Orvel Dean Dilsaver

Wm Cott M.D.

Witnesses To Mark:
{

Applications for Enrollment of Creek Newborn
Act of 1905 Volume III

Subscribed and sworn to before me this 20th day of March, 1905.

                        J.C. Stone
                        Notary Public.

BIRTH AFFIDAVIT.

DEPARTMENT OF THE INTERIOR.
COMMISSION TO THE FIVE CIVILIZED TRIBES.

IN RE APPLICATION FOR ENROLLMENT, as a citizen of the CREEK Nation, of Orvel Dean Dillsaver, born on the 17 day of June, 1902

Name of Father:	Mode Dillsaver	a citizen of the	U.S.	Nation.
Name of Mother:	Missouri Dillsaver	a citizen of the	Creek	Nation.

                Postoffice   Okmulgee

AFFIDAVIT OF MOTHER.

UNITED STATES OF AMERICA, Indian Territory,
    WESTERN   DISTRICT.

    I, Missouri Dillsaver, on oath state that I am 21 years of age and a citizen by blood, of the Creek Nation; that I am the lawful wife of Mode Dillsaver, who is a citizen, by ----- of the U. S. Nation; that a male child was born to me on 17 day of June, 1902, that said child has been named Orvel Dean Dillsaver, and is now living.

                        Misouri[sic] Dilsaver[sic]

Witnesses To Mark:

    Subscribed and sworn to before me this 17" day of Mar., 1905.

                        J. McDermott
                        Notary Public.

Applications for Enrollment of Creek Newborn
Act of 1905   Volume III

I Nancy Cloud on oath states[sic] that I am 34 yrs. old that on March 22. 190<u>4</u> a male child was born to me and is named Anderson Bigpond and is now living name of Father John Bigpond a citizen of the Creek Nation name of mother Nancy Cloud a citzen[sic] of the Creek Nation

Witness to mark
  Ada Ferry
  E.L Davis

                        her
                Nancy x Cloud
                      mark

        Subscribed and sworn to before me this 15 day of March 1905
                                     J.H. Hamilton   Notary public
    my commission[sic] expires Oct 7, 1906

Mid Wife

I Lizzie Allen wife of Jeese[sic] Allen on oath states that on July 24, 1901, I attended on Nancy Cloud and a girl child was born to her and has been named Susie Bigpond I also attended Nancy Cloud on March 22, 1904 and a male child was born to her and had been named Anderson Bigpond and both of them is now living.

                              her
                      Lizzie x Allen midwife

Witness to mark   mark
  Ada Ferry
  E.L Davis

Subscribed and sworn to before me this 15 day of March 1905.
                            J.H.Hamilton
                                        Notary public
    my commission[sic] expires Oct. 7, 1906.

BIRTH AFFIDAVIT.

(See duplicate)

Department of the Interior,
COMMISSION TO THE FIVE CIVILIZED TRIBES.

IN RE APPLICATION FOR ENROLLMENT, as a citizen of the Creek Nation, of Anderson Bigpond , born on the 22 day of March , 1904

Name of Father:	John Bigpond	a citizen of the	Creek Nation.
Name of Mother:	Nancy " (Cloud)	a citizen of the	Creek Nation.

                        Postoffice   Bristow, IT

Applications for Enrollment of Creek Newborn
Act of 1905 Volume III

AFFIDAVIT OF MOTHER. (Child present)

UNITED STATES OF AMERICA, Indian Territory, }
   Western   DISTRICT.

    I, Nancy Bigpond , on oath state that I am 29 years of age and a citizen by blood, of the Creek Nation; that I am the lawful wife of John Bigpond , who is a citizen, by blood of the Creek Nation; that a male child was born to me on 22 day of Mar , 1904 , that said child has been named Anderson Bigpond , and is now living.

                                      her
                           Nancy x Bigpond
Witnesses To Mark: mark
{ EC Griesel
  Jesse McDermott

    Subscribed and sworn to before me this 21 day of April , 1905.

                               J. McDermott
   (Seal)   Notary Public.

AFFIDAVIT OF ATTENDING PHYSICIAN OR MID-WIFE.

UNITED STATES OF AMERICA, Indian Territory, }
   Western   DISTRICT.

    I, Lizzie Allen , a midwife , on oath state that I attended on Mrs. Nancy Bigpond , wife of John Bigpond on the 22" day of March , 1904 ; that there was born to her on said date a male child; that said child is now living and is said to have been named Anderson Bigpond

                                      her
                           Lizzie x Allen
Witnesses To Mark: mark
{ EC Griesel
  Jesse McDermott

    Subscribed and sworn to before me this 21" day of April, 1905.

                               J. McDermott
   Seal   Notary Public.

Applications for Enrollment of Creek Newborn
Act of 1905 Volume III

BIRTH AFFIDAVIT.

See old affidavit list

Department of the Interior,
COMMISSION TO THE FIVE CIVILIZED TRIBES.

IN RE APPLICATION FOR ENROLLMENT, as a citizen of the Creek Nation, of Susie Bigpond, born on the 24" day of July, 1901

Name of Father: John Bigpond   a citizen of the   Creek   Nation. Auchee
Name of Mother: Nancy " (Cloud)   a citizen of the   Creek   Nation. Auchee

Postoffice   Bristow, IT

AFFIDAVIT OF MOTHER.   (Child present)

UNITED STATES OF AMERICA, Indian Territory,
Western   DISTRICT.

I, Nancy Bigpond, on oath state that I am 29 years of age and a citizen by blood, of the Creek Nation; that I am the lawful wife of John Bigpond, who is a citizen, by blood of the Creek Nation; that a female child was born to me on 24" day July, 1901, that said child has been named Susie Bigpond, and is now living.

her
Nancy x Bigpond
mark

Witnesses To Mark:
  EC Griesel
  Jesse McDermott

Subscribed and sworn to before me this 21 day of April, 1905.

J. McDermott
(Seal)   Notary Public.

AFFIDAVIT OF ATTENDING PHYSICIAN OR MID-WIFE.

UNITED STATES OF AMERICA, Indian Territory,
Western   DISTRICT.

I, Lizzie Allen, a midwife, on oath state that I attended on Mrs. Nancy Bigpond, wife of John Bigpond on the 24 day of July, 1901; that there was born to her on said date a female child; that said child is now living and is said to have been named Susie Bigpond

her
Lizzie x Allen
mark

Applications for Enrollment of Creek Newborn
Act of 1905   Volume III

Witnesses To Mark:
{ EC Griesel
{ Jesse McDermott

Subscribed and sworn to before me this 21 day of April, 1905.

                           J. McDermott
                           Notary Public.

SUPPLEMENTAL PROOF.

DEPARTMENT OF THE INTERIOR,
COMMISSION TO THE FIVE CIVILIZED TRIBES.

IN RE Application for Enrollment, as a citizen of the Creek (or Muskogee) Nation, of Susie Bigpond , born on the 24 day of July , 1901

Name of Father:	John Bigpond	a citizen of the	Creek	Nation.
Name of Mother:	Nancy Cloud	a citizen of the	Creek	Nation.

              Postoffice   Bristow I.T.

Child Brought in Mar 16-05. Gr.

AFFIDAVIT OF PARENT.
(To be made if child is now living)

UNITED STATES OF AMERICA,
    Indian Territory,
Western   DISTRICT.

     I, Nancy Cloud, on oath state that I am 34 years of age and a citizen by Blood , of the Creek (or Muskogee) Nation; that I am the mother of Susie Bigpond a female child who was born on the 24 day of July , 1901, that said child is now living.

                          her
                   Nancy x Bigpond
Witnesses To Mark: mark
{ J.W. Vaughan
{ Ada Ferry

Subscribed and sworn to before me this 15 *day of* March, *1905.*

                        J.H. Hamilton
                        Notary Public.
                        My commission expires
                        Oct. 7 1906

Applications for Enrollment of Creek Newborn
Act of 1905 Volume III

AFFIDAVIT OF PARENT.
(To be made if child is now living)

UNITED STATES OF AMERICA,
    Indian Territory,
Western   DISTRICT.

I, , on oath state that I am   years of age and a citizen by   of the Creek (or Muskogee) Nation; that I am the   of   a   child who was born on the   day of , 190, that said child died on the   day of   , 190.

Witnesses To Mark:

Subscribed and sworn to before me this 15 day of March, 1905.

                          J.H. Hamilton
                          Notary Public.

BIRTH AFFIDAVIT.

DEPARTMENT OF THE INTERIOR,
COMMISSION TO THE FIVE CIVILIZED TRIBES.

IN RE Application for Enrollment, as a citizen of the Creek Nation, of Susie Bigpond, born on the 24 day of July, 1901

Name of Father:	John Bigpond	a citizen of the	Creek	Nation.
Name of Mother:	Nancy Bigpond	a citizen of the	Creek	Nation.

                Postoffice   Bristow, I.T.

AFFIDAVIT OF MOTHER.

UNITED STATES OF AMERICA, Indian Territory,
    Northern   DISTRICT.

I, Nancy Bigpond , on oath state that I am 30 years of age and a citizen by blood , of the Creek   Nation; that I am the lawful wife of John Bigpond , who is a citizen, by blood of the Creek   Nation; that a female child was born to me on 24 day of $[sic] July, 1901 , that said child has been named Susie Bigpond , and is now living.

                          Her
                     Nancy x Bigpond
Witnesses To Mark: mark
    E Castain
    John G. Lieber

Applications for Enrollment of Creek Newborn
Act of 1905 Volume III

Subscribed and sworn to before me this 27 *day of* Sept , *190*1.

          John G. Lieber
          Notary Public.

AFFIDAVIT OF ATTENDING PHYSICIAN OR MID-WIFE.

UNITED STATES OF AMERICA, Indian Territory, ⎫
  Northern   DISTRICT. ⎬
            ⎭

  I, John Bigpond ~~, a ,~~ on oath state that I attended on ~~Mrs~~. my wife, Nancy , ~~wife of~~ Bigpond on the 24 day of July , 1901 ; that there was born to her on said date a female child; that said child is now living and is said to have been named Susie Bigpond
            His
         John x Bigpond
Witnesses To Mark: mark
 ⎰ E Castain
 ⎱ John G. Lieber

Subscribed and sworn to before me this 27 *day of* Sept , *190*1.

          John G. Lieber
          Notary Public.

BIRTH AFFIDAVIT.
DEPARTMENT OF THE INTERIOR.
COMMISSION TO THE FIVE CIVILIZED TRIBES.

  IN RE APPLICATION FOR ENROLLMENT, as a citizen of the CREEK Nation, of Tully Mae Wallace , born on the 23 day of January , 1903

           non
Name of Father: W. A. Wallace a ^ citizen of the *(blank)* Nation.
Name of Mother: Ella Wallace   a citizen of the Creek Nation.

        Postoffice Eufaula Ind. Ter.

Applications for Enrollment of Creek Newborn
Act of 1905   Volume III

(child present 3-13-05.)

AFFIDAVIT OF MOTHER.

UNITED STATES OF AMERICA, Indian Territory, ⎫
   Western   **DISTRICT.** ⎭

    I, Ella Wallace , on oath state that I am 28 years of age and a citizen by Blood , of the Creek   Nation; that I am the lawful wife of W. A. Wallace   , who is a non citizen, by *(blank)* of the *(blank)* Nation; that a Female child was born to me on 23 day of January , 1903 , that said child has been named Tully Mae Wallace , and is now living.

                                                   Ella Wallace

Witnesses To Mark:
{

    Subscribed and sworn to before me this 11 day of March , 1905.

                                   (Illegible) Washington
                                             Notary Public.

My Commission expires July 8th, 1906.

AFFIDAVIT OF ATTENDING PHYSICIAN OR MID-WIFE.

UNITED STATES OF AMERICA, Indian Territory, ⎫
   Western   **DISTRICT.** ⎭

    I, George W. West   , a Physician   , on oath state that I attended on Mrs. Ella Wallace , wife of W. A. Wallace on the 23 day of January , 1903 ; that there was born to her on said date a Female child; that said child is now living and is said to have been named Tully Mae Wallace

                                            Geo. W. West M.D.

Witnesses To Mark:
{

    Subscribed and sworn to before me this 11 day of March , 1905.

                                   (Illegible) Washington
                                             Notary Public.

My Commission expires July 8th, 1906.

Applications for Enrollment of Creek Newborn
Act of 1905 Volume III

BIRTH AFFIDAVIT.

DEPARTMENT OF THE INTERIOR.
COMMISSION TO THE FIVE CIVILIZED TRIBES.

IN RE APPLICATION FOR ENROLLMENT, as a citizen of the CREEK Nation, of William R. Jacobs, born on the 4th day of August, 1904

Name of Father:	Newman F. Jacobs	a citizen of the	Creek	Nation.
Name of Mother:	Ella L. Jacobs	a citizen of the	Creek	Nation.

Postoffice Holdenville I.T.

AFFIDAVIT OF MOTHER.

UNITED STATES OF AMERICA, Indian Territory,
WESTERN DISTRICT.

I, Ella L. Jacobs, on oath state that I am 21 years of age and a citizen by Blood, of the Creek Nation; that I am the lawful wife of Newman F. Jacobs, who is a citizen, by Blood of the Creek Nation; that a Male child was born to me on 4th day of August, 1904, that said child has been named William R. Jacobs, and is now living.

Ella L Jacobs

Witnesses To Mark:

Subscribed and sworn to before me this 11th day of March, 1905.

My Com expires May 16th 1908   LMMiller
                                        Notary Public.

AFFIDAVIT OF ATTENDING PHYSICIAN OR MID-WIFE.

UNITED STATES OF AMERICA, Indian Territory,
Western DISTRICT.

I, Mrs. Jennie C. Jacobs, a midwife, on oath state that I attended on Mrs. Ella L. Jacobs, wife of Newman F. Jacobs on the 4 day of August, 1904; that there was born to her on said date a male child; that said child is now living and is said to have been named William R. Jacobs

                                        her
                        Mrs. Jennie C. Jacobs x
Witnesses To Mark: mark
  Sam H. Miller
  John A Jacobs

Applications for Enrollment of Creek Newborn
Act of 1905   Volume III

Subscribed and sworn to before me this 11th day of March , 1905.

My Com expires May 16th 1908   LMMiller
                                           Notary Public.

BIRTH AFFIDAVIT.

DEPARTMENT OF THE INTERIOR.
COMMISSION TO THE FIVE CIVILIZED TRIBES.

IN RE APPLICATION FOR ENROLLMENT, as a citizen of the CREEK Nation, of Samuel H. Miller Jr. , born on the 26 day of September , 1902

Name of Father:	Louis M. Miller	a citizen of the	Creek	Nation.
Name of Mother:	Lillie Miller	a citizen of the	Creek	Nation.

Postoffice   Holdenville, I.T.

AFFIDAVIT OF MOTHER.

UNITED STATES OF AMERICA, Indian Territory,
WESTERN   DISTRICT.

I, Lillie Miller , on oath state that I am 30 years of age and a citizen by Blood , of the Creek Nation; that I am the lawful wife of Louis M. Miller , who is a citizen, by Blood of the Creek Nation; that a Male child was born to me on 26 day of September, 1902 , that said child has been named Samuel H. Miller Jr. , and is now living.

                                           Lillie Miller

Witnesses To Mark:

{

Subscribed and sworn to before me this 11th day of March , 1905.

                                           W. S. Haston
                                           Notary Public.
                                           My com ex May 30, 1907.

Applications for Enrollment of Creek Newborn
Act of 1905 Volume III

AFFIDAVIT OF ATTENDING PHYSICIAN OR MID-WIFE.

UNITED STATES OF AMERICA, Indian Territory,
Western DISTRICT.

I, Mrs. Annie Yargee , a Midwife , on oath state that I attended on Mrs. Lillie Miller , wife of Louis M. Miller on the 26 day of September , 1902 ; that there was born to her on said date a male child; that said child is now living and is said to have been named Samuel H. Miller, Jr.

Annie Yargee

Witnesses To Mark:

Subscribed and sworn to before me this 11th day of March , 1905.

W. S. Haston
Notary Public.
My com ex May 30, 1907.

NC 199.

Muskogee, Indian Territory, May 20, 1905.

Daniel N. Bard,
Checotah, Indian Territory.

Dear Sir:

In the matter of the application for the enrollment of your minor children, Daniel Lee and Oda May Bard, as a citizen of the Creek Nation, you are advised that the Commission requires the affidavit of the midwife or physician in attendance at the birth of said children.

There are herewith enclosed two blank forms of birth affidavits, and in executing same care should be exercised to see that all blanks are properly filled, all names written in full and in the event that the persons signing the affidavits are unable to write, signature by mark must be attested by two witnesses. Each affidavit must be executed before a Notary Public and the notarial seal and signature of the officer must be attached to each separate affidavit.

Respectfully,

BC.

Chairman.

Applications for Enrollment of Creek Newborn
Act of 1905 Volume III

BIRTH AFFIDAVIT.

DEPARTMENT OF THE INTERIOR.
COMMISSION TO THE FIVE CIVILIZED TRIBES.

IN RE APPLICATION FOR ENROLLMENT, as a citizen of the CREEK Nation, of Daniel Lee Bard, born on the 19 day of Dec. , 1901

Name of Father:	Daniel N. Bard	a citizen of the Creek	Nation.
Name of Mother:	Emma "	a citizen of the U.S.	Nation.

Postoffice Checotah

Child Present Gr.

AFFIDAVIT OF MOTHER.

UNITED STATES OF AMERICA, Indian Territory,
WESTERN   DISTRICT.

I, Emma Bard , on oath state that I am 28 years of age and a citizen by ----- , of the U.S. Nation; that I am the lawful wife of Daniel N. Bard , who is a citizen, by blood of the Creek Nation; that a male child was born to me on 19 day of Dec , 1901 , that said child has been named Daniel Lee Bard , and is now living.

                    Her
                Emma x Bard
Witnesses To Mark: mark
  { J Y Miller
    EC Griesel

Subscribed and sworn to before me this 13 day of March , 1905.

                Edw C Griesel
                    Notary Public.

AFFIDAVIT OF ATTENDING PHYSICIAN OR MID-WIFE.

UNITED STATES OF AMERICA, Indian Territory,
   Western   DISTRICT.

                                  husband
I, Daniel N. Bard , a ----- , on oath state that I ~~attended on~~ Mrs. Emma Bard , ~~wife of~~ on the 19 day of Dec. , 1901 ; that there was born to her on said date a male child; that said child is now living and is said to have been named Daniel Lee Bard

                Daniel N Bard

Witnesses To Mark:
  {

Applications for Enrollment of Creek Newborn
Act of 1905 Volume III

Subscribed and sworn to before me this 13 day of March, 1905.

                          Edw C Griesel
                          Notary Public.

BIRTH AFFIDAVIT.

DEPARTMENT OF THE INTERIOR.
COMMISSION TO THE FIVE CIVILIZED TRIBES.

IN RE APPLICATION FOR ENROLLMENT, as a citizen of the CREEK Nation, of Oda May Bard, born on the 15 day of Jan., 1904

Name of Father:	Daniel N. Bard	a citizen of the	Creek	Nation.
Name of Mother:	Emma "	a citizen of the	U.S.	Nation.

                Postoffice   Checotah

Child Present - Gr.

            AFFIDAVIT OF ~~MOTHER~~. Father

UNITED STATES OF AMERICA, Indian Territory,
    WESTERN   DISTRICT.

    I, Daniel N Bard, on oath state that I am 35 years of age and a citizen by blood, of the Creek Nation; that I am the lawful ~~wife~~ husband of Emma Bard, who is a citizen, by ----- of the U.S. Nation; that a female child was born to me on 15 day of Jan, 1904, that said child has been named Oda May Bard, and is now living.

                        Daniel N Bard

Witnesses To Mark:
{

Subscribed and sworn to before me this 13 day of March, 1905.

                        Edw C Griesel
                        Notary Public.

                        mother of child
        AFFIDAVIT OF ~~ATTENDING PHYSICIAN OR MID-WIFE~~.

UNITED STATES OF AMERICA, Indian Territory,
    Western   DISTRICT.

    I, Emma Bard, ~~a , on oath state that I attended on Mrs.~~, wife of Daniel N Bard on the 15 day of Jan, 1904; that there was born to ~~her~~ me on said date a female child; that said child is now living and is said to have been named Oda May Bard

Applications for Enrollment of Creek Newborn
Act of 1905 Volume III

                                       Her
                                 Emma x Bard

Witnesses To Mark: mark
  { JY Miller
    EC Griesel

Subscribed and sworn to before me this 13 day of March, 1905.

                                      Edw C Griesel
                                          Notary Public.

BIRTH AFFIDAVIT.

DEPARTMENT OF THE INTERIOR.
COMMISSION TO THE FIVE CIVILIZED TRIBES.

IN RE APPLICATION FOR ENROLLMENT, as a citizen of the Creek Nation, of Oda May Bard, born on the 15th day of January, 1904

Name of Father:	Daniel N. Bard	a citizen of the Creek Nation. Coweta
Name of Mother:	Emma "	a citizen of the United States Nation.

                            Postoffice   Checotah, I.T.

AFFIDAVIT OF ATTENDING PHYSICIAN OR MID-WIFE.

UNITED STATES OF AMERICA, Indian Territory,
      Western   DISTRICT.

I, Rachel Thornsberry, a mid-wife, on oath state that I attended on Mrs. Emma Bard, wife of Daniel N. Bard on the 15th day of January, 1904; that there was born to her on said date a female child; that said child was living March 4, 1905, and is said to have been named Oda May Bard

                                    Rachel x Thornsberry

Witnesses To Mark:
  { *(Illegible)* McIntosh
    Roley C McIntosh

Subscribed and sworn to before me this 27th day of May, 1905.

                                    Charles Buford
My commission expires July 3rd 1906   Notary Public.

Applications for Enrollment of Creek Newborn
Act of 1905   Volume III

BIRTH AFFIDAVIT.

DEPARTMENT OF THE INTERIOR.
COMMISSION TO THE FIVE CIVILIZED TRIBES.

IN RE APPLICATION FOR ENROLLMENT, as a citizen of the Creek Nation, of Daniel Lee Bard, born on the 19th day of December, 1901

Name of Father:	Daniel N. Bard	a citizen of the Creek Nation.
Name of Mother:	Emma Bard	a citizen of the United States Nation.

Postoffice   Checotah, Ind. Ter.

AFFIDAVIT OF ATTENDING PHYSICIAN OR MID-WIFE.

UNITED STATES OF AMERICA, Indian Territory,
Western   DISTRICT.

I, Kate Sharp, a mid-wife, on oath state that I attended on Mrs. Emma Bard, wife of Daniel N. Bard on the 19th day of December, 1901; that there was born to her on said date a male child; that said child is now living and is said to have been named Daniel Lee Bard

Kate Sharp

Witnesses To Mark:

Subscribed and sworn to before me this 29th day of May, 1905.

Charles Buford

My commission expires July 3rd 1906   Notary Public.

BIRTH AFFIDAVIT.

DEPARTMENT OF THE INTERIOR.
COMMISSION TO THE FIVE CIVILIZED TRIBES.

IN RE APPLICATION FOR ENROLLMENT, as a citizen of the Creek Nation, of Stella Raabe, born on the 20th day of October, 1901

Name of Father:	Chris Raabe	a citizen of the U.S. Nation.
Name of Mother:	Ida May Raabe	a citizen of the Creek Nation.

Postoffice   Bristow I.T.

Applications for Enrollment of Creek Newborn
Act of 1905 Volume III

AFFIDAVIT OF MOTHER.

UNITED STATES OF AMERICA, Indian Territory, ⎫
   Northern   DISTRICT. ⎭

    I, Ida May Raabe, on oath state that I am 19 years of age and a citizen by Blood, of the Creek Nation; that I am the lawful wife of Chris Raabe, who is a citizen, by *(blank)* of the U.S. Nation; that a Female child was born to me on 20th day of October, 1901, that said child has been named Stella, and is now living.

                                   Ida May Raabe

Witnesses To Mark:
{

    Subscribed and sworn to before me this 14th day of June, 1902.

                                     J.W. Flynn
                                          Notary Public.

AFFIDAVIT OF ATTENDING PHYSICIAN OR MID-WIFE.

UNITED STATES OF AMERICA, Indian Territory, ⎫
   Northern   DISTRICT. ⎭

    I, Bell Dixon, a *(blank)*, on oath state that I attended on Mrs. Ida May Raabe, wife of Chris Raabe on the 20th day of October, 1901; that there was born to her on said date a Female child; that said child is now living and is said to have been named Stella Raabe

                                bell[sic] Dixon x

Witnesses To Mark:
{

    Subscribed and sworn to before me this 14th day of June, 1902.

                                          Notary Public.

                    Department of the Interior
                            D[sic]
            Commission to the five Civilized Tribes.

    In re application for enrollment, as a citizen of the Creek Nation of Stella Raabe, born on the 20th day of, October, 1901.
Name of the father; Chris Raabe, a non-citizen, of Creek Nation.
Name of the Mother; Ida May Raabe, a citizen of the Creek Nation.
                                   Post Office, Olive I.T.

Applications for Enrollment of Creek Newborn
Act of 1905   Volume III

Child Present - Mar 17-05 Gr.

Affidavit of Mother.

United States of America,
    Western District,   ss.
    Indian Territory.

    I, Ida May Raabe, on oath state that I am, twenty years of age and a citizen by blood, of the Creek Nation, that I am the lawful wife of Chris Raabe, who is a non-citizen of the Creek Nation; that a female child was born to me on 20th day of October, 1901, that said child has been named Stella Raabe, and is now living.

Ida May Raabe

    Witness to Mark.

Subscribed and sworn to before me this 17th day of March 1905.

My Commission Expires Nov 29-1908   Edw C Griesel
                                                          Notary Public.

Affidavit of attending Physician, or Mid-wife.

United States of America,
    Western District,   ss.
    Indian Territory.

    I Mary Lindsay, a nurse and midwife, on oath state that I attended on Mrs. Ida May Raabe , wife of Chris Raabe on the 4th day of June, 1904 ; that there was born to her on said date a female child; that said child is now living and is said to have been named Celia Raabe.

Mary Lindsay

Witness to Mark.

Subscribed and sworn to before me this 16th day of March 1905.

(Name Illegible)

My Commission Expires July 8, 1906   Notary Public.

Applications for Enrollment of Creek Newborn
Act of 1905 Volume III

Department of the Interior
D[sic]
Commission to the five Civilized Tribes.

In re application for enrollment, as a citizen of the Creek Nation of Celia Raabe, born on the 4th day of, June, 1904.
Name of the father;   Chris Raabe , a non-citizen, of Creek Nation.
Name of the Mother; Ida May Raabe, a citizen of the Creek Nation.
Post Office, Olive I.T.
Child Present - Mar 17-05 Gr.

Affidavit of Mother.

United States of America,
　Western District,　　ss.
　Indian Territory.

I, Ida May Raabe, on oath state that I am, twenty years of age and a citizen by blood, of the Creek Nation, that I am the lawful wife of Chris Raabe, who is a non-citizen of the Creek Nation; that a female child was born to me on 4th day of June, 1901, that said child has been named Celia Raabe, and is now living.

Ida May Raabe

Witness to Mark.

Subscribed and sworn to before me this 17th day of March 1905.

Edw C Griesel
My Commission Expires Nov 29-1908　　　　Notary Public.

Affidavit of attending Physician, or Mid-wife.

United States of America,
　Western District,　　ss.
　Indian Territory.

I Mary Lindsay, a nurse and midwife, on oath state that I attended on Mrs. Ida May Raabe , wife of Chris Raabe on the 20th day of October, 1901 ; that there was born to her on said date a female child; that said child is now living and is said to have been named Stella Raabe.

Mary Lindsay

Witness to Mark.

Applications for Enrollment of Creek Newborn
Act of 1905   Volume III

Subscribed and sworn to before me this 16th day of March 1905.

(Name Illegible)

My Commission Expires July 8, 1906   Notary Public.

BIRTH AFFIDAVIT.

DEPARTMENT OF THE INTERIOR.
COMMISSION TO THE FIVE CIVILIZED TRIBES.

IN RE APPLICATION FOR ENROLLMENT, as a citizen of the Creek Nation, of Woods Cooper Rogers, born on the 29 day of Nov., 1903

Name of Father:	Wm Penn Rogers	a citizen of the	Creek	Nation.
Name of Mother:	Augusta Rogers	a ^ citizen of the non	"	Nation.

Postoffice   Checotah

child present

AFFIDAVIT OF MOTHER.

UNITED STATES OF AMERICA, Indian Territory,
Western   DISTRICT.

I, Augusta Rogers, on oath state that I am 23 years of age and a citizen by -----, of the U.S. Nation; that I am the lawful wife of Wm Penn Rogers, who is a citizen, by blood of the Creek Nation; that a male child was born to me on 29" day of Nov., 1903, that said child has been named Woods Cooper Rogers, and was living March 4, 1905.

                                             Augusta Rogers

Witnesses To Mark:
{

Subscribed and sworn to before me this 8" day of April, 1905.

                                             Edw C Griesel
                                             Notary Public.

Applications for Enrollment of Creek Newborn
Act of 1905   Volume III

AFFIDAVIT OF ATTENDING PHYSICIAN OR MID-WIFE.

UNITED STATES OF AMERICA, Indian Territory,
　　Western　　DISTRICT.

I, A J Pollard, a Physician, on oath state that I attended on Mrs. Augusta Rogers, wife of Wm P Rogers on the 29th day of November, 1903 ; that there was born to her on said date a male child; that said child was living March 4, 1905, and is said to have been named Woods Cooper Rogers

　　　　　　　　　　　　　　A.J. Pollard M.D.

Witnesses To Mark:

{

Subscribed and sworn to before me this 21st day of March, 1905.

　　　　　　　　　　　　　　F S Aurd
　　　　　　　　　　　　　　　　Notary Public.
My Commission Expires January 13, 1907

BIRTH AFFIDAVIT.

DEPARTMENT OF THE INTERIOR.
COMMISSION TO THE FIVE CIVILIZED TRIBES.

IN RE APPLICATION FOR ENROLLMENT, as a citizen of the CREEK Nation, of Woods C. Rogers, born on the 29 day of Nov., 1903

Name of Father:	Wm P Rogers	a citizen of the	Creek	Nation.
Name of Mother:	Augusta "	a citizen of the	U.S.	Nation.

　　　　　　　　　　Postoffice　　Checotah

AFFIDAVIT OF MOTHER.

UNITED STATES OF AMERICA, Indian Territory,
　　WESTERN　　DISTRICT.

I, Wm P Rogers, on oath state that I am 34 years of age and a citizen by blood, of the Creek Nation; that I am the lawful ~~wife~~ husb of Augusta Rogers, who is a citizen, by ----- of the U.S. Nation; that a male child was born to me on 29 day of Nov., 1903, that said child has been named Woods C Rogers, and is now living.

　　　　　　　　　　　　　　William P. Rogers

Witnesses To Mark:

{

Applications for Enrollment of Creek Newborn
Act of 1905 Volume III

Subscribed and sworn to before me this 13" day of March, 1905.

           Edw C Griesel
           Notary Public.

DEPARTMENT OF THE INTERIOR.

COMMISSION TO THE FIVE CIVILIZED TRIBES.

In Re Application for enrollment, as a citizen of the Creek Nation of Woods Cooper Rogers, born on the 29" day of November 1903.

Name of Father; William Penn Rogers a citizen of the Creek Nation.
Name of Mother; Augusta Rogers a non-citizen of the Creek Nation.

           PostOffice Checotah, I.T.

Affidavit of Attending Physician.

United States of America,
Indian Territory,
Western District.

 I, A. J. Pollard, a Physician, on oath state that I attended on Mrs. Augusta Rogers, wife of William Penn Rogers on the 29" day of November 1903 that there was born to her on said date a male child that said child is now living and is said to have been named Woods Cooper Rogers

           A. J. Pollard, M. D.

           Z. I. J. Holt

BIRTH AFFIDAVIT.

DEPARTMENT OF THE INTERIOR.
COMMISSION TO THE FIVE CIVILIZED TRIBES.

 IN RE APPLICATION FOR ENROLLMENT, as a citizen of the CREEK Nation, of John Rogers, born on the 11 day of Feb. , 1905

| Name of Father: | Wm P. Rogers | a citizen of the | Creek | Nation. |
| Name of Mother: | Augusta " | a citizen of the | U. S. | Nation. |

         Postoffice   Checotah I.T.

Applications for Enrollment of Creek Newborn
Act of 1905   Volume III

AFFIDAVIT OF MOTHER.

UNITED STATES OF AMERICA, Indian Territory,
  WESTERN   DISTRICT.

I, Wm P Rogers, on oath state that I am 34 years of age and a citizen by blood, of the Creek Nation; that I am the lawful ~~wife~~ hus of Augusta Rogers, who is a citizen, by ----- of the U. S. Nation; that a male child was born to me on 11 day of Feb., 1905, that said child has been named John Rogers, and is now living.

William P. Rogers

Witnesses To Mark:
{

Subscribed and sworn to before me this 13 day of March, 1905.

Edw C Griesel
Notary Public.

BIRTH AFFIDAVIT.

DEPARTMENT OF THE INTERIOR.
COMMISSION TO THE FIVE CIVILIZED TRIBES.

IN RE APPLICATION FOR ENROLLMENT, as a citizen of the Creek Nation, of John Rogers, born on the 11 day of Feby., 1905

| Name of Father: | Wm Penn Rogers | a citizen of the | Creek | Nation. |
| Name of Mother: | Augusta Rogers | a ^non citizen of the | Creek | Nation. |

Postoffice   Checotah

(child present)

AFFIDAVIT OF MOTHER.

UNITED STATES OF AMERICA, Indian Territory,
  Western   DISTRICT.

I, Augusta Rogers, on oath state that I am 23 years of age and a citizen by -----, of the U.S. Nation; that I am the lawful wife of Wm Penn Rogers, who is a citizen, by blood of the Creek Nation; that a male child was born to me on 11" day of Feby., 1905, that said child has been named John Rogers, and is now living.

Augusta Rogers

Applications for Enrollment of Creek Newborn
Act of 1905 Volume III

Witnesses To Mark:
{

Subscribed and sworn to before me this 8" day of April, 1905.

Edw C Griesel
Notary Public.

AFFIDAVIT OF ATTENDING PHYSICIAN OR MID-WIFE.

UNITED STATES OF AMERICA, Indian Territory,
Western DISTRICT. }

I, A.J. Pollard, a Physician, on oath state that I attended on Mrs. Augusta Rogers, wife of Wm P Rogers on the 11th day of February, 1905; that there was born to her on said date a male child; that said child was living March 4, 1905, and is said to have been named John Rogers

AJ Pollard M.D.

Witnesses To Mark:
{

Subscribed and sworn to before me this 21st day of March, 1905.

F S Aurd
Notary Public.

My Commission Expires January 13, 1907

Department of the Interior
D[sic]
Commission to the five Civilized Tribes.

In re application for enrollment, as a citizen of the Creek Nation of Albert Emmet Barney, born on the 20th day of, November, 1904

Name of the father; Albert Barney, a non-citizen, of Creek Nation.
Name of the Mother; Bessie Barney (nee Carlile), a citizen of the Creek Nation.

Post Office, Bristow I.T.

Applications for Enrollment of Creek Newborn
Act of 1905   Volume III

(Child Present - 3-17-05)

Affidavit of Mother.

United States of America,
    Western District,   ss.
    Indian Territory.

    I, Bessie Barney, on oath state that I am, 17 years of age and a citizen by blood, of the Creek Nation, that I am the lawful wife of Albert Barney, who is a non-citizen of the Creek Nation; that a male child was born to me on 20th day of November, 1904, that said child has been named Albert Emmet Barney, and is now living. That my maiden [sic] before marriage was Bessie Carlile.

                                        Her
                              Bessie x Barney
Witness to Mark.   mark
Irwin Donovan
EC Griesel

Subscribed and sworn to before me this 17th day of March 1905.

                                      Edw C Griesel
My Commission Expires Nov 29-08   Notary Public.

Affidavit of attending Physician, or Mid-wife.

United States of America,
    Western District,   ss.
    Indian Territory.

    I Lizzie Earley, a midwife, on oath state that I attended on Mrs. Bessie Barney, wife of Homer[sic] Barney on the 20th day of November, 1904 ; that there was born to her on said date a male child; that said child is now living and is said to have been named Albert Emmet Barney

                                      Lizzie Earley
Witness to Mark.

Subscribed and sworn to before me this 16th day of March 1905.

                                    (Name Illegible)
My Commission Expires July 8, 1906   Notary Public.

Applications for Enrollment of Creek Newborn
Act of 1905 Volume III

NC 203.

Muskogee, Indian Territory, May 20, 1905.

G. L. Baughman,
    Hitchitee, Indian Territory.

Dear Sir:

    In the matter of the application for the enrollment of your minor children, Melvin W. and Gold C. Baughman, as citizens of the Creek Nation, you are advised that the Commission requires the affidavit of the midwife or physician in attendance at the birth of said child.

    There are herewith enclosed two blank forms of birth affidavits, and in executing same care should be exercised to see that all blanks are properly filled, all names written in full and in the event that the persons signing the affidavits are unable to write, signature by mark must be attested by two witnesses. Each affidavit must be executed before a Notary Public and the notarial seal and signature of the officer must be attached to each separate affidavit.

                Respectfully,

BC.   Chairman.

BIRTH AFFIDAVIT.

DEPARTMENT OF THE INTERIOR.
COMMISSION TO THE FIVE CIVILIZED TRIBES.

    IN RE APPLICATION FOR ENROLLMENT, as a citizen of the Creek Nation, of Gold C. Baughman, born on the 21 day of January, 1905

| Name of Father: | G L Baughman | a citizen of the | U.S. | Nation. |
| Name of Mother: | Sarah Baughman | a citizen of the | Creek | Nation. |

                Postoffice   Hitchitee, I.T.

AFFIDAVIT OF MOTHER.

UNITED STATES OF AMERICA, Indian Territory, ⎫
    Western   DISTRICT. ⎬

    I, Sarah Baughman , on oath state that I am 24 years of age and a citizen by Blood , of the Creek Nation; that I am the lawful wife of G. L. Baughman , who is a citizen, by *(blank)* of the U.S. Nation; that a male child was born to me on 21 day

Applications for Enrollment of Creek Newborn
Act of 1905   Volume III

of January, 1905, that said child has been named Gold C. Baughman, and was living March 4, 1905.

Miss Sarah Baughman

Witnesses To Mark:
{

Subscribed and sworn to before me this 12 day of July, 1905.

Joseph C. Moron
Notary Public.

My Commission Expires Feb 29-1908

AFFIDAVIT OF ATTENDING PHYSICIAN OR MID-WIFE.

UNITED STATES OF AMERICA, Indian Territory, }
Western   DISTRICT.

I, Ida Greenleaf, a midwife, on oath state that I attended on Mrs. Sarah Baughman, wife of G. L. Baughman on the 21 day of January, 1905; that there was born to her on said date a male child; that said child was living March 4, 1905, and is said to have been named Gold C. Baughman

Ida Greenleaf

Witnesses To Mark:
{

Subscribed and sworn to before me this 12 day of July, 1905.

Joseph C. Moron
Notary Public.

My Commission Expires
Feb 29-1908

(The above affidavit copied again)

BIRTH AFFIDAVIT.
DEPARTMENT OF THE INTERIOR.
COMMISSION TO THE FIVE CIVILIZED TRIBES.

IN RE APPLICATION FOR ENROLLMENT, as a citizen of the Creek Nation, of Malvin W. Baughman, born on the 4 day of Dec, 1902

Name of Father:	G L Baughman	a citizen of the	U.S.	Nation.
Name of Mother:	Sarah Baughman	a citizen of the	Creek	Nation.

Applications for Enrollment of Creek Newborn
Act of 1905   Volume III

Postoffice   Hitchitee, I.T.

AFFIDAVIT OF MOTHER.

UNITED STATES OF AMERICA, Indian Territory,
Western   DISTRICT.

I, Sarah Baughman , on oath state that I am 24 years of age and a citizen by Blood , of the Creek Nation; that I am the lawful wife of G. L. Baughman , who is a citizen, by *(blank)* of the U.S. Nation; that a male child was born to me on 4th day of December , 1902 , that said child has been named Malvin W Baughman , and was living March 4, 1905.

Miss Sarah Baughman

Witnesses To Mark:

Subscribed and sworn to before me this 12 day of July , 1905.

Joseph C. Moron
Notary Public.

My Commission Expires Feb 29-1908

AFFIDAVIT OF ATTENDING PHYSICIAN OR MID-WIFE.

UNITED STATES OF AMERICA, Indian Territory,
Western   DISTRICT.

I, Sarah Greenleaf , a midwife , on oath state that I attended on Mrs. Sarah Baughman , wife of G. L. Baughman on the 4th day of December , 1902 ; that there was born to her on said date a male child; that said child was living March 4, 1905, and is said to have been named Malvin W. Baughman

her
Sarah x Greenleaf
mark

Witnesses To Mark:
 Emma *(Illegible)*
 Annie *(Illegible)*

Subscribed and sworn to before me this 11 day of July , 1905.

Joseph C. Moron
Notary Public.

My Commission Expires
Feb 29-1908

Applications for Enrollment of Creek Newborn
Act of 1905   Volume III

BIRTH AFFIDAVIT.

DEPARTMENT OF THE INTERIOR.
COMMISSION TO THE FIVE CIVILIZED TRIBES.

IN RE APPLICATION FOR ENROLLMENT, as a citizen of the CREEK Nation, of Melvin W. Baughman, born on the 4 day of ~~Jan~~ Dec, 1902

Name of Father: G L Baughman   a citizen of the   U.S.   Nation.
Name of Mother: Sarah   "   a citizen of the   Creek   Nation.

Postoffice   Hitchite[sic]

Child Present Gr.

AFFIDAVIT OF MOTHER.

UNITED STATES OF AMERICA, Indian Territory, ⎱
    WESTERN   DISTRICT.   ⎰

I, Sarah Baughman , on oath state that I am 24 years of age and a citizen by blood, of the Creek Nation; that I am the lawful wife of G. L. Baughman , who is a citizen, by ----- of the U.S. Nation; that a male   child was born to me on 4 day of ~~Jan~~ Dec , 1902 , that said child has been named   Melvin W Baughman , and is now living.

                                Sarah Baughman

Witnesses To Mark:

{

Subscribed and sworn to before me this 13" day of March , 1905.

                              Edw C Griesel
                                Notary Public.

BIRTH AFFIDAVIT.

DEPARTMENT OF THE INTERIOR.
COMMISSION TO THE FIVE CIVILIZED TRIBES.

IN RE APPLICATION FOR ENROLLMENT, as a citizen of the CREEK Nation, of Gold C. Baughman Jr., born on the 21 day of Jan, 1905

Name of Father: G L Baughman   a citizen of the   ~~Creek~~ U.S. Nation.
Name of Mother: Sarah   "   a citizen of the   Creek   Nation.

                       Postoffice   Hitchite[sic]

Applications for Enrollment of Creek Newborn
Act of 1905   Volume III

(Child present) HGH

AFFIDAVIT OF MOTHER.

UNITED STATES OF AMERICA, Indian Territory, }
    WESTERN   DISTRICT.

    I, Sarah Baughman, on oath state that I am 24 years of age and a citizen by blood, of the Creek Nation; that I am the lawful wife of G. L. Baughman, who is a citizen, by ----- of the U.S. Nation; that a male child was born to me on 21 day of Jan., 1905, that said child has been named Gold C. Baughman Jr., and is now living.

                                    Sarah Baughman

Witnesses To Mark:
{

    Subscribed and sworn to before me this 13" day of March, 1905.

                                      Edw C Griesel
                                      Notary Public.

AFFIDAVIT OF ATTENDING PHYSICIAN OR MID-WIFE.

UNITED STATES OF AMERICA, Indian Territory, }
    Western   DISTRICT.

    I, G. L. Baughman, a -----, on oath state that I attended on Mrs. Sarah Baughman my, wife of ------ on the 21 day of July Jan, 1905; that there was born to her on said date a male child; that said child is now living and is said to have been named Gold C. Baughman Jr

                                    G. L. Baughman

Witnesses To Mark:
{

    Subscribed and sworn to before me this 13" day of March, 1905.

                                      Edw C Griesel
                                      Notary Public.

Applications for Enrollment of Creek Newborn
Act of 1905   Volume III

BIRTH AFFIDAVIT.

DEPARTMENT OF THE INTERIOR.
COMMISSION TO THE FIVE CIVILIZED TRIBES.

IN RE APPLICATION FOR ENROLLMENT, as a citizen of the CREEK Nation, of Daniel W. Brown, born on the 11 day of July, 1902

Name of Father:	Gold C. Brown	a citizen of the	U.S.	Nation.
Name of Mother:	Zenia "	a citizen of the	Creek	Nation.

Postoffice   Checotah

(child present) HGH

AFFIDAVIT OF MOTHER.

UNITED STATES OF AMERICA, Indian Territory,
WESTERN   DISTRICT.

I, Zenia Brown, on oath state that I am 38 years of age and a citizen by blood, of the Creek Nation; that I am the lawful wife of Gold C. Brown, who is a citizen, by ----- of the U.S. Nation; that a male child was born to me on 11 day of July, 1902, that said child has been named Daniel W. Brown, and is now living.

Zenia Brown

Witnesses To Mark:
{

Subscribed and sworn to before me this 13" day of March, 1905.

Edw C Griesel
Notary Public.

AFFIDAVIT OF ATTENDING PHYSICIAN OR MID-WIFE.

UNITED STATES OF AMERICA, Indian Territory,
Western   DISTRICT.

I, Hettie M. Hicks, a midwife, on oath state that I attended on Mrs. Zenia Brown, wife of Gold C. Brown on the 11 day of July, 1902 ; that there was born to her on said date a male child; that said child is now living and is said to have been named Daniel W. Brown

Hettie M. Hicks

Witnesses To Mark:
{

Applications for Enrollment of Creek Newborn
Act of 1905   Volume III

Subscribed and sworn to before me this 13" day of March, 1905.

                                  Edw C Griesel
                                  Notary Public.

BIRTH AFFIDAVIT.

DEPARTMENT OF THE INTERIOR.
COMMISSION TO THE FIVE CIVILIZED TRIBES.

IN RE APPLICATION FOR ENROLLMENT, as a citizen of the Creek Nation, of Browder F. Bruce, born on the 23 day of February, 1904

Name of Father: Moten Bruce   a ~~citizen of the~~ non citizen Nation.
Name of Mother: Thebe[sic] Bruce   a citizen of the Creek Nation[sic]Nation.

                        Postoffice   Bristow I.T.

AFFIDAVIT OF MOTHER.

UNITED STATES OF AMERICA, Indian Territory,
    Western   **DISTRICT.**

    I, Pheba Bruce, on oath state that I am 18 years of age and a citizen by Blood, of the Creek Nation; that I am the lawful wife of Moten Bruce, who is a non citizen, by *(blank)* of the Creek Nation; that a male child was born to me on 23rd day of February, 1904, that said child has been named Browder F. Bruce, and is now living. and affiant further says her maiden name was Pheba Perryman

                                  Pheba Bruce

Witnesses To ~~Mark~~: signature
   { John W Overstreet
   { C. C. DauCartos

Subscribed and sworn to before me this 15th day of March, 1905.

                             John W Overstreet
Western Dist I.T.   Notary Public.

Applications for Enrollment of Creek Newborn
Act of 1905 Volume III

AFFIDAVIT OF ATTENDING PHYSICIAN OR MID-WIFE.

UNITED STATES OF AMERICA, Indian Territory, }
    Western   DISTRICT.

    I, Mahala Perrin, a Midwife, on oath state that I attended on Mrs. Thebe[sic] Bruce, wife of Moten Bruce on the 23rd day of February, 1904; that there was born to her on said date a male child; that said child is now living and is said to have been named Browder F. Bruce

                                 Mahaley Perrin

Witnesses To Mark:
{ John W Overstreet
{ C. C. DauCartos

    Subscribed and sworn to before me this 19th day of Mch, 1905.

                              John W Overstreet
Western Dist I.T.   Notary Public.

BIRTH AFFIDAVIT.

DEPARTMENT OF THE INTERIOR.
COMMISSION TO THE FIVE CIVILIZED TRIBES.

    IN RE APPLICATION FOR ENROLLMENT, as a citizen of the CREEK Nation, of Browder F. Bruce, born on the 23 day of Feb, 1904

Name of Father:	Moten R. Bruce	a citizen of the	U.S.	Nation.
Name of Mother:	Pheba Bruce	a citizen of the	Creek	Nation.

                        Postoffice   Bristow

AFFIDAVIT OF ~~MOTHER~~. Father

UNITED STATES OF AMERICA, Indian Territory, }
    WESTERN   DISTRICT.

    I, Moten R. Bruce, on oath state that I am 22 years of age and a citizen by -----, of the U.S. Nation; that I am the lawful ~~wife~~ husb of Phoebe Bruce, who is a citizen, by blood of the Creek Nation; that a male child was born to me on 23 day of Feb., 1904, that said child has been named Browder F. Bruce, and is now living.

                                 Moten R. Bruce

Witnesses To Mark:
{
{

Applications for Enrollment of Creek Newborn
Act of 1905   Volume III

Subscribed and sworn to before me this 18 day of March, 1905.

                Edw C Griesel
                Notary Public.

BIRTH AFFIDAVIT.

DEPARTMENT OF THE INTERIOR.
COMMISSION TO THE FIVE CIVILIZED TRIBES.

IN RE APPLICATION FOR ENROLLMENT, as a citizen of the CREEK Nation, of Ethel Bough, born on the 27 day of October, 1904

Name of Father:	Arthur Bough	a citizen of the	U.S.	Nation.
Name of Mother:	Emma Bough	a citizen of the	Creek	Nation.

                Postoffice   Broken Arrow

Child present J.D.

AFFIDAVIT OF MOTHER.

UNITED STATES OF AMERICA, Indian Territory,
    WESTERN   DISTRICT.

    I, Emma Bough, on oath state that I am 22 years of age and a citizen by blood, of the Creek Nation; that I am the lawful wife of Arthur Bough, who is a citizen, by ----- of the U.S. Nation; that a female child was born to me on 27 day of October, 1904, that said child has been named Ethel Bough, and is now living.

                Her
              Emma x Bough
Witnesses To Mark: mark
  { H.G. Hains
    EC Griesel

Subscribed and sworn to before me this 18 day of March, 1905.

                Edw C Griesel
                Notary Public.

Applications for Enrollment of Creek Newborn
Act of 1905 Volume III

AFFIDAVIT OF ATTENDING ~~PHYSICIAN~~ OR MID-WIFE.

UNITED STATES OF AMERICA, Indian Territory,
WESTERN DISTRICT.

I, Rachel Bough , a Mid Wife , on oath state that I attended on Mrs. Emma Bough , wife of Arthur Bough on the 27 day of Oct , 1904; that there was born to her on said date a female child; that said child is now living and is said to have been named Ethel Bough

                                    Her
                            Rachel x Bough

Witnesses To Mark: mark
{ H.G. Hains
  EC Griesel

Subscribed and sworn to before me this 18 day of March, 1905.

                                Edw C Griesel
                                Notary Public.

BIRTH AFFIDAVIT.

DEPARTMENT OF THE INTERIOR.
COMMISSION TO THE FIVE CIVILIZED TRIBES.

IN RE APPLICATION FOR ENROLLMENT, as a citizen of the CREEK Nation, of Henry Bough, born on the 8 day of October , 1902

Name of Father:	Arthur Bough	a citizen of the	U.S.	Nation.
Name of Mother:	Emma Bough	a citizen of the	Creek	Nation.

                        Postoffice   Broken Arrow

Child present J.D.

AFFIDAVIT OF MOTHER.

UNITED STATES OF AMERICA, Indian Territory,
WESTERN DISTRICT.

I, Emma Bough , on oath state that I am 22 years of age and a citizen by blood , of the Creek Nation; that I am the lawful wife of Arthur Bough , who is a citizen, by ----- of the U.S. Nation; that a male child was born to me on 8 day of October , 1902 , that said child has been named Henry Bough , and is now living.

                                Her
                        Emma x Bough

Witnesses To Mark: mark
{ H.G. Hains
  EC Griesel

Applications for Enrollment of Creek Newborn
Act of 1905   Volume III

Subscribed and sworn to before me this 18 day of March , 1905.

        Edw C Griesel
        Notary Public.

AFFIDAVIT OF ATTENDING ~~PHYSICIAN~~ OR MID-WIFE.

UNITED STATES OF AMERICA, Indian Territory, ⎫
  WESTERN DISTRICT. ⎬
           ⎭

  I, Rachel Bough , a Midwife , on oath state that I attended on Mrs. Emma Bough , wife of Arthur Bough on the 8 day of Oct , 1902; that there was born to her on said date a male child; that said child is now living and is said to have been named Henry Bough

        Her
        Rachel x Bough
Witnesses To Mark: mark
 { H.G. Hains
  EC Griesel

Subscribed and sworn to before me this 18 day of March, 1905.

        Edw C Griesel
        Notary Public.

NC-207

DEPARTMENT OF THE INTERIOR,
COMMISSIONER TO THE FIVE CIVILIZED TRIBES.

Muskogee, Indian Territory, December 16, 1905.

  In the matter of the application for the enrollment of Manuel Sarty as a citizen by blood of the Creek Nation.

  Hepsey McGilbray, being sworn, testified as follows (through Jesse McDermott, Official Interpreter):

EXAMINATION BY THE COMMISSIONER:
Q What is your name? A Hepsey McGilbray.
Q How old are you? A I don't know that.

  Witness appears to be about 19 or 20 years of age. Roll No. 1399.

Q What is your postoffice? A Mellette.

Applications for Enrollment of Creek Newborn
Act of 1905   Volume III

Q Have you a child named Manuel Sarty? A No, I haven't.
Q Were you ever married to Rolley Sarty? A No.
Q Do you know a person named Hepsey McGilbray who was married to Rolley Sarty? A No.

Jennison Wallace, being sworn, testified a follows (through Jesse McDermott, Official Interpreter):

BY THE COMMISSIONER:
Q Do you know this woman who has just testified? A No sir, I don't.
Q Do you know anyone named Hepsey who married Rolley Sarty? A Yes, I know a lady by the name Hepsey McGilbray who lives near Coweta.
Q Did she marry Rolley Sarty A Yes sir, he is her husband.
Q You think a letter addressed to her at Coweta would reach her? A Yes sir.
Q What was the name of that Hepsey McGilbray's father? A Captain McGilbray.
Q What Creek Indian Town did she belong to? A I don't know that.

The Hepsey McGilbray referred to by the witness is identified on Creek Indian card, Field No. 2833, and her name is contained in the partial list of citizens by blood of the Creek Nation approved by the Secretary of the Interior March 28, 1902, opposite Roll No. 8019.

INDIAN TERRITORY, Western District.
I, J. Y. Miller, a stenographer to the Commissioner to the Five Civilized Tribes, do hereby certify that the above and foregoing is a true and complete translation of my notes as same appear in my stenographic report of this case.

JY Miller

Sworn to and subscribed before me
this the 20th day of December,
1905.

J McDermott
Notary Public.

BIRTH AFFIDAVIT.

DEPARTMENT OF THE INTERIOR.
COMMISSION TO THE FIVE CIVILIZED TRIBES.

IN RE APPLICATION FOR ENROLLMENT, as a citizen of the CREEK Nation, of Manuel Sarty, born on the 3 day of March , 1904

Name of Father:	Rollie Sarty	a citizen of the	Creek	Nation.
Name of Mother:	Hepsey "	a citizen of the	"	Nation.

Postoffice   Weer

Applications for Enrollment of Creek Newborn
Act of 1905 Volume III

(child present)

AFFIDAVIT OF MOTHER.

UNITED STATES OF AMERICA, Indian Territory, }
WESTERN DISTRICT. }

I, Hepsey Sarty, on oath state that I am 20 years of age and a citizen by blood, of the Creek Nation; that I am the lawful wife of Rollie Sarty, who is a citizen, by blood of the Creek Nation; that a male child was born to me on 3 day of March, 1904, that said child has been named Manuel Sarty, and is now living.

          Her
        Hepsey x Sarty
Witnesses To Mark: mark
{ H.G. Hains
{ EC Griesel

Subscribed and sworn to before me this 18" day of March, 1905.

        Edw C Griesel
         Notary Public.

BIRTH AFFIDAVIT.

DEPARTMENT OF THE INTERIOR.
COMMISSION TO THE FIVE CIVILIZED TRIBES.

IN RE APPLICATION FOR ENROLLMENT, as a citizen of the Creek Nation, of Manuel Sarty, born on the 3rd day of March, 1904

Name of Father:	Roley Sarty	a citizen of the	Creek	Nation.
Name of Mother:	Hapsy[sic] Sarty	a citizen of the	Creek	Nation.

      Postoffice ~~Coweta~~ Weer

(child present)

AFFIDAVIT OF MOTHER.

UNITED STATES OF AMERICA, Indian Territory, }
Western DISTRICT. }

I, Hapsey[sic] Sarty, on oath state that I am 20 Twenty years of age and a citizen by blood, of the Creek Nation; that I am the lawful wife of Roley Sarty, who is a citizen, by blood of the Creek Nation; that a male child was born to me on 3rd day of March, 1904, that said child has been named Manuel Sarty, and is now living.

        Hapsy Sarty

Applications for Enrollment of Creek Newborn
Act of 1905   Volume III

Witnesses To Mark:
  { James B. Pike

Subscribed and sworn to before me this 20th day of March , 1905.

B J Beavers
Notary Public.

My commission expires <u>Dec 19-1908</u>

AFFIDAVIT OF ATTENDING PHYSICIAN OR MID-WIFE.

UNITED STATES OF AMERICA, Indian Territory,
  Western   DISTRICT.

I, Susan Sarty , a midwife , on oath state that I attended on Mrs. Hapsy Sarty , wife of Roley Sarty on the 3rd day of March , 1904 ; that there was born to her on said date a male child; that said child is now living and is said to have been named Manuel Sarty

her
Susan x Sarty
mark

Witnesses To Mark:
  { James B. Pike
  { Cornelius Boudinot

Subscribed and sworn to before me this 20th day of March , 1905.

B J Beavers
Notary Public.

My commission expires Dec 19-1908

N.C. 207

Muskogee, Indian Territory, September 15, 1905.

Hepsie Sarty,
  Care Rollie Sarty,
    Weer, Indian Territory.

Dear Madam:

In the matter of the application for the enrollment of your minor children, Emanuel Sarty and Martin Gambler, as citizens of the Creek Nation, you are advised that you will be allowed fifteen days from date hereof within which to appear before the office of the Commissioner to the Five Civilized Tribes in Muskogee, Indian Territory, for the purpose of being examined under oath.

Applications for Enrollment of Creek Newborn
Act of 1905   Volume III

This matter should receive your prompt attention.

        Respectfully,

              Acting Commissioner.

NC-207

          Muskogee, Indian Territory, December 23, 1905.

Hepsey McGilbra[sic]
  Weer, Indian Territory.

Dear Madam:

  There are on file at this Office the affidavits of Hepsey Sarty, mother, and Susan Sarty, midwife, in the matter of the application for the enrollment of Manuel Sarty, born March 3, 1904, as a citizen of the Creek Nation.

  You are requested to advise this Office whether or not you have a minor child named Manuel Sarty, born on the above named date. The father of said child appears to be Rollie Sarty.

  You are also requested to advise this Office as to the names of your parents and other members of your family, your maiden name, the Creek Indian Town to which you belong, and, if possible, your name and roll number as same appear on your allotment certificate or deeds to land in the Creek Nation, to enable this Office to identify you on its rolls of Creek citizens.

  This matter should receive your immediate attention.

        Respectfully,

              Commissioner.

Applications for Enrollment of Creek Newborn
Act of 1905 Volume III

BIRTH AFFIDAVIT.

DEPARTMENT OF THE INTERIOR,
COMMISSION TO THE FIVE CIVILIZED TRIBES.

IN RE Application for Enrollment, as a citizen of the Creek Nation, of James Evans Jr., born on the 19th day of February, 1905

Name of Father:	James Evans	a citizen of the	Creek Nation.
Name of Mother: Stella Evans <u>nee</u> Sanger		a citizen of the	Creek Nation.

Postoffice   Oak-ta-ha Ind. Ty.

AFFIDAVIT OF MOTHER.

UNITED STATES OF AMERICA, Indian Territory, }
    Western   DISTRICT.

I, James Evans, on oath state that I am 23 years of age and a citizen by blood, of the Creek Nation; that Stella Evans nee Sanger my late wife was 24 years old and my ~~that I am the~~ lawful wife ~~of~~ also she was , ~~who is~~ a citizen, by blood of the Creek Nation; that a male child was born to ~~me~~ us on the 19th day of February, 1905, that said child has been named James Evans Jr, and is now living. that the said mother of said child died on the 14th of March 1905.

James Evans

Witnesses To Mark:
{

Subscribed and sworn to before me this 18th *day of* March, *1905.*

Z.T. Walrand *(difficult to read)*
Notary Public.
Com. Exps 1906-7-1

AFFIDAVIT OF ATTENDING PHYSICIAN OR MID-WIFE.

UNITED STATES OF AMERICA, Indian Territory, }
    Western   DISTRICT.

I, A.J. Snelson M.D., a Physician, on oath state that I attended on Mrs. Stella Evans (nee Sanger), wife of James Evans on the 19th day of February, 1905; that there was born to her on said date a male child; that said child is now living and is said to have been named James Evans Jr.

A.J. Snelson

Witnesses To Mark:
{

Applications for Enrollment of Creek Newborn
Act of 1905   Volume III

Subscribed and sworn to before me this 21st *day of* March, *1905.*

A.M. Darling
Notary Public.
Com. Exps *(illegible)*

BIRTH AFFIDAVIT.
DEPARTMENT OF THE INTERIOR,
COMMISSION TO THE FIVE CIVILIZED TRIBES.

IN RE Application for Enrollment, as a citizen of the Creek Nation, of Phidelta Lee Evans, born on the *(blank)* day of June, 1903

Name of Father: James Evans   a citizen of the   Creek   Nation.
Name of Mother: Stella Evans <u>nee</u> Sanger   a citizen of the   Creek   Nation.

Postoffice   Oak-ta-ha Ind. Ty.

AFFIDAVIT OF <s>MOTHER</s>.
father

UNITED STATES OF AMERICA, Indian Territory,
    Western   DISTRICT. }

I, James Evans , on oath state that I am 23 years of age and a citizen by blood , of the Creek   Nation; <s>that I am</s> that Stella Evans nee Sanger, who was the lawful wife of this affiant and she was <s>who is</s> a citizen, by blood of the Creek   Nation; aged 24 years at time of her death that a   female   child was born to <s>me</s> us on *(blank)* day of June , 1903 , that said child has been named Phidelta Lee Evans , and is now living. The said mother, my said wife died on the 14th day of March 1905.

James Evans

Witnesses To Mark:
    {

Subscribed and sworn to before me this 18th *day of* March *, 1905.*

Z.T. Walrond *(difficult to read)*
Notary Public.
Term exps 1906-7-1

Applications for Enrollment of Creek Newborn
Act of 1905 Volume III

AFFIDAVIT OF ATTENDING PHYSICIAN OR MID-WIFE.

UNITED STATES OF AMERICA, Indian Territory, }
  Western DISTRICT.

  I, Louisa J. Cain , a midwife , on oath state that I attended on Mrs. Stella Evans (nee Sanger) , wife of James Evans on the 28 day of June , 1903 ; that there was born to her on said date a female child; that said child is now living and is said to have been named Phidelta Lee Evans

           Louisa J Cain

Witnesses To Mark:
 { Chas F. Cain
  R. Lowrey

Subscribed and sworn to before me this 24th *day of* March, *1905*.

         W.A. Cain
          Notary Public.
         Com. expires July 24 190?

BIRTH AFFIDAVIT.
DEPARTMENT OF THE INTERIOR.
COMMISSION TO THE FIVE CIVILIZED TRIBES.

  IN RE APPLICATION FOR ENROLLMENT, as a citizen of the CREEK Nation, of Phidelta Lee Evans, born on the 28th day of June , 1903

Name of Father:	James Evans	a citizen of the	Creek	Nation.
Name of Mother:	Stella Evans <u>nee</u> Sanger	a citizen of the	Creek	Nation.

      Postoffice Oak-ta-ha Ind. Ty.

AFFIDAVIT OF MOTHER.

UNITED STATES OF AMERICA, Indian Territory, }
  WESTERN DISTRICT.

  I, James Evans, on oath state that I am 23 years of age and a citizen by blood , of the Creek Nation; that I ~~am~~ was the lawful ~~wife~~ husband of Stella Evans nee Sanger , who ~~is~~ was a citizen, by blood of the Creek Nation; and who died on the 14" day of February[sic] 1905 that a female child was born to ~~me~~ us on 28th day of June , 1903 , that said child has been named Phidelta Lee Evans , and is now living.

         J. A. Evans

Applications for Enrollment of Creek Newborn
Act of 1905   Volume III

Witnesses To Mark:
{ Z T Walrond

    Subscribed and sworn to before me this 25th day of March , 1905.

                              Z.T. Walrond
                                    Notary Public.
                              Com. exps July 1" 1906

DEPARTMENT OF THE INTERIOR,
COMMISSIONER TO THE FIVE CIVILIZED TRIBES.

REFER IN REPLY TO THE FOLLOWING:
NC-208

                        Muskogee, Indian Territory, **August 4, 1905.**

James Evans,
    Oktaha, Indian Territory.

Dear Sir:

    You are hereby advised that on **July 28, 1905** , the Secretary of the Interior approved the enrollment of your minor child, **Phidelta Lee Evans** , as a citizen by blood of the **Creek** Nation, and that the name of said child appears upon the roll of new born citizens of the **Creek** Nation as Number **142** .

    The child is now entitled to an allotment, and application therefor should be made without delay at the Land Office for the Nation in which the prospective allotment is located.

    An entire allotment for said child must be selected at the time of the original application.

                        Respectively,

                                    Commissioner.

Applications for Enrollment of Creek Newborn
Act of 1905   Volume III

DEPARTMENT OF THE INTERIOR,
COMMISSIONER TO THE FIVE CIVILIZED TRIBES.

REFER IN REPLY TO THE FOLLOWING:

NC-208

Muskogee, Indian Territory, **August 4, 1905.**

James Evans,
    Oktaha, Indian Territory.

Dear Sir:

You are hereby advised that on **July 28, 1905**, the Secretary of the Interior approved the enrollment of your minor child, **James Evans, Jr.**, as a citizen by blood of the **Creek** Nation, and that the name of said child appears upon the roll of new born citizens of the **Creek** Nation as Number **143**.

The child is now entitled to an allotment, and application therefor should be made without delay at the Land Office for the Nation in which the prospective allotment is located.

An entire allotment for said child must be selected at the time of the original application.

        Respectively,

                Commissioner.

United States of America   ⎫
  Indian Territory,   ⎬ ss.
  Western District.   ⎭

Sallie Coon being first duly sworn, on her oath, deposes and says: My name is Sallie Coon, my age is 29 years, my Postoffice is Checotah I.T. I am a Citizen by blood of the Creek Nation; I am the wife of Fred C. Coon, a white man; I am the mother of Oda M. Coon, born November 13th 1904 at our home, about 6 miles South East of Checotah, I.T; Oda M. Coon is my youngest child, a girl, and is living at the present time. Lydia Wells, was the mid wife present at the birth of this child.

Witness Charles Buford   Sallie Coon

Subscribed and sworn to before me this 13th day of March 1905.

My commission expires July 3rd 1906.   Charles Buford
                                                  Notary Public.

Applications for Enrollment of Creek Newborn
Act of 1905 Volume III

United States of America
  Indian Territory, } ss.
  Western District.

    Lydia Wells, being first duly sworn on her oath deposes and says: My name is Lydia Wells, I am 55 years old, I live 6 miles S.E. of Checotah I.T. My Post office is Checotah I.T; I have been well acquainted with Fred C. Coon and Sallie Coon for more than the last 10 years. Fred C. Coon is a white man, Sallie Coon, his wife, is a Citizen by blood of the Creek Nation. I am a mid wife and in my capacity as such attended Mrs. Sallie Coon before, during and after the birth of her youngest child, a girl, born November 13th 1904 at the home of its parents 6 miles South East of Checotah I.T. This child has been given the name of Oda M. Coon and is living at the present time; I saw the child last this very day.

        Witness to mark.   her
W.R. Allen   Checotah I.T.   Lydia x Wells
A A Smith   mark

Subscribed and sworn to before me this 13th day of March AD 1905

                                            Charles Buford
My commission expires July 3rd 1906   Notary Public.

DEPARTMENT OF THE INTERIOR,
COMMISSIONER TO THE FIVE CIVILIZED TRIBES.

REFER IN REPLY TO THE FOLLOWING:
NC-209

                            Muskogee, Indian Territory, **August 4, 1905.**

Sallie Coon,
       Care of Fred C. Coon,
              Checotah, Indian Territory.
Dear Madam:

    You are hereby advised that on **July 28, 1905**, the Secretary of the Interior approved the enrollment of your minor child, **Oda M. Coon**, as a citizen by blood of the **Creek** Nation, and that the name of said child appears upon the roll of new born citizens of the **Creek** Nation as Number **144**.

    The child is now entitled to an allotment, and application therefor should be made without delay at the Land Office for the Nation in which the prospective allotment is located.

    An entire allotment for said child must be selected at the time of the original application.

                    Respectively,

                                  Commissioner.

Applications for Enrollment of Creek Newborn
Act of 1905 Volume III

DEPARTMENT OF THE INTERIOR,
COMMISSIONER TO THE FIVE CIVILIZED TRIBES.

REFER IN REPLY TO THE FOLLOWING:
NC-210

Muskogee, Indian Territory, **August 4, 1905.**

Myrtle M. Goode,
    Care of George Goode,
        Mounds, Indian Territory.

Dear Madam:

    You are hereby advised that on **July 28, 1905**, the Secretary of the Interior approved the enrollment of your minor child, **Rowena Goode**, as a citizen by blood of the **Creek** Nation, and that the name of said child appears upon the roll of new born citizens of the **Creek** Nation as Number **145**.

    The child is now entitled to an allotment, and application therefor should be made without delay at the Land Office for the Nation in which the prospective allotment is located.

    An entire allotment for said child must be selected at the time of the original application.

                   Respectively,

                           Commissioner.

BIRTH AFFIDAVIT.

DEPARTMENT OF THE INTERIOR.
COMMISSION TO THE FIVE CIVILIZED TRIBES.

    IN RE APPLICATION FOR ENROLLMENT, as a citizen of the Creek Nation, of Rowena Goode, born on the 1st day of February, 1903

Name of Father:	George Goode	a citizen of the	Creek	Nation.
Name of Mother:	Myrtle M "	a citizen of the	Creek	Nation.

                    Postoffice   Mounds

Applications for Enrollment of Creek Newborn
Act of 1905   Volume III

AFFIDAVIT OF MOTHER.

UNITED STATES OF AMERICA, Indian Territory, }
   Western   DISTRICT.

   I, Myrtle M. Goode , on oath state that I am 22 years of age and a citizen by blood , of the Creek Nation; that I am the lawful wife of George Goode , who is a citizen, by marriage of the Creek Nation; that a Female child was born to me on 1st day of February, 1903, that said child has been named Rowena Goode, and is now living.

Myrtle M Goode

Witnesses To ~~Mark~~: signature
{ Fle Garner
  J J Deere

   Subscribed and sworn to before me this 14th day of March , 1905.

F.E. (Illegible)

My Commission expires July 21-1908.   Notary Public.

AFFIDAVIT OF ATTENDING PHYSICIAN OR MID-WIFE.

UNITED STATES OF AMERICA, Indian Territory, }
   Western   DISTRICT.

   I, M.E. Hill , a Mid wife , on oath state that I attended on Mrs. Myrtle M Goode , wife of George Goode on the 1st day of February , 1903 ; that there was born to her on said date a Female child; that said child is now living and is said to have been named Rowena Goode

her
M.E. + Hill
mark

Witnesses To Mark:
{ Fle Garner
  J J Deere

   Subscribed and sworn to before me this 14th day of March , 1905.

F.E. (Illegible)

My Commission expires July 21-1908.   Notary Public.

Applications for Enrollment of Creek Newborn
Act of 1905   Volume III

BIRTH AFFIDAVIT.

DEPARTMENT OF THE INTERIOR.
COMMISSION TO THE FIVE CIVILIZED TRIBES.

IN RE APPLICATION FOR ENROLLMENT, as a citizen of the CREEK Nation, of Rowena Goode, born on the 1 day of Feb , 1903

Name of Father:	George Goode	a citizen of the U.S.	Nation.
Name of Mother:	Myrtle M "	a citizen of the Creek	Nation.

Postoffice   Mounds

(Child present) HGH

AFFIDAVIT OF MOTHER.

UNITED STATES OF AMERICA, Indian Territory, }
WESTERN   DISTRICT.

I, Myrtle M. Goode , on oath state that I am 22 years of age and a citizen by blood , of the Creek Nation; that I am the lawful wife of George Goode , who is a citizen, by ----- of the U.S. Nation; that a female child was born to me on 1 day of Feb , 1903, that said child has been named Rowena Goode, and is now living.

Myrtle M Goode

Witnesses To Mark:
{

Subscribed and sworn to before me this 13 day of March , 1905.

Edw C Griesel
Notary Public.

DEPARTMENT OF THE INTERIOR,
COMMISSIONER TO THE FIVE CIVILIZED TRIBES.

REFER IN REPLY TO THE FOLLOWING:

NC-211

Muskogee, Indian Territory, **August 4, 1905.**

Emma H. Puryear,
   Care of Frank M. Puryear,
      Mounds, Indian Territory.

Dear Madam:

You are hereby advised that on **July 28, 1905** , the Secretary of the Interior approved the enrollment of your minor child, **William H. Puryear** , as a citizen by

Applications for Enrollment of Creek Newborn
Act of 1905 Volume III

blood of the **Creek** Nation, and that the name of said child appears upon the roll of new born citizens of the **Creek** Nation as Number **146** .

The child is now entitled to an allotment, and application therefor should be made without delay at the Land Office for the Nation in which the prospective allotment is located.

An entire allotment for said child must be selected at the time of the original application.

Respectively,

Commissioner.

BIRTH AFFIDAVIT.

DEPARTMENT OF THE INTERIOR.
COMMISSION TO THE FIVE CIVILIZED TRIBES.

IN RE APPLICATION FOR ENROLLMENT, as a citizen of the Creek Nation, of William H. Puryear , born on the 27 day of Sept , 1904

Name of Father:	Frank M Puryear	a citizen of the	U.S.	Nation.
Name of Mother:	Emma H Puryear	a citizen of the	Creek	Nation.

Postoffice   Mounds Ind. Terry

AFFIDAVIT OF MOTHER.

UNITED STATES OF AMERICA, Indian Territory,
Western   DISTRICT.

I, Emma H Puryear , on oath state that I am 26 years of age and a citizen by blood , of the Creek Nation; that I am the lawful wife of Frank M Puryear , who is a non-citizen, by *(blank)* of the Creek Nation; that a male child was born to me on 27th day of September , 1904 , that said child has been named William H Puryear , and is now living.

Emma H Puryear

Witnesses To Mark:

Subscribed and sworn to before me this 11th day of March , 1905.

D J Red

Notary Public.

Applications for Enrollment of Creek Newborn
Act of 1905   Volume III

AFFIDAVIT OF ATTENDING PHYSICIAN OR MID-WIFE.

UNITED STATES OF AMERICA, Indian Territory, }
    Western   DISTRICT.

I, J. W. Bronaugh , a physician , on oath state that I attended on Mrs. Emma H Puryear , wife of Frank M Puryear on the 27th day of September , 1904 ; that there was born to her on said date a male child; that said child is now living and is said to have been named William H. Puryear

                              J. W. Bronaugh M.D.

Witnesses To Mark:
    { George *(Illegible)*
      Elmer Finley

Subscribed and sworn to before me this 11th day of March, 1905.

                          D J Red
                                Notary Public.

BIRTH AFFIDAVIT.

DEPARTMENT OF THE INTERIOR.
COMMISSION TO THE FIVE CIVILIZED TRIBES.

IN RE APPLICATION FOR ENROLLMENT, as a citizen of the CREEK Nation, of Wm H. Puryear , born on the 27 day of Sept. , 1904

| Name of Father: | Frank M Puryear | a citizen of the | U.S. | Nation. |
| Name of Mother: | Emma H " | a citizen of the | Creek | Nation. |

                    Postoffice   Mounds

(child present) HGH

AFFIDAVIT OF MOTHER.

UNITED STATES OF AMERICA, Indian Territory, }
    WESTERN   DISTRICT.

I, Emma H. Puryear , on oath state that I am 26 years of age and a citizen by blood , of the Creek Nation; that I am the lawful wife of Frank M. Puryear , who is a citizen, by ----- of the U.S. Nation; that a male child was born to me on 27 day of Sept. , 1904 , that said child has been named William H. Puryear , and is now living.

                            Emma H Puryear

Witnesses To Mark:
    {

Applications for Enrollment of Creek Newborn
Act of 1905   Volume III

Subscribed and sworn to before me this 13" day of March , 1905.

> Edw C Griesel
> Notary Public.

DEPARTMENT OF THE INTERIOR,
COMMISSION TO THE FIVE CIVILIZED TRIBES.

IN RE APPLICATION FOR ENROLLMENT, as citizens of the Creek Nation of Howard H. Henry, born on the 18th day of March, 1902, and Edith Clara Henry, born on the first day of January, 1904, Name of father James P. Henry, a citizen of the Creek Nation, name of mother Carrie Henry, not a citizen of the Creek nation[sic], Post office, Henryetta Indian Territory.

United States of America,   )
Indian Territory,   )
Western Judicial District.   )
)   AFFIDAVIT OF MOTHER.

I, Carraie Heanry, on oath state that I am thirty years of age and not a citizen by blood of the Creek Nation; that I am the lawful wife of James P. Henry, who is a citizen, by blood of the Creek Nation; that a male child was born to me on the 18th day March, 1902; that said child has been named Howard H. Henry; and that a female child was born to me on the 1st day of Janury[sic] 1904; that said child has been named Edith Clara Henry; that both of said children are now living.

> Carrie Henry.

Subscribed and sworn to before me this 13th day of March 1905.

> William B. Morgan
> Notary Public.

My Commission expires Aril 22nd, 1908.

AFFIDAVIT OF ATTENDING PHYSICIAN.

UNITED STATES OF AMERICA,   )
INDIAN TERRITORY,   ) ss.
WESTERN JUDICIAL DISTRICT.   )

I, Charles E. Scharnagel, a regular practicing physician, on oath state tha[sic] I attended on Mrs Carraie Henry, wife of James P. Henry, on the 18th day of March 1902; that there was born to her on said date a male child; that said child is now living and is said to have been been[sic] named Howard H. Henry; and that on the first day of January,

Applications for Enrollment of Creek Newborn
Act of 1905   Volume III

1904, I attended on Mrs. Carraie Henry, wife of James P. Henry, and that there was born to her on said date a female child; that said child is now living and is said to have been named Edith Clara Henry.

Chas E. Scharnagel M.D.

Subscribed and sworn to before me this 13th day of March 1905.

William B. Morgan
Notary Public.

My Commission expires Aril 22nd, 1908.

Father's Roll No. I. 4430.

MARRIAGE LICENSE

"'

UNITED STATES OF AMERICA,   )
   INDIAN TERRITORY ,   )
   Northern District.   ) ss   No. 1326
)

TO ANY PERSON AUTHORIZED BY LAW TO SOLEMNIZE MARRIAGE--Greeting:

YOU ARE HEREBY COMMANDED TO Solemnize the Rite and publish the Banns of Matrimony between Mr. J. P. Henry, of Senora, in the Indian Territory, aged 24 years, and Miss Carrie C. Harper, of Senora, in the Indian Territory, aged 22 years, according to law, and do you officially sign and return this license to the parties therein named.

WITNESS my hand and official seal at Muscogee, Indian Territory this 16" day of Sept. A. D. 1898.

(Signed) J. A. Winston.
Clerk of the U. S.
Court

By (Signed) W. P. Young, Deputy

CERTIFICATE OF MARRIAGE.

" " "

UNITED STATES OF AMERICA,   )
   INDIAN TERRITORY,   )
   Northern District.   ) ss
)

Applications for Enrollment of Creek Newborn
Act of 1905   Volume III

I, J. A. Winston, Clerk U.S. Court, DO HEREBY CERTIFY, that on the 16" day of Sept. A. D. 1898, I did duly and according to law as commanded in the foregoing License, solemnize the Rite and publish the Banns of Matrimony between the parties therein named.

WITNESS my hand this 16" day of Sept A. D. 1898.

My credentials are recorded in the office of the Clerk of the United States Court, Indian Territory, Northern District, Book --- Page ----.

J. A. Winston, Clerk
By W. P. Young, D. C.

I, Harriett E. Arbuckle on oath state that the above and foregoing is a true and correct copy of same.

Harriett E. Arbuckle

Subscribed and sworn to before me this 7, day of March, 1906.

J. McDermott
Notary Public.

CERTIFICATE OF RECORD.

UNITED STATES OF AMERICA,)
    INDIAN TERRITORY,   ) ss
Northern District.   )

I, James A. WINSTON, Clerk of the United States Court in the Northern District, Indian Territory, do hereby certify that the instrument hereto attached was field[sic] for record in my office the 16 day of Sept 1898, at -----M and duly recorded in Book ---------- marriage Record, Page 146.

WITNESS my hand and seal of said Court at Muscogee in said Territory, this 17 day of Sept A. D. 1898.

Jas A. Winston Clerk

By ------------------------------Deputy.

NC 212.

Muskogee, Indian Territory, July 5, 1905.

Carrie Henry,
    Henryetta, Indian Territory.

Dear Madam:

Applications for Enrollment of Creek Newborn
Act of 1905   Volume III

In the matter of the application for the enrollment of your minor children, Howard H. and Edith Clair[sic] Henry, as citizens of the Creek Nation, you are advised that there is no proof at this office of your marriage to the father of said children, James P. Henry, a citizen of the Creek Nation.

A certified copy of your marriage license or other satisfactory proof of your marriage to said James P. Henry should be forwarded at once to this office.

Respectfully,

Commissioner.

N. C. 212.

JWH

Muskogee, Indian Territory, January 29, 1907.

C. E. Kilmer,
   Coweta, Indian Territory.

Dear Sir :--

Your attention is invited to the following provision of the Act of Congress approved April 26, 1906:

> "Provided, that the rolls of the tribes affected by this Act shall be fully completed on or before the fourth day of March, nineteen hundred and seven, and the Secretary of the Interior shall have no jurisdiction to approve the enrollment of any person after said date."

In view of the above and inasmuch as you appear to be the notary public in the case, you are urged to notify Retta Sarty, wife of Jasper Sarty, and alleged mother of Lena Sarty, to write this office at once, stating her maiden name, the names of her parents, the Creek Indian town to which she belongs and if possible, her roll number as same appears on her certificates or deeds to land in the Creek Nation.

Letters written to said Retta Sarty for this purpose have been ignored and in the event that you cannot induce her to answer and furnish said information, you are requested to do so yourself if you can secure the information.

Respectfully,

Commissioner.

Applications for Enrollment of Creek Newborn
Act of 1905   Volume III

BIRTH AFFIDAVIT.

DEPARTMENT OF THE INTERIOR.
COMMISSION TO THE FIVE CIVILIZED TRIBES.

IN RE APPLICATION FOR ENROLLMENT, as a citizen of the CREEK Nation, of Lena Canard , born on the 26 day of Nov. , 1902

Name of Father:	Martin Canard	a citizen of the	Creek	Nation.
Name of Mother:	Annie Lovett	a citizen of the C[sic]	"	Nation.

Postoffice   Coweta, I. T.

(child present) HGH

AFFIDAVIT OF MOTHER.

UNITED STATES OF AMERICA, Indian Territory, }
    WESTERN   DISTRICT.

I, Annie Lovett , on oath state that I am 25 years of age and a citizen by blood , of the Creek Nation; that I am not the lawful wife of Martin Canard , who is a citizen, by blood of the Creek Nation; that a female child was born to me on 26 day of Nov. , 1903 , that said child has been named Lena Canard , and is now living.

                                   Annie Lovett

Witnesses To Mark:
{

Subscribed and sworn to before me this 11 day of March , 1905.

My Commission   J. McDermott
Expires July 25" 1907   Notary Public.

AFFIDAVIT OF ATTENDING PHYSICIAN OR MID-WIFE.

UNITED STATES OF AMERICA, Indian Territory, }
    Western   DISTRICT.

I, Kizzie Lovett , a midwife , on oath state that I attended on ~~Mrs~~. Annie Lovett , ~~wife of~~——— on the 26 day of Nov. , 1903 ; that there was born to her on said date a female child; that said child is now living and is said to have been named Lena Canard

                                      her
                              Kizzie x Lovett
Witnesses To Mark: mark
  { H.G. Hains
     J. McDermott

Applications for Enrollment of Creek Newborn
Act of 1905   Volume III

Subscribed and sworn to before me this 11 day of March, 1905.

My Com
Ex July 25" 1907

J. McDermott
Notary Public.

DEPARTMENT OF THE INTERIOR,
COMMISSIONER TO THE FIVE CIVILIZED TRIBES.

REFER IN REPLY TO THE FOLLOWING:

NC-214

Muskogee, Indian Territory, **August 4, 1905.**

Barney Tiger,
   Wetumka, Indian Territory.

Dear Sir:

You are hereby advised that on **July 28, 1905**, the Secretary of the Interior approved the enrollment of your minor child, **Ewnah J. Tiger**, as a citizen by blood of the **Creek** Nation, and that the name of said child appears upon the roll of new born citizens of the **Creek** Nation as Number **148**.

The child is now entitled to an allotment, and application therefor should be made without delay at the Land Office for the Nation in which the prospective allotment is located.

An entire allotment for said child must be selected at the time of the original application.

Respectfully,

Commissioner.

BIRTH AFFIDAVIT.

DEPARTMENT OF THE INTERIOR.
COMMISSION TO THE FIVE CIVILIZED TRIBES.

IN RE APPLICATION FOR ENROLLMENT, as a citizen of the CREEK Nation, of Ewnah J. Tiger, born on the 13 day of July, 1903

Name of Father:	Barney Tiger	a citizen of the	Creek	Nation.
Name of Mother:	Katie Tiger	a citizen of the	Creek	Nation.

Postoffice   Wetumka, Ind. Terr.

Applications for Enrollment of Creek Newborn
Act of 1905 Volume III

AFFIDAVIT OF MOTHER.

UNITED STATES OF AMERICA, Indian Territory, }
WESTERN DISTRICT.

    I, Katie Tiger , on oath state that I am twenty-five years of age and a citizen by blood, of the Creek Nation; that I am the lawful wife of Barney Tiger , who is a citizen, by blood of the Creek Nation; that a male child was born to me on 13th. day of July , 1903 , that said child has been named Ewnah J. Tiger , and is now living.

                                            Katie Tiger

Witnesses To Mark:
{

    Subscribed and sworn to before me this 16 day of March , 1905.
    My com. exp. June 13, 1908.

                                            Jas. P. Atkins
                                                Notary Public.

AFFIDAVIT OF ATTENDING PHYSICIAN OR MID-WIFE.

UNITED STATES OF AMERICA, Indian Territory, }
    Western DISTRICT.

    I, Lucy Stewart , a Mid-wife , on oath state that I attended on Mrs. Katie Tiger , wife of Barney Tiger on the 13th. day of July , 1903 ; that there was born to her on said date a male child; that said child is now living and is said to have been named Ewnah J. Tiger

                                            her
                                  Lucy x Stewart

Witnesses To Mark: mark
{ Cleveland P. Hicks Wetumka I.T.
  William D. Atkins, Wetumka I.T.

    Subscribed and sworn to before me this 16 day of March, 1905.

                                            Jas. P. Atkins
                                            Notary Public.
My com. exp. June 13, 1908.

Applications for Enrollment of Creek Newborn
Act of 1905 Volume III

DEPARTMENT OF THE INTERIOR,
COMMISSIONER TO THE FIVE CIVILIZED TRIBES.

REFER IN REPLY TO THE FOLLOWING:

NC-215

Muskogee, Indian Territory, **August 4, 1905.**

George Perryman,
    Tulsa, Indian Territory.

Dear Sir:

    You are hereby advised that on **July 28, 1905**, the Secretary of the Interior approved the enrollment of your minor child, **Okema Perryman**, as a citizen by blood of the **Creek** Nation, and that the name of said child appears upon the roll of new born citizens of the **Creek** Nation as Number **149**.

    The child is now entitled to an allotment, and application therefor should be made without delay at the Land Office for the Nation in which the prospective allotment is located.

    An entire allotment for said child must be selected at the time of the original application.

                      Respectively,

                                        Commissioner.

BIRTH AFFIDAVIT.

DEPARTMENT OF THE INTERIOR.
COMMISSION TO THE FIVE CIVILIZED TRIBES.

    IN RE APPLICATION FOR ENROLLMENT, as a citizen of the Creek Nation, of Okema Perryman, born on the 16 day of May, 1904

Name of Father:	George Perryman	a citizen of the	Creek	Nation.
Name of Mother:	Ophia Perryman	a citizen of the	U. S.	Nation.

                        Postoffice   Tulsa

                    AFFIDAVIT OF ~~MOTHER~~. Father

                                        Child <u>Present.</u>

UNITED STATES OF AMERICA, Indian Territory, ⎫
    G[sic]   DISTRICT. ⎭

    I, George Perryman, on oath state that I am 21 years of age and a citizen by blood, of the Creek Nation; that I am the lawful ~~wife~~ Husband of Ophia Perryman, who is a citizen, by ----- of the U.S. Nation; that a female child was born to me on

Applications for Enrollment of Creek Newborn
Act of 1905   Volume III

16 day of May , 1904 , that said child has been named Okema Perryman , and was living March 4, 1905.

George B Perryman

Witnesses To Mark:
{

Subscribed and sworn to before me this 4 day of May, 1905.

Edw C Griesel
Notary Public.

BIRTH AFFIDAVIT.
DEPARTMENT OF THE INTERIOR.
COMMISSION TO THE FIVE CIVILIZED TRIBES.

IN RE APPLICATION FOR ENROLLMENT, as a citizen of the Creek Nation, of Okema Perryman, born on the 16th day of May , 1904

Name of Father: George Perryman   a citizen of the   Creek   Nation.
Name of Mother: Ophia Perryman a non-citizen   ~~a citizen~~ of the   Creek   Nation.

Postoffice   Tulsa, Indian Territory.

AFFIDAVIT OF MOTHER. Child Brought in
?/5/05

UNITED STATES OF AMERICA, Indian Territory, }
Western   DISTRICT.

I, Ophia Perryman , on oath state that I am 21 years of age and ~~a citizen by~~ a non-citizen , of the Creek Nation; that I am the lawful wife of George Perryman , who is a citizen, by blood of the Creek Nation; that a female child was born to me on 16th day of May , 1904 , that said child has been named Okema Perryman , and was living March 4, 1905.

Ophia Perryman

Witnesses To Mark:
{   W.H. Thompson
    J.A. Kinyon

Subscribed and sworn to before me this 13 day of March , 1905.

My commission expires Dec 18-1908   W.D Abbott
Notary Public.

Applications for Enrollment of Creek Newborn
Act of 1905   Volume III

AFFIDAVIT OF ATTENDING PHYSICIAN OR MID-WIFE.

UNITED STATES OF AMERICA, Indian Territory, ⎱
    Western   DISTRICT.   ⎰

    I, Dr. T. E. Shepard , a Physician , on oath state that I attended on Mrs. Ophia Perryman , wife of George Perryman on the 16th day of May , 1904 ; that there was born to her on said date a female child; that said child was living March 4, 1905, and is said to have been named Okema Perryman

                                         T.E. Shepard

Witnesses To Mark:
   {

    Subscribed and sworn to before me this 13th day of March, 1905.

                                  W.D. Abbott
My commission expires Dec 18-1908   Notary Public.

DEPARTMENT OF THE INTERIOR,
COMMISSIONER TO THE FIVE CIVILIZED TRIBES.

REFER IN REPLY TO THE FOLLOWING:
NC-217

                            Muskogee, Indian Territory, **August 4, 1905.**

Isaac Johnson,
      Weer, Indian Territory.

Dear Sir:

    You are hereby advised that on **July 28, 1905** , the Secretary of the Interior approved the enrollment of your minor child, **Miley Johnson** , as a citizen by blood of the **Creek** Nation, and that the name of said child appears upon the roll of new born citizens of the **Creek** Nation as Number **150** .

    The child is now entitled to an allotment, and application therefor should be made without delay at the Land Office for the Nation in which the prospective allotment is located.

    An entire allotment for said child must be selected at the time of the original application.

                        Respectively,

                                      Commissioner.

Applications for Enrollment of Creek Newborn
Act of 1905   Volume III

BIRTH AFFIDAVIT.

DEPARTMENT OF THE INTERIOR.
COMMISSION TO THE FIVE CIVILIZED TRIBES.

IN RE APPLICATION FOR ENROLLMENT, as a citizen of the CREEK Nation, of Scott Johnson, born on the 8 day of Nov., 1902

Name of Father:	Isaac Johnson	a citizen of the	Creek	Nation.
Name of Mother:	Nicey "	a citizen of the	"	Nation.

Postoffice   Weer, I.T.

AFFIDAVIT OF ~~MOTHER~~. Father

UNITED STATES OF AMERICA, Indian Territory,
WESTERN   DISTRICT.

I, Isaac Johnson, on oath state that I am 28 years of age and a citizen by ~~Freedman~~ blood, of the Creek Nation; that I am the lawful ~~wife~~ hus of Nicey Johnson, who is a citizen, by ~~Freedman~~ blood of the Creek Nation; that a male child was born to me on 8 day of Nov., 1902, that said child has been named Scott Johnson, and ~~is now living~~. died July 8, 1903

I F Johnson

Witnesses To Mark:

Subscribed and sworn to before me this 11 day of March, 1905.

My Commission   J. McDermott
Expires July 25" 1907   Notary Public.

N. C. 217   J.L.D

DEPARTMENT OF THE INTERIOR
COMMISSIONER TO THE FIVE CIVILIZED TRIBES.

In the matter of the application for the enrollment of Scott Johnson, deceased, as a citizen by blood of the Creek Nation.

. . . .

STATEMENT AND ORDER.

The record in this case shows that on March 11, 1905, application was made, in affidavit form, for the enrollment of Scott Johnson, deceased, as a citizen by blood of the Creek Nation, under the provisions of the act of Congress approved March 3, 1905.

Applications for Enrollment of Creek Newborn
Act of 1905   Volume III

It appears that the affidavit filed in this matter that said Scott Johnson, deceased, was born November 8, 1902, and died July 8, 1903.

The act of Congress approved March 3, 1905, (33 Stats., 1048), provides:

"That the Commission to the Five Civilized Tribes is authorized for sixty days after the date of the approval of this act to receive and consider applications for enrollment, of children, <u>born subsequent to May twenty-fifth, nineteen hundred and one, and prior to March fourth, nineteen hundred and five, and living on said latter date,</u> to citizens of the Creek tribe of Indians whose enrollment has been approved by the Secretary of the Interior prior to the approval of this act; and to enroll and make allotments to such children."

It is, therefore, ordered that the application for the enrollment of Scott Johnson, deceased, as a citizen by blood of the Creek Nation, be, and the same is, hereby dismissed.

Tams Bixby Commissioner.

Muskogee, Indian Territory.
JAN 4 1907

BIRTH AFFIDAVIT.

DEPARTMENT OF THE INTERIOR.
COMMISSION TO THE FIVE CIVILIZED TRIBES.

IN RE APPLICATION FOR ENROLLMENT, as a citizen of the CREEK Nation, of Miley Johnson, born on the 8 day of May, 1904

Name of Father:	Isaac Johnson	a citizen of the	Creek	Nation.
Name of Mother:	Nicey "	a citizen of the	"	Nation.

Postoffice   Weer, I.T.

AFFIDAVIT OF ~~MOTHER~~.
father

UNITED STATES OF AMERICA, Indian Territory,
WESTERN   DISTRICT.

I, Isaac Johnson, on oath state that I am 28 years of age and a citizen by blood, of the Creek Nation; that I am the lawful ~~wife~~ hus of Nicey Johnson, who is a citizen, by blood of the Creek Nation; that a female child was born to me on 8 day of May, 1904, that said child has been named Miley Johnson, and is now living.

I F Johnson

Witnesses To Mark:

Applications for Enrollment of Creek Newborn
Act of 1905 Volume III

Subscribed and sworn to before me this 11 day of March, 1905.

                              J. McDermott
                              Notary Public.

BIRTH AFFIDAVIT.

DEPARTMENT OF THE INTERIOR.
COMMISSION TO THE FIVE CIVILIZED TRIBES.

IN RE APPLICATION FOR ENROLLMENT, as a citizen of the Creek Nation, of Miley Johnson, born on the 8th day of May, 1904

Name of Father:	Isaac Johnson	a citizen of the Creek	Nation.
Name of Mother:	Nicey Johnson	a citizen of the Creek	Nation.

                    Postoffice   Weer, I.T.

AFFIDAVIT OF MOTHER.

UNITED STATES OF AMERICA, Indian Territory,
    Western   DISTRICT.

    I, Nicey Johnson, on oath state that I am 35 years of age and a citizen by Blood, of the Creek Nation; that I am the lawful wife of Isaac Johnson, who is a citizen, by blood of the Creek Nation; that a female child was born to me on 8th day of May, 1904, that said child has been named Miley Johnson, and is now living.

                                      her
                            Nicey Johnson x
Witnesses To Mark: mark
    B P Johnson
    Francis Asbury

    Subscribed and sworn to before me this 20th day of March, 1905.

                            CW Lumpkin
                            Notary Public.
Com xpires[sic] Jny 9-1906

Applications for Enrollment of Creek Newborn
Act of 1905   Volume III

AFFIDAVIT OF ATTENDING PHYSICIAN OR MID-WIFE.

UNITED STATES OF AMERICA, Indian Territory,
Western   DISTRICT.

I, Jennie Berryhill, a *(blank)*, on oath state that I attended on Mrs. Nicey Johnson, wife of Isaac Johnson on the 8th day of May, 1904; that there was born to her on said date a   female   child; that said child is now living and is said to have been named Miley Johnson

                                                            her
                                  Jennie Berryhill   x
Witnesses To Mark: mark
  { B P Johnson
    Francis Asbury

Subscribed and sworn to before me this 28 day of March, 1905.

                                      CW Lumpkin
                                          Notary Public.

Com xpires[sic]
    Jny 9-1906

DEPARTMENT OF THE INTERIOR,
COMMISSIONER TO THE FIVE CIVILIZED TRIBES.

REFER IN REPLY TO THE FOLLOWING:
NC-218

                            Muskogee, Indian Territory,   **August 4, 1905.**

Jessie Parker,
    Care of William E. Parker,
        Tulsa, Indian Territory.

Dear Madam:

You are hereby advised that on **July 28, 1905**, the Secretary of the Interior approved the enrollment of your minor child, **Charles Edward Parker**, as a citizen by blood of the **Creek** Nation, and that the name of said child appears upon the roll of new born citizens of the **Creek** Nation as Number **151**.

The child is now entitled to an allotment, and application therefor should be made without delay at the Land Office for the Nation in which the prospective allotment is located.

An entire allotment for said child must be selected at the time of the original application.

Applications for Enrollment of Creek Newborn
Act of 1905   Volume III

Respectively,

Commissioner.

BIRTH AFFIDAVIT.

DEPARTMENT OF THE INTERIOR,
COMMISSION TO THE FIVE CIVILIZED TRIBES.

IN RE Application for Enrollment, as a citizen of the Creek Nation, of Charles Edward Parker, born on the 10th day of June, 1904

Name of Father: William E. Parker   a citizen of the ~~(illegible)   Nation~~.
Name of Mother: Jessie Parker (nee Carey)   a citizen of the   Creek   Nation.

Postoffice   Tulsa, Ind. Ter

AFFIDAVIT OF MOTHER.

UNITED STATES OF AMERICA, Indian Territory,
     Western   DISTRICT.

I, Jessie Parker (nee Carey), on oath state that I am Twenty years of age and a citizen by blood, of the Creek Nation; that I am the lawful wife of William E. Parker, who is a citizen, by marriage of the Creek Nation; that a male child was born to me on 10th day of June, 1904, that said child has been named Charles Edward Parker, and is now living.

Jessie Parker

Witnesses To Mark:
{

Subscribed and sworn to before me this 13th *day of* March, *190*5.

Com Exp. 7/2/1906   Luther Mann
                                    Notary Public.

AFFIDAVIT OF ATTENDING PHYSICIAN OR MID-WIFE.

UNITED STATES OF AMERICA, Indian Territory,
     Western   DISTRICT.

I, W H *(Illegible)*   , a physician, on oath state that I attended on Mrs. Jessie Parker, wife of William E. Parker on the *(blocked out)* day of June, 1904; that there was born to her on said date a male child; that said child is now living and is said to have been named Charles Edward Parker

225

Applications for Enrollment of Creek Newborn
Act of 1905   Volume III

                         W.H. *(Illegible)*

Witnesses To Mark:

{

Subscribed and sworn to before me this 15 *day of* March, *1905.*

     Com Exp. 7/2/1906   Luther Mann
                                         Notary Public.

DEPARTMENT OF THE INTERIOR,
COMMISSIONER TO THE FIVE CIVILIZED TRIBES.

REFER IN REPLY TO THE FOLLOWING:
NC-219

                        Muskogee, Indian Territory, **August 4, 1905.**

William G. Bruner,
     Tulsa, Indian Territory.

Dear Sir:

       You are hereby advised that on **July 28, 1905**, the Secretary of the Interior approved the enrollment of your minor child, **Flora Bruner**, as a citizen by blood of the **Creek** Nation, and that the name of said child appears upon the roll of new born citizens of the **Creek** Nation as Number **152**.

       The child is now entitled to an allotment, and application therefor should be made without delay at the Land Office for the Nation in which the prospective allotment is located.

       An entire allotment for said child must be selected at the time of the original application.

                       Respectively,

                                     Commissioner.

BIRTH AFFIDAVIT.
                     DEPARTMENT OF THE INTERIOR.
              COMMISSION TO THE FIVE CIVILIZED TRIBES.

       IN RE APPLICATION FOR ENROLLMENT, as a citizen of the Creek Nation, of Flora Bruner, born on the 9" day of November, 1904

Name of Father:	William G. Bruner	a citizen of the	Creek	Nation.
Name of Mother:	Jennie Bruner	a citizen of the	Creek	Nation.

Applications for Enrollment of Creek Newborn
Act of 1905   Volume III

Postoffice   Inesa Ind Ter

AFFIDAVIT OF MOTHER.

UNITED STATES OF AMERICA, Indian Territory,
Western   DISTRICT.

I, Jennie Bruner , on oath state that I am 25 years of age and a citizen by Blood, of the Creek Nation; that I am the lawful wife of William G. Bruner , who is a citizen, by Blood of the Creek Nation; that a Female child was born to me on 9" day of November , 1904 , that said child has been named Flora Bruner , and was living March 4, 1905.

              her
            Jennie x Bruner

Witnesses To Mark: mark
{ Robert E Lynch Inesa I.T.
  Eric O. Albert

Subscribed and sworn to before me this 13" day of March , 1905.

My Com Ex 7/3/1906   Robert E Lynch
              Notary Public.

AFFIDAVIT OF ATTENDING PHYSICIAN OR MID-WIFE.

UNITED STATES OF AMERICA, Indian Territory,
Western   DISTRICT.

I, Sarah Smith , a Mid wife , on oath state that I attended on Mrs. Jennie Bruner, wife of William G. Bruner on the 9 day of November , 1904 ; that there was born to her on said date a female child; that said child was living March 4, 1905, and is said to have been named Flora Bruner

              Her
            Sarah x Smith

Witnesses To Mark: mark
{ Robert E. Lynch Inesa I.T.
  Eric O. Albert

Subscribed and sworn to before me this 28 day of March, 1905.

My Com Ex 7/3/1906   Robert E Lynch
              Notary Public.

Applications for Enrollment of Creek Newborn
Act of 1905   Volume III

DEPARTMENT OF THE INTERIOR,
COMMISSIONER TO THE FIVE CIVILIZED TRIBES.

REFER IN REPLY TO THE FOLLOWING:
NC-220

Muskogee, Indian Territory, **August 4, 1905.**

Walter Posey,
    Wagoner, Indian Territory.

Dear Sir:

You are hereby advised that on **July 28, 1905**, the Secretary of the Interior approved the enrollment of your minor child, **Terry O. Posey**, as a citizen by blood of the **Creek** Nation, and that the name of said child appears upon the roll of new born citizens of the **Creek** Nation as Number **153**.

The child is now entitled to an allotment, and application therefor should be made without delay at the Land Office for the Nation in which the prospective allotment is located.

An entire allotment for said child must be selected at the time of the original application.

          Respectively,

                    Commissioner.

BIRTH AFFIDAVIT.

DEPARTMENT OF THE INTERIOR.
COMMISSION TO THE FIVE CIVILIZED TRIBES.

IN RE APPLICATION FOR ENROLLMENT, as a citizen of the Creek Nation, of Terry O. Posey, born on the 9th day of March, 1903

Name of Father: Walter Posey   a citizen of the   Creek   Nation.
Name of Mother: Mary L. Posey   a citizen of the United States Nation.

              Postoffice   Wagoner I.T.

AFFIDAVIT OF MOTHER.

UNITED STATES OF AMERICA, Indian Territory, ⎫
    Western Judicial   DISTRICT. ⎭

I, Mary L. Posey, on oath state that I am 31 years of age and a citizen by Marriage, of the Creek Nation; that I am the lawful wife of Walter Posey, who is a citizen, by Blood of the Creek Nation; that a male child was born to me on 9th

Applications for Enrollment of Creek Newborn
Act of 1905   Volume III

day of March, 1903, that said child has been named Terry O. Posey, and was living March 4, 1905.

                                          Mary L. Posey

Witnesses To Mark:
{

Subscribed and sworn to before me this 14 day of March, 1905.

                                          H R Bonner
                                              Notary Public.

AFFIDAVIT OF ATTENDING PHYSICIAN OR MID-WIFE.

UNITED STATES OF AMERICA, Indian Territory,
    Western Judicial   DISTRICT.

    I, G W Jobe, a Physician, on oath state that I attended on Mrs. Mary L Posey, wife of Walter Posey on the 9th day of March, 1903; that there was born to her on said date a male child; that said child was living March 4, 1905, and is said to have been named Terry O. Posey

                                          G.W. Jobe M.D.

Witnesses To Mark:
{

Subscribed and sworn to before me this 14 day of March, 1905.

                                          H R Bonner
My Com Ex. July 1st 1906.   Notary Public.

DEPARTMENT OF THE INTERIOR,
COMMISSIONER TO THE FIVE CIVILIZED TRIBES.

REFER IN REPLY TO THE FOLLOWING:

NC-221

                                  Muskogee, Indian Territory, **August 4, 1905.**

Arty Alexander,
      Okmulgee, Indian Territory.

Dear Sir:

    You are hereby advised that on **July 28, 1905**, the Secretary of the Interior approved the enrollment of your minor child, **Mary Alexander**, as a citizen by blood of the **Creek** Nation, and that the name of said child appears upon the roll of new born citizens of the **Creek** Nation as Number **154**.

Applications for Enrollment of Creek Newborn
Act of 1905   Volume III

The child is now entitled to an allotment, and application therefor should be made without delay at the Land Office for the Nation in which the prospective allotment is located.

An entire allotment for said child must be selected at the time of the original application.

Respectively,

Commissioner.

Proof of Mother's Death.

United States of America,)
Indian Territory,   ) ss.
Western District.   )

I, Artie Alexander, on oath state that I am about 48 years of age and a citizen by blood of the Creek Nation, that Nancy Alexander, deceased, the[sic] was a citizen by blood of the Creek Nation, was my wife till the time of her death, that on the 24th day of February, 1903, there was born to the said Nancy Alexander, deceased, a female child, that said child is now living and is named Mary Alexander, that said Nancy Alexander died on the 24th. day of February, 1903 a few hours after the birth of said Mary Alexander, that I am father of said Mary Alexander.

his
Artie x Alexander
mark

Witness:
    Wm C Newman
    E.E. Hardridge

Subscribed and sworn to before me this eighth day March, 1905.

J C Stone
Notary Public.

My commission expires Apr 24th 1907

United States of America,)
)
Indian Territory,   ) ss.
)
Western District.   )

I, Harry Micco, on oath state that I am about 45 years of age and a citizen of the Creek Nation by blood, that I am brother of said Nancy Alexander, that she, the said

Applications for Enrollment of Creek Newborn
Act of 1905   Volume III

Nancy Alexander, died on or about the 24th. day of February, 1903, only a short time after the birth of her female child, now living and named Mary Alexander.

                                            his
                                  Harry x Micco
                                         mark

Witness:
      Wm C Newman
      E.E. Hardridge

Subscribed and sworn to before me this eighth day March, 1905.

                                        J C Stone
                                                        Notary Public.

My commission expires Apr 24th 1907

BIRTH AFFIDAVIT.

DEPARTMENT OF THE INTERIOR.
COMMISSION TO THE FIVE CIVILIZED TRIBES.

      IN RE APPLICATION FOR ENROLLMENT, as a citizen of the CREEK Nation, of Mary Alexander, born on the 24th day of February, 1903

| Name of Father: | Artie Alexander | a citizen of the | Creek | Nation. |
| Name of Mother: | Nancy Alexander | a citizen of the | Creek | Nation. |

                                Postoffice   Okmulgee

                       AFFIDAVIT OF ~~MOTHER~~. Father

UNITED STATES OF AMERICA, Indian Territory,
      WESTERN   DISTRICT.

     I, Artie Alexander , on oath state that I am *(blank)* years of age and a citizen by blood , of the Creek Nation; that I am the lawful ~~wife~~ hus of Nancy Alexander (dec'd), who is a citizen, by blood of the Creek Nation; that a *(blank)* child was born to me on 24 day of Feb , 1903 , that said child has been named Mary Alexander , and is now living.

                                          his
                                    Artie x Alexander
Witnesses To Mark: mark
      { Jesse McDermott
      { HG Hains

Applications for Enrollment of Creek Newborn
Act of 1905   Volume III

Subscribed and sworn to before me this 10 day of March, 1905.

My Commission   J. McDermott
Ex July 25" 1905[sic]   Notary Public.

AFFIDAVIT OF ATTENDING PHYSICIAN OR MID-WIFE.

UNITED STATES OF AMERICA, Indian Territory,
    WESTERN   DISTRICT.

I, William M. Cott M.D. , a Physician , on oath state that I attended on Mrs. Nancy Alexander , wife of Artie Alexander on the 24 day of February , 1903 ; that there was born to her on said date a female child; that said child is now living and is said to have been named Mary Alexander

William M Cott, M.D.

Witnesses To Mark:
{

Subscribed and sworn to before me this 9th day of March, 1905.

J.O. Stone
Notary Public.

DEPARTMENT OF THE INTERIOR,
COMMISSIONER TO THE FIVE CIVILIZED TRIBES.

REFER IN REPLY TO THE FOLLOWING:
NC-222

Muskogee, Indian Territory, **August 4, 1905.**

Edna Pike,
    Care of Vester Pike,
        Dustin, Indian Territory.

Dear Sir:

You are hereby advised that on **July 28, 1905** , the Secretary of the Interior approved the enrollment of your minor child, **Fay Pike**, as a citizen by blood of the **Creek** Nation, and that the name of said child appears upon the roll of new born citizens of the **Creek** Nation as Number **155** .

The child is now entitled to an allotment, and application therefor should be made without delay at the Land Office for the Nation in which the prospective allotment is located.

Applications for Enrollment of Creek Newborn
Act of 1905 Volume III

An entire allotment for said child must be selected at the time of the original application.

Respectively,

Commissioner.

BIRTH AFFIDAVIT.

DEPARTMENT OF THE INTERIOR.
COMMISSION TO THE FIVE CIVILIZED TRIBES.

IN RE APPLICATION FOR ENROLLMENT, as a citizen of the Creek Nation, of Fay Pike, born on the 11 day of July, 1904

Name of Father: Vester Pike   a citizen of the United States Nation.
Name of Mother: Edna Pike   a citizen of the   Creek   Nation.

Postoffice   Dustin Ind Ter

AFFIDAVIT OF MOTHER.

UNITED STATES OF AMERICA, Indian Territory,
Western   DISTRICT.

I, Edna Pike, on oath state that I am 18 years of age and a citizen by birth, of the Creek Nation; that I am the lawful wife of Vester Pike, who is a citizen, by birth of the United States Nation; that a female child was born to me on 11 day of July, 1904, that said child has been named Fay, and was living March 4, 1905.

Edna Pike

Witnesses To Mark:

Subscribed and sworn to before me this 4 day of April, 1905.

E E Lewis

Com Expires 5/20-1907   Notary Public.

AFFIDAVIT OF ATTENDING PHYSICIAN OR MID-WIFE.

UNITED STATES OF AMERICA, Indian Territory,
Western   DISTRICT.

I, J.W. Robertson, a Physician, on oath state that I attended on Mrs. Edna Pike, wife of Vester Pike on the 11th day of July, 1904; that there was born to her on

Applications for Enrollment of Creek Newborn
Act of 1905   Volume III

said date a   female   child; that said child was living March 4, 1905, and is said to have been named Fay Pike

J. W. Robertson M.D.

Witnesses To Mark:

{

   Subscribed and sworn to before me this 4 day of April , 1905.

E E Lewis

Com Expires 5/20-1907   Notary Public.

BIRTH AFFIDAVIT.

DEPARTMENT OF THE INTERIOR.
COMMISSION TO THE FIVE CIVILIZED TRIBES.

IN RE APPLICATION FOR ENROLLMENT, as a citizen of the CREEK Nation, of Fay Pike , born on the 11 day of July , 1904

Name of Father:	Vester Pike	a citizen of the U. S.	Nation.
Name of Mother:	Edna "	a citizen of the Creek	Nation.

Postoffice   Dustin

(Child present) HGH

AFFIDAVIT OF MOTHER.

UNITED STATES OF AMERICA, Indian Territory, }
       WESTERN   DISTRICT.

   I, Edna Pike , on oath state that I am 18 years of age and a citizen by blood , of the Creek   Nation; that I am the lawful wife of Vester Pike , who is a citizen, by birth of the Creek   Nation; that a female   child was born to me on 11   day of July , 1904 , that said child has been named Fay Pike , and is now living.

Edna Pike

Witnesses To Mark:

{

   Subscribed and sworn to before me this 11 day of March , 1905.

My Com   J. McDermott
Ex July 25" 1907   Notary Public.

Applications for Enrollment of Creek Newborn
Act of 1905   Volume III

(NOTE: The misplaced letter below should be with the Birth Affidavit and correspondence of the child on page 246 of this book; a copy has been placed there by this author.)

NC 226[sic].

Muskogee, Indian Territory, May 20, 1905.

Mary Bright,
    Fry, Indian Territory.

Dear Madam:

    There is on file with the Commission an affidavit executed by you relative to the birth of your minor child, Thelma Beatrice Bright. The Commission is unable to identify you on its rolls under the name of Bright, and you are requested to furnish the Commission with your name, the names of your parents, the Indian Town to which you belong, and if possible, the number which appears on your deed for land in the Creek Nation.

    Respectfully,

    Chairman.

DEPARTMENT OF THE INTERIOR,
COMMISSIONER TO THE FIVE CIVILIZED TRIBES.

REFER IN REPLY TO THE FOLLOWING:
NC-223

Muskogee, Indian Territory, **August 4, 1905.**

John M. Posey,
    Wagoner, Indian Territory.

Dear Sir:

    You are hereby advised that on **July 28, 1905**, the Secretary of the Interior approved the enrollment of your minor child, **Hugh F. Posey**, as a citizen by blood of the **Creek** Nation, and that the name of said child appears upon the roll of new born citizens of the **Creek** Nation as Number **156**.

    The child is now entitled to an allotment, and application therefor should be made without delay at the Land Office for the Nation in which the prospective allotment is located.

    An entire allotment for said child must be selected at the time of the original application.

Applications for Enrollment of Creek Newborn
Act of 1905   Volume III

Respectively,

Commissioner.

BIRTH AFFIDAVIT.

DEPARTMENT OF THE INTERIOR.
COMMISSION TO THE FIVE CIVILIZED TRIBES.

IN RE APPLICATION FOR ENROLLMENT, as a citizen of the Creek Nation, of Hugh F. Posey, born on the 20th day of May, 1903

Name of Father:	John M Posey	a citizen of the	Creek	Nation.
Name of Mother:	Laura E. Posey	a citizen of the	*(blank)*	Nation.

Postoffice   Wagoner, Ind. Ter.

AFFIDAVIT OF MOTHER.

UNITED STATES OF AMERICA, Indian Territory,
Western Judicial   DISTRICT.

I, Laura E. Posey, on oath state that I am 38 years of age and a citizen by Marriage, of the Creek Nation; that I am the lawful wife of John M. Posey, who is a citizen, by Blood of the Creek Nation; that a male child was born to me on 20th day of May, 1903, that said child has been named Hugh F. Posey, and was living March 4, 1905.

Laura E. Posey

Witnesses To Mark:

Subscribed and sworn to before me this 14 day of March, 1905.

H R Bonner
My Com Ex. July 1st 1906.   Notary Public.

AFFIDAVIT OF ATTENDING PHYSICIAN OR MID-WIFE.

UNITED STATES OF AMERICA, Indian Territory,
Western Judicial   DISTRICT.

I, G W Jobe, a Physician, on oath state that I attended on Mrs. Laura E Posey, wife of John M Posey on the 20 day of May, 1903; that there was born to her on said date a male child; that said child was living March 4, 1905, and is said to have been named Hugh F Posey

Applications for Enrollment of Creek Newborn
Act of 1905   Volume III

GW Jobe M.D.

Witnesses To Mark:

{ Subscribed and sworn to before me this 14 day of March , 1905.

My Com Ex. July 1ˢᵗ 1906.

H R Bonner
Notary Public.

Okemah I.T. July 12 – 1905

Know all men, by these present, witnessth:- On this the 12ᵗʰ day of July 1905 Personally appeared before me a Notary Public in and for the Western Judicial Dist. Ind. Terr. J.E. Foster personally well known to me and makes the following sworn affidavit. That I am the identical person named in the Marriage License issued to me on Jan. 12 – 1902, and that my name appears on the Creek Indian Roll No. 5215 as Edward Foster. That I was married to Grace M. Satterbee on the 26ᵗʰ day of Jan. 1902 at Fentress Ind Terr. by C.A. Polk, Minister.

J.E. Foster

Subscribed and sworn to before me this undersigned a Notary Public for the Western District Ind. Terr. on this the 12ᵗʰ day of July 1905.

Geo. D. *(Illegible)*

My Commission Expires Aug. 2-1906.

CERTIFICATE OF RECORD.

𝔘nited 𝔖tates of 𝔄merica,
Indian Territory,   } ss.
Northern District.

I, *CHARLES A. DAVIDSON*, Clerk of the United States Court in the Northern District, Indian Territory, do hereby certify that the instrument hereto attached was filed for record in my office the   7   day of   Apr   1902 ~~at   M.~~, and duly recorded in Book   26 , Marriage Record, Page   321

WITNESS my hand and seal of said Court at Muscogee, in said Territory, this   10   day of   Apr   A. D. 190 2

Chas. A. Davidson   Clerk.
By   Deputy.

Applications for Enrollment of Creek Newborn
Act of 1905   Volume III

(The above Certificate was given three times)

MARRIAGE LICENSE

United States of America, ⎫
  Indian Territory,   ⎬ ss.   No. **1736**
  Northern District.   ⎭

To Any Person Authorized by Law to Solemnize Marriage---Greeting:

You are Hereby Commanded to Solemnize the Rite and publish the Banns of Matrimony between Mr.   J. E. Foster   of   Fentress , in the Indian Territory, aged   22   years and Miss Grace M Satterbee   of   Fentress   in the Indian Territory aged   16   years according to law, and do you officially sign and return this License to the parties therein named.
                                   Wewoka
    WITNESS my hand and official seal at ~~Muscogee~~ Indian Territory this   12"   day of   January   A.D. 190 2
                             Chas. A. Davidson
                                 Clerk of the U.S. Court
By   M. F. Manville   Deputy

CERTIFICATE OF MARRIAGE.

United States of America, ⎫
  Indian Territory,   ⎬ ss.
  Northern District.   ⎭

    I,   C A Polk   , a Minister of the Gospel, DO HEREBY CERTIFY that on the   26   day of   January   A. D. 1902, I did duly and according to law as commanded in the foregoing License, solemnize the Rite and publish the Banns of Matrimony between the parties therein named.

    WITNESS my hand this   20   day of   Jan   A. D. 1902

    My credentials are recorded in the office of the Clerk of the United States Court, Indian Territory, Northern District, Book   C , Page   110   .

Applications for Enrollment of Creek Newborn
Act of 1905   Volume III

C A Polk
A Minister of the Gospel

Note—This License and Certificate of Marriage must be returned to the Office of the Clerk of the United States Court in the Northern District, Indian Territory, from whence it was issued, within sixty days from the date thereof, or the party to whom the license was issued will be liable in the amount of the One Hundred Dollars ($100.00)

BIRTH AFFIDAVIT.

DEPARTMENT OF THE INTERIOR.
COMMISSION TO THE FIVE CIVILIZED TRIBES.

IN RE APPLICATION FOR ENROLLMENT, as a citizen of the Muskogee Nation, of John W. Foster, born on the 1 day of Feb , 1903

Name of Father:	Edward Foster	a citizen of the Muskogee	Nation.
Name of Mother:	Grace M. Foster	a citizen of the U. S.	Nation.

Postoffice   Morse I.T.

AFFIDAVIT OF MOTHER.

UNITED STATES OF AMERICA, Indian Territory,
Western   DISTRICT.

I, Grace M. Foster , on oath state that I am 19 years of age and a citizen by *(blank)* , of the United States ~~Nation~~; that I am the lawful wife of Edward Foster , who is a citizen, by blood of the Muskogee Nation; that a male child was born to me on 1 day of Feb. , 1903 , that said child has been named John W. Foster , and was living March 4, 1905.

Grace M. Foster

Witnesses To Mark:
{

Subscribed and sworn to before me this 15 day of March , 1905.

C. C. Eskridge
My Commission Expires March 5th, 1908.   Notary Public.

AFFIDAVIT OF ATTENDING PHYSICIAN OR MID-WIFE.

UNITED STATES OF AMERICA, Indian Territory,
Western   DISTRICT.

I, Sarah A. Storms , a Mid-wife , on oath state that I attended on Mrs. Grace M. Foster , wife of Edward Foster on the 1 day of Feb. , 1903 ; that there was born to

Applications for Enrollment of Creek Newborn
Act of 1905   Volume III

her on said date a   male   child; that said child was living March 4, 1905, and is said to have been named John W. Foster

Sarah A Storms

Witnesses To Mark:

{ Subscribed and sworn to before me this 15 day of March, 1905.

C. C. Eskridge
Notary Public.

My Commission Expires March 5th, 1908.

NC 224.

Muskogee, Indian Territory, July 7, 1905.

Grace N[sic]. Foster,
   Morse, Indian Territory.

Dear Madam:

In the matter of the application for the enrollment of your minor child, John W. Foster, as a citizen of the Creek Nation, you are advised that proof of your marriage to Edward Foster, the father of said child, is required.

A certified copy of your marriage license or other satisfactory proof of your marriage should be forwarded to the office of the Commissioner to the Five Civilized Tribes.

Respectfully,

Commissioner.

BIRTH AFFIDAVIT.

DEPARTMENT OF THE INTERIOR.
COMMISSION TO THE FIVE CIVILIZED TRIBES.

IN RE APPLICATION FOR ENROLLMENT, as a citizen of the CREEK Nation, of Jeff Francis, born on the 30 day of May, 1904

Name of Father:	Robert Francis	a citizen of the	Creek	Nation.
Name of Mother:	Millie Francis	a citizen of the	Creek	Nation.

Postoffice   Eufaula

Applications for Enrollment of Creek Newborn
Act of 1905   Volume III

AFFIDAVIT OF MOTHER.

UNITED STATES OF AMERICA, Indian Territory,
    WESTERN   DISTRICT.

    I, Robert Francis , on oath state that I am 29 years of age and a citizen by blood, of the   Creek Nation; that I am the lawful ~~wife~~ husband of Millie Francis , who is a citizen, by blood of the   Creek Nation; that a male   child was born to me on 30 day of   May , 1904 , that said child has been named Jeff Francis , and is now living.

                                        Robert Francis

Witnesses To Mark:

{

    Subscribed and sworn to before me this 28 day of March, 1905.

My Commission   J. McDermott
Expires July 25" 1907   Notary Public.

Department of the Interior,
COMMISSION TO THE FIVE CIVILIZED TRIBES.

    IN RE APPLICATION FOR ENROLLMENT, as a citizen of the Creek Nation, of Jeff Francis , born on the 31 day of May , 1904

Name of Father: Robert Francis   a citizen of the   Creek   Nation.
Hickory Ground Town
Name of Mother: Millie Francis   a citizen of the   Creek   Nation.
Ketchopataky Town

                          Postoffice,   Eufaula, Ind. Ter.

AFFIDAVIT OF MOTHER.

UNITED STATES OF AMERICA,
    Indian Territory.   Child is present
    Western   District.

    I, Millie Francis , on oath state that I am about 31 years of age and a citizen by blood , of the Creek   Nation; that I am the lawful wife of Robert Francis , who is a citizen, by blood of the Creek Nation; that a male   child was born to me on 31   day of May , 1904 , that said child has been named Jeff Francis , and is now living.

Applications for Enrollment of Creek Newborn
Act of 1905 Volume III

Millie Francis

WITNESSES TO MARK:
{ Alex Posey

Subscribed and sworn to before me this 3 *day of* April, 1905.

Drennan C Skaggs
NOTARY PUBLIC

AFFIDAVIT OF ATTENDING PHYSICIAN OR MID-WIFE.

UNITED STATES OF AMERICA,
Indian Territory.
Western   District.

I, Cinda Polk , a midwife , on oath state that I attended on Mrs. Millie Francis , wife of Robert Francis on the 31 day of May , 1904 ; that there was born to her on said date a male child; that said child is now was living on March 4, 1905 and is said to have been named Jeff Francis

her
Cinda x Polk
mark

WITNESSES TO MARK:
{ Alex Posey
  DC Skaggs

Subscribed and sworn to before me this 3 *day of* April, 1905.

Drennan C Skaggs
NOTARY PUBLIC

BIRTH AFFIDAVIT.

DEPARTMENT OF THE INTERIOR.
COMMISSION TO THE FIVE CIVILIZED TRIBES.

IN RE APPLICATION FOR ENROLLMENT, as a citizen of the CREEK Nation, of Bettie Francis, born on the 15 day of March , 1903

Name of Father:	Robert Francis	a citizen of the	Creek	Nation.
Name of Mother:	Millie Francis	a citizen of the	Creek	Nation.

Postoffice   Eufaula, I.T.

Applications for Enrollment of Creek Newborn
Act of 1905   Volume III

AFFIDAVIT OF MOTHER.

UNITED STATES OF AMERICA, Indian Territory,
WESTERN   DISTRICT.

I, Robert Francis , on oath state that I am ~~32~~ 29 years of age and a citizen by blood, of the Creek Nation; that I am the lawful ~~wife~~ husband of Millie Francis , who is a citizen, by blood of the Creek Nation; that a female child was born to me on 15 day of March , 1903 , that said child has been named Bettie Francis , and is now living.

                                    Robert Francis
Witnesses To Mark:
{

Subscribed and sworn to before me this 11th day of Mar., 1905.

My Commission   J. McDermott
Expires July 25" 1907   Notary Public.

Department of the Interior,
COMMISSION TO THE FIVE CIVILIZED TRIBES.

IN RE APPLICATION FOR ENROLLMENT, as a citizen of the Creek Nation, of Bettie Francis , born on the 15 day of March , 1903

Name of Father: Robert Francis   a citizen of the   Creek   Nation.
Hickory Ground
Name of Mother: Millie Francis   a citizen of the   Creek   Nation.
Ketchopataky Town
                        Postoffice,   Eufaula, Ind. Ter.

AFFIDAVIT OF MOTHER.

UNITED STATES OF AMERICA,
    Indian Territory.   Child is present
    Western   District.

I, Millie Francis , on oath state that I am about 31 years of age and a citizen by blood , of the Creek Nation; that I am the lawful wife of Robert Francis , who is a citizen, by blood of the Creek Nation; that a female child was born to me on 15 day of March , 1903 , that said child has been named Bettie Francis , and ~~is now~~ was living. on March 4, 1905

                                    Millie Francis

Applications for Enrollment of Creek Newborn
Act of 1905   Volume III

WITNESSES TO MARK:
{ Alex Posey

Subscribed and sworn to before me this 3 *day of* April, *1905.*

Drennan C Skaggs
NOTARY PUBLIC

AFFIDAVIT OF ATTENDING PHYSICIAN OR MID-WIFE.

UNITED STATES OF AMERICA,
    Indian Territory.
    Western   District.

I, Cinda Polk , a midwife , on oath state that I attended on Mrs. Millie Francis , wife of Robert Francis on the 15 day of March , 1903 ; that there was born to her on said date a female child; that said child was living March 4, 1905 March 4, 1905 ~~is now living~~ and is said to have been named Bettie Francis

                                       her
                                  Cinda x Polk
WITNESSES TO MARK: mark
{ Alex Posey
  DC Skaggs

Subscribed and sworn to before me this 3 *day of* April, *1905.*

Drennan C Skaggs
NOTARY PUBLIC

NC 225.

Muskogee, Indian Territory, May 20, 1905.

Robert Francis,
    Eufaula, Indian Territory.

Dear Sir:

   In the matter of the application for the enrollment of your minor children, Bettie and Jeff Francis, as citizens of the Creek Nation, you are advised that the Commission requires the affidavits of the mother and midwife or physician in attendance at the birth of said children.

   There are herewith enclosed two blank forms of birth affidavit, and in executing same care should be exercised to see that all blanks are properly filled, all names written in full and in the event that the persons signing the affidavits are unable to write,

Applications for Enrollment of Creek Newborn
Act of 1905 Volume III

signature by mark must be attested by two witnesses. Each affidavit must be executed before a Notary Public and the notarial seal and signature of the officer must be attached to each separate affidavit.

Respectfully,

BC.   Chairman.

(NOTE: The letter below was misplaced with the Birth Affidavit and correspondence on page 236 of this book; this letter has been placed here by this author.)

NC 226[sic].

Muskogee, Indian Territory, May 20, 1905.

Mary Bright,
    Fry, Indian Territory.

Dear Madam:

    There is on file with the Commission an affidavit executed by you relative to the birth of your minor child, Thelma Beatrice Bright. The Commission is unable to identify you on its rolls under the name of Bright, and you are requested to furnish the Commission with your name, the names of your parents, the Indian Town to which you belong, and if possible, the number which appears on your deed for land in the Creek Nation.

Respectfully,

Chairman.

BIRTH AFFIDAVIT.

DEPARTMENT OF THE INTERIOR.
COMMISSION TO THE FIVE CIVILIZED TRIBES.

    IN RE APPLICATION FOR ENROLLMENT, as a citizen of the Creek Nation, of Thelma Beatrice Bright, born on the 12th day of December, 1903

| Name of Father: | Luke O. Bright | not a citizen of the | Creek Nation. |
| Name of Mother: | Mary Bright | a citizen of the | Creek Nation. |

Postoffice   Fry, Ind. Ter.

Applications for Enrollment of Creek Newborn
Act of 1905   Volume III

AFFIDAVIT OF MOTHER.

UNITED STATES OF AMERICA, Indian Territory,
  Western   DISTRICT.

I, Mary Bright , on oath state that I am 23 years of age and a citizen by blood , of the Creek Nation; that I am the lawful wife of Luke O. Bright , who is not a citizen, by *(blank)* of the Creek Nation; that a female child was born to me on 12th day of December, 1903 , that said child has been named Thelma Beatrice Bright , and was living March 4, 1905.

Mary Bright

Witnesses To Mark:
  { George W. Stanclift Bixby I T
  { Roy Thompson Bixby I.T.

Subscribed and sworn to before me this 14th day of March , 1905.

Francis R. Brennan
Notary Public.

AFFIDAVIT OF ATTENDING PHYSICIAN OR MID-WIFE.

UNITED STATES OF AMERICA, Indian Territory,
  Western   DISTRICT.

I, Lizzie Teague , a mid-wife , on oath state that I attended on Mrs. Mary Bright , wife of Luke O. Bright on the 12th day of December , 1903 ; that there was born to her on said date a female child; that said child was living March 4, 1905, and is said to have been named Thelma Beatrice Bright

Lizzie Teague

Witnesses To Mark:
  { George W. Stanclift   Bixby I T
  { Roy Thompson   Bixby I.T.

Subscribed and sworn to before me this 14th day of March , 1905.

Francis R. Brennan
Notary Public.

Applications for Enrollment of Creek Newborn
Act of 1905   Volume III

(The letter below is typed as was given on microfilm.)

C 226   COPY

Fry P. O. Ind Ty May 23, 1905

Commission to the five Civilized Tribes

    Your letter of the 20th to hand in Reply to questions asked will try to make it plain when I filed my name was <u>Mary Richard.</u> My mothers name when filed was, Anna Brummet my Fathers name was W. A. McKim, a white man. I have two Brothers, William & R. A. McKim one Sister her name Hattie Inscho. I have a son his name on deed Leon Dewitt Bright. My Homestead Deed-39.
Commission No-6306
Allotment Deed 40. Com. No. 6307 File No. 3068,
My Deed was signed by P. Porter. The 12 day of Dec 1902. Approved by the Secretary Jan. 27-1903, & filed for Record on the 4 day of February 1904, allotment Deed Recorded in Book 6 Page 228.
Homestead Deed Recorded in Book F. Page 228.
Creek Indian Roll No. 2144
Oh yes and we all belong to the town Big Springs I think I have said a plenty so you will have no more trouble looking it up. Can you inform me now when the land Office will be open for filing these minor children I am very respt.

(Signed) Mary Bright

DEPARTMENT OF THE INTERIOR,
COMMISSIONER TO THE FIVE CIVILIZED TRIBES.

REFER IN REPLY TO THE FOLLOWING:
NC-226

Muskogee, Indian Territory, **August 4, 1905.**

Mary Bright,
    Care of Luke O. Bright,
        Fry, Indian Territory.

Dear Madam:

    You are hereby advised that on **July 28, 1905**, the Secretary of the Interior approved the enrollment of your minor child, **Thelma Beatrice Bright**, as a citizen by blood of the **Creek** Nation, and that the name of said child appears upon the roll of new born citizens of the **Creek** Nation as Number **169**.

    The child is now entitled to an allotment, and application therefor should be made without delay at the Land Office for the Nation in which the prospective allotment is located.

Applications for Enrollment of Creek Newborn
Act of 1905 Volume III

An entire allotment for said child must be selected at the time of the original application.

Respectively,

Commissioner.

DEPARTMENT OF THE INTERIOR,
COMMISSIONER TO THE FIVE CIVILIZED TRIBES.

REFER IN REPLY TO THE FOLLOWING:

NC-227

Muskogee, Indian Territory, **August 4, 1905.**

Timmie Fife,
    Sapulpa, Indian Territory.

Dear Sir:

You are hereby advised that on **July 28, 1905**, the Secretary of the Interior approved the enrollment of your minor child, **Dawes Fife**, as a citizen by blood of the **Creek** Nation, and that the name of said child appears upon the roll of new born citizens of the **Creek** Nation as Number **157**.

The child is now entitled to an allotment, and application therefor should be made without delay at the Land Office for the Nation in which the prospective allotment is located.

An entire allotment for said child must be selected at the time of the original application.

Respectively,

Commissioner.

AFFIDAVIT OF ATTENDING PHYSICIAN OR MID-WIFE.

UNITED STATES OF AMERICA, Indian Territory,
    Western   DISTRICT.

I, H. O. Lyford, a Physician, on oath state that I attended on Mrs. Sarah Fife, wife of Timmie Fife on the 10th day of Aug, 1903; that there was born to her on said date a male child; that said child is now living and is said to have been named Dawes Fife

                        H. O. Lyford, M.D.

Witnesses To Mark:

Applications for Enrollment of Creek Newborn
Act of 1905 Volume III

Subscribed and sworn to before me this 15th day of March, 1905.

My Commission expires 10/20-1906   Joseph Brown
                                                              Notary Public.

BIRTH AFFIDAVIT.

DEPARTMENT OF THE INTERIOR.
COMMISSION TO THE FIVE CIVILIZED TRIBES.

IN RE APPLICATION FOR ENROLLMENT, as a citizen of the CREEK Nation, of Dawes Fife, born on the 10 day of Aug , 1903

Name of Father:	Timmie Fife	a citizen of the	Creek	Nation.
Name of Mother:	Sarah "	a citizen of the	"	Nation.

                          Postoffice   Sapulpa, I. T.

(Child present) HGH

AFFIDAVIT OF MOTHER.

UNITED STATES OF AMERICA, Indian Territory, ⎫
    WESTERN   DISTRICT. ⎦

I, Sarah Fife , on oath state that I am 38 years of age and a citizen by blood , of the Creek Nation; that I am the lawful wife of Timmie Fife , who is a citizen, by blood of the Creek Nation; that a boy child was born to me on 10 day of Aug , 1903 , that said child has been named Dawes Fife , and is now living.

                                                     her
                                       Sarah x Fife
Witnesses To Mark: mark
⎰ Zera Ellen Parrish
⎱ Jesse McDermott

Subscribed and sworn to before me this 10 day of March , 1905.

My Commission   J. McDermott
Ex July 25" 1907   Notary Public.

Applications for Enrollment of Creek Newborn
Act of 1905   Volume III

DEPARTMENT OF THE INTERIOR,
COMMISSIONER TO THE FIVE CIVILIZED TRIBES.

REFER IN REPLY TO THE FOLLOWING:

NC-228

Muskogee, Indian Territory, **August 4, 1905.**

Annie Cooper,
    Care E. E. Cooper,
        Broken Arrow, Indian Territory.

Dear Madam:

You are hereby advised that on **July 28, 1905**, the Secretary of the Interior approved the enrollment of your minor child, **Florence Cooper**, as a citizen by blood of the **Creek** Nation, and that the name of said child appears upon the roll of new born citizens of the **Creek** Nation as Number **158**.

The child is now entitled to an allotment, and application therefor should be made without delay at the Land Office for the Nation in which the prospective allotment is located.

An entire allotment for said child must be selected at the time of the original application.

                Respectively,

                            Commissioner.

BIRTH AFFIDAVIT.

DEPARTMENT OF THE INTERIOR.
COMMISSION TO THE FIVE CIVILIZED TRIBES.

IN RE APPLICATION FOR ENROLLMENT, as a citizen of the CREEK Nation, of Florence Cooper, born on the 22 day of October, 1903

Name of Father:	E. E. Cooper	a citizen of the	U. S.	Nation.
Name of Mother:	Annie Cooper	a citizen of the	Creek	Nation.

                Postoffice   Broken Arrow

AFFIDAVIT OF ~~MOTHER~~. Father

UNITED STATES OF AMERICA, Indian Territory, }
    WESTERN   DISTRICT.}

I, E. E. Cooper, on oath state that I am 31 years of age and a citizen by -----, of the U. S. Nation; that I am the lawful ~~wife~~ husband of Annie Cooper, who is a

Applications for Enrollment of Creek Newborn
Act of 1905   Volume III

citizen, by blood of the Creek Nation; that a female child was born to me on 22 day of October , 1903, that said child has been named Florence Cooper , and is now living.

E. E. Cooper

Witnesses To Mark:
{

Subscribed and sworn to before me this 10 day of March , 1905.

My Commission   J. McDermott
Ex July 25" 1907   Notary Public.

BIRTH AFFIDAVIT.

DEPARTMENT OF THE INTERIOR.
COMMISSION TO THE FIVE CIVILIZED TRIBES.

IN RE APPLICATION FOR ENROLLMENT, as a citizen of the Creek Nation, of Florence Cooper, born on the 22 day of October , 1903

Name of Father:	E. E. Cooper	a citizen of the	U. S.	Nation.
Name of Mother:	Annie "	a citizen of the	Creek	Nation.

Postoffice   Broken Arrow

Child Present Gr.

AFFIDAVIT OF MOTHER.

UNITED STATES OF AMERICA, Indian Territory, }
    Western   DISTRICT.

I, Annie Cooper , on oath state that I am 30 years of age and a citizen by blood, of the Creek Nation; that I am the lawful wife of E E Cooper , who is a citizen, by ----- of the U S. Nation; that a Female child was born to me on 22 day of Oct , 1903, that said child has been named Florence Cooper , and is now living.

                               Her
                     Annie x Cooper
Witnesses To Mark: mark
{ HG Hains
  EC Griesel

Subscribed and sworn to before me this 17 day of March , 1905.

                            Edw C Griesel
                               Notary Public.

Applications for Enrollment of Creek Newborn
Act of 1905   Volume III

AFFIDAVIT OF ATTENDING ~~PHYSICIAN~~ OR MID-WIFE.

UNITED STATES OF AMERICA, Indian Territory,
    Western   DISTRICT.

    I, Sukey Hains , a Mid Wife , on oath state that I attended on Mrs. Annie Cooper , wife of E E Cooper on the 22 day of Oct , 1903 ; that there was born to her on said date a female child; that said child is now living and is said to have been named Florence Cooper

                                 Her
                         Sukey x Hains
Witnesses To Mark: mark
  { E E Cooper
    EC Griesel

    Subscribed and sworn to before me this 17 day of Mar , 1905.

                          Edw C Griesel
                          Notary Public.

DEPARTMENT OF THE INTERIOR,
COMMISSIONER TO THE FIVE CIVILIZED TRIBES.

REFER IN REPLY TO THE FOLLOWING:

NC-229

                      Muskogee, Indian Territory, **August 4, 1905.**

Katie Turnbow,
     Care of Aaron Turnbow,
          Checotah, Indian Territory.

Dear Madam:

    You are hereby advised that on **July 28, 1905** , the Secretary of the Interior approved the enrollment of your minor child, **James Henry Tunbow** , as a citizen by blood of the **Creek** Nation, and that the name of said child appears upon the roll of new born citizens of the **Creek** Nation as Number **159** .

    The child is now entitled to an allotment, and application therefor should be made without delay at the Land Office for the Nation in which the prospective allotment is located.

    An entire allotment for said child must be selected at the time of the original application.

                      Respectively,

                                Commissioner.

Applications for Enrollment of Creek Newborn
Act of 1905   Volume III

DEPARTMENT OF THE INTERIOR,
COMMISSIONER TO THE FIVE CIVILIZED TRIBES.

REFER IN REPLY TO THE FOLLOWING:
NC-229

Muskogee, Indian Territory, **August 4, 1905.**

Katie Turnbow,
    Care of Aaron Turnbow,
        Checotah, Indian Territory.

Dear Madam:

    You are hereby advised that on **July 28, 1905**, the Secretary of the Interior approved the enrollment of your minor child, **Charlie Turnbow**, as a citizen by blood of the **Creek** Nation, and that the name of said child appears upon the roll of new born citizens of the **Creek** Nation as Number **160**.

    The child is now entitled to an allotment, and application therefor should be made without delay at the Land Office for the Nation in which the prospective allotment is located.

    An entire allotment for said child must be selected at the time of the original application.

        Respectively,

                Commissioner.

BIRTH AFFIDAVIT.

DEPARTMENT OF THE INTERIOR.
COMMISSION TO THE FIVE CIVILIZED TRIBES.

    IN RE APPLICATION FOR ENROLLMENT, as a citizen of the Creek Nation, of James Henry Turnbow, born on the 26 day of February, 1903

Name of Father:	Aaron Turnbow	a citizen of the United States Nation.
Name of Mother:	Katie Turnbow	a citizen of the Creek Nation.

        Postoffice   Checotah, Ind. Ter.

AFFIDAVIT OF MOTHER.

UNITED STATES OF AMERICA, Indian Territory, ⎫
    Western   DISTRICT. ⎭

    I, Katie Turnbow, on oath state that I am 19 years of age and a citizen by blood , of the Creek Nation[sic] Nation; that I am the lawful wife of Aaron Turnbow , who

Applications for Enrollment of Creek Newborn
Act of 1905   Volume III

is a citizen, by *(blank)* of the United States Nation; that a male child was born to me on 26 day of February , 1903 , that said child has been named James Henry Turnbow, and was living March 4, 1905.

            Katie Turnbow

Witnesses To Mark:
{ Chas R Freeman
 Ernie V. Freeman

  Subscribed and sworn to before me this 18th day of March , 1905.

            A A Smith
My Commission Expires Feb. 24, 1907.   Notary Public.

AFFIDAVIT OF ATTENDING PHYSICIAN OR MID-WIFE.

UNITED STATES OF AMERICA, Indian Territory,
  Western DISTRICT.

  I, Eliza Dagley , a *(blank)* , on oath state that I attended on Mrs. Katie Turnbow, wife of Aaron Turnbow on the 26 day of February , 1903 ; that there was born to her on said date a male child; that said child was living March 4, 1905, and is said to have been named James Henry Turnbow

            her
          Eliza Dagley x
Witnesses To Mark: mark
{ Chas R Freeman
 Ernie V. Freeman

  Subscribed and sworn to before me this 18th day of March , 1905.

            A A Smith
My Commission Expires Feb. 24, 1907.   Notary Public.

BIRTH AFFIDAVIT.

DEPARTMENT OF THE INTERIOR.
COMMISSION TO THE FIVE CIVILIZED TRIBES.

  IN RE APPLICATION FOR ENROLLMENT, as a citizen of the Creek Nation, of Charlie Turnbow, born on the 26 day of September, 1904

Name of Father:	Aaron Turnbow	a citizen of the United States Nation.
Name of Mother:	Katie Turnbow	a citizen of the Creek Nation.

        Postoffice Checotah, Ind. Ter.

Applications for Enrollment of Creek Newborn
Act of 1905 Volume III

AFFIDAVIT OF MOTHER.

UNITED STATES OF AMERICA, Indian Territory,
Western DISTRICT.

I, Katie Turnbow , on oath state that I am 19 years of age and a citizen by Blood , of the Creek Nation; that I am the lawful wife of Aaron Turnbow , who is a citizen, by *(blank)* of the United States Nation; that a male child was born to me on 26 day of September , 1904 , that said child has been named Charlie Turnbow, and was living March 4, 1905.

Katie Turnbow

Witnesses To Mark:
{ Chas R Freeman
{ Ernie V. Freeman

Subscribed and sworn to before me this 18th day of March , 1905.

A A Smith

My Commission Expires Feb. 24, 1907.   Notary Public.

AFFIDAVIT OF ATTENDING PHYSICIAN OR MID-WIFE.

UNITED STATES OF AMERICA, Indian Territory,
Western DISTRICT.

I, Matilda Turnbow , a *(blank)* , on oath state that I attended on Mrs. Katie Turnbow , wife of Aaron Turnbow on the 26 day of September , 1904 ; that there was born to her on said date a male child; that said child was living March 4, 1905, and is said to have been named Charlie Turnbow

her
Matilda x Turnbow
mark

Witnesses To Mark:
{ Chas R Freeman
{ Ernie V. Freeman

Subscribed and sworn to before me this 18th day of March , 1905.

A A Smith

My Commission Expires Feb. 24, 1907.   Notary Public.

Applications for Enrollment of Creek Newborn
Act of 1905   Volume III

BIRTH AFFIDAVIT.

DEPARTMENT OF THE INTERIOR.
COMMISSION TO THE FIVE CIVILIZED TRIBES.

IN RE APPLICATION FOR ENROLLMENT, as a citizen of the CREEK Nation, of Ruby Burgess, born on the 8 day of April, 1902

Name of Father:	Ed Burgess	a citizen of the	Creek	Nation.
Name of Mother:	Inay Burgess	a citizen of the	Creek	Nation.

Postoffice   Kellyville I.T.

AFFIDAVIT OF MOTHER.

UNITED STATES OF AMERICA, Indian Territory,
WESTERN   DISTRICT.

I, Inay Burgess, on oath state that I am 26 years of age and a citizen by Blood, of the Creek Nation; that I am the lawful wife of Ed Burgess, who is a citizen, by Blood of the Creek Nation; that a female child was born to me on 8 day of April, 1902, that said child has been named Ruby Burgess, and is now living.

Inay Burgess

Witnesses To Mark:
{

Subscribed and sworn to before me this 24 day of March, 1905.

My commission expires   W.W. Holder
Sept. 8, 1906   Notary Public.

AFFIDAVIT OF ATTENDING PHYSICIAN OR MID-WIFE.

UNITED STATES OF AMERICA, Indian Territory,
Western   DISTRICT.

I, Mary Huffine, a mid-wife, on oath state that I attended on Mrs. Inay Burgess, wife of Ed Burgess on the 8 day of April, 1902; that there was born to her on said date a female child; that said child is now living and is said to have been named Ruby Burgess

Mary Huffine

Witnesses To Mark:
{

Applications for Enrollment of Creek Newborn
Act of 1905   Volume III

Subscribed and sworn to before me this 24 day of March, 1905.

    My commission expires   W.W. Holder
    Sept. 8, 1906   Notary Public.

BIRTH AFFIDAVIT.

DEPARTMENT OF THE INTERIOR.
COMMISSION TO THE FIVE CIVILIZED TRIBES.

IN RE APPLICATION FOR ENROLLMENT, as a citizen of the CREEK Nation, of Ruby Burgess, born on the 8 day of April, 1902

Name of Father:	Ed Burgess	a citizen of the	Creek	Nation.
Name of Mother:	May "	a citizen of the	"	Nation.

        Postoffice   Sapulpa

(child present)

AFFIDAVIT OF MOTHER.

UNITED STATES OF AMERICA, Indian Territory,
    WESTERN   DISTRICT.

    I, May Burgess, on oath state that I am 26 years of age and a citizen by blood, of the Creek Nation; that I am the lawful wife of Ed Burgess, who is a citizen, by blood of the Creek Nation; that a female child was born to me on 8 day of April, 1902, that said child has been named Ruby Burgess, and is now living.

                                          May Burgess

Witnesses To Mark:

    Subscribed and sworn to before me this 20 day of March, 1905.

                                      Edw C Griesel
                                      Notary Public.

Applications for Enrollment of Creek Newborn
Act of 1905   Volume III

BIRTH AFFIDAVIT.

DEPARTMENT OF THE INTERIOR.
COMMISSION TO THE FIVE CIVILIZED TRIBES.

IN RE APPLICATION FOR ENROLLMENT, as a citizen of the Creek Nation, of William McHenry Bible, born on the 4 day of July, 1902

Name of Father:	Lewis Bible	a citizen of the	Creek	Nation.
Name of Mother:	Mulsie Bible	a citizen of the	Creek	Nation.

Postoffice   Broken Arrow, Ind. Ter.

AFFIDAVIT OF MOTHER.

UNITED STATES OF AMERICA, Indian Territory,
Western   DISTRICT.

I, Mulsie Bible, on oath state that I am 28 years of age and a citizen by Blood, of the Creek Nation; that I am the lawful wife of Lewis Bible, who is a citizen, by Blood of the Creek Nation; that a male child was born to me on 4 day of July, 1902, that said child has been named William Mchenry[sic] Bible, and was living March 4, 1905.

Mulsie Bible

Witnesses To Mark:
{

Subscribed and sworn to before me this 6 day of April, 1905.

W.G. Cooper
Notary Public.

Com Ex 10/25-1906

AFFIDAVIT OF ATTENDING PHYSICIAN OR MID-WIFE.

UNITED STATES OF AMERICA, Indian Territory,
Western   DISTRICT.

I, Rosa Chisholm, a Mid-Wife, on oath state that I attended on Mrs. Mulsie Bible, wife of Lewis Bible on the 4 day of July, 1902; that there was born to her on said date a Male child; that said child was living March 4, 1905, and is said to have been named William Mchenry Bible.

Rosa Chisholm

Witnesses To Mark:
{

Applications for Enrollment of Creek Newborn
Act of 1905   Volume III

Subscribed and sworn to before me this 6 day of April, 1905.

W.G. Cooper
Notary Public.

Com Ex 10/25-1906

BIRTH AFFIDAVIT.

DEPARTMENT OF THE INTERIOR.
COMMISSION TO THE FIVE CIVILIZED TRIBES.

IN RE APPLICATION FOR ENROLLMENT, as a citizen of the Creek Nation, of David Bible, born on the 16 day of July, 1904

Name of Father:	Lewis Bible	a citizen of the	Creek	Nation.
Name of Mother:	Mulsie "	a citizen of the	"	Nation.

Postoffice   Fry

AFFIDAVIT OF ~~MOTHER~~. Father

UNITED STATES OF AMERICA, Indian Territory,
    WESTERN   DISTRICT.

    I, Lewis Bible, on oath state that I am 27 years of age and a citizen by blood, of the Creek Nation; that I am the lawful ~~wife~~ hus of Mulsie Bible, who is a citizen, by blood of the Creek Nation; that a male child was born to me on 16 day of July, 1904, that said child has been named David Bible, and is now living.

Lewis Bible

Witnesses To Mark:

Subscribed and sworn to before me this 10 day of March, 1905.

Edw C Griesel
Notary Public.

Applications for Enrollment of Creek Newborn
Act of 1905   Volume III

BIRTH AFFIDAVIT.

DEPARTMENT OF THE INTERIOR.
COMMISSION TO THE FIVE CIVILIZED TRIBES.

IN RE APPLICATION FOR ENROLLMENT, as a citizen of the Creek Nation, of David Bible, born on the 16 day of July, 1904

Name of Father:	Lewis Bible	a citizen of the	Creek Nation.
Name of Mother:	Mulsie Bible	a citizen of the	Creek Nation.

Postoffice   Broken Arrow, Ind. Ter.

AFFIDAVIT OF MOTHER.

UNITED STATES OF AMERICA, Indian Territory,
Western   DISTRICT.

I, Mulsie Bible, on oath state that I am 28 years of age and a citizen by Blood, of the Creek Nation; that I am the lawful wife of Lewis Bible, who is a citizen, by Blood of the Creek Nation; that a male child was born to me on 16 day of July, 1904, that said child has been named David Bible, and was living March 4, 1905.

Mulsie Bible

Witnesses To Mark:
{

Subscribed and sworn to before me this 6 day of April, 1905.

W.G. Cooper
Notary Public.

Com Exp Oct 25 1906

AFFIDAVIT OF ATTENDING PHYSICIAN OR MID-WIFE.

UNITED STATES OF AMERICA, Indian Territory,
Western   DISTRICT.

I, Rosa Chisholm, a Mid-Wife, on oath state that I attended on Mrs. Mulsie Bible, wife of Lewis Bible on the 16 day of July, 1904; that there was born to her on said date a Male child; that said child was living March 4, 1905, and is said to have been named David Bible.

Rosa Chisholm

Witnesses To Mark:
{

Applications for Enrollment of Creek Newborn
Act of 1905   Volume III

Subscribed and sworn to before me this 6 day of   April , 1905.

                                       W.G. Cooper
                                           Notary Public.

Com Exp 10/25-1906

BIRTH AFFIDAVIT.

DEPARTMENT OF THE INTERIOR.
COMMISSION TO THE FIVE CIVILIZED TRIBES.

IN RE APPLICATION FOR ENROLLMENT, as a citizen of the CREEK Nation, of Wm McKinley[sic] Bible , born on the 4 day of July , 1902

Name of Father:	Lewis Bible	a citizen of the	Creek	Nation.
Name of Mother:	Mulsie "	a citizen of the	"	Nation.

                            Postoffice   Fry

AFFIDAVIT OF ~~MOTHER.~~ father

UNITED STATES OF AMERICA, Indian Territory, ⎫
     WESTERN   DISTRICT.⎭

    I, Lewis Bible , on oath state that I am 27   years of age and a citizen by blood , of the   Creek   Nation; that I am the lawful ~~wife~~ hus of Mulsie Bible , who is a citizen, by blood   of the   Creek   Nation; that a   male   child was born to me on 4 day of July , 1902 , that said child has been named   Wm McKinley Bible   , and is now living.

                                     Lewis Bible

Witnesses To Mark:

   {

    Subscribed and sworn to before me this 10 day of March, 1905.

                                   Edw C Griesel
                                     Notary Public.

Applications for Enrollment of Creek Newborn
Act of 1905   Volume III

DEPARTMENT OF THE INTERIOR,	REFER IN REPLY TO THE FOLLOWING:
COMMISSIONER TO THE FIVE CIVILIZED TRIBES.	NC-232

Muskogee, Indian Territory, **August 4, 1905.**

Dave Tiger,
    Coweta, Indian Territory.

Dear Sir:

    You are hereby advised that on **July 28, 1905**, the Secretary of the Interior approved the enrollment of your minor child, **Edward Tiger**, as a citizen by blood of the **Creek** Nation, and that the name of said child appears upon the roll of new born citizens of the **Creek** Nation as Number **162**.

    The child is now entitled to an allotment, and application therefor should be made without delay at the Land Office for the Nation in which the prospective allotment is located.

    An entire allotment for said child must be selected at the time of the original application.

                          Respectively,

                                  Commissioner.

DEPARTMENT OF THE INTERIOR,	REFER IN REPLY TO THE FOLLOWING:
COMMISSIONER TO THE FIVE CIVILIZED TRIBES.	NC-232

Muskogee, Indian Territory, **August 4, 1905.**

Dave Tiger,
    Coweta, Indian Territory.

Dear Sir:

    You are hereby advised that on **July 28, 1905**, the Secretary of the Interior approved the enrollment of your minor child, **George Tiger**, as a citizen by blood of the **Creek** Nation, and that the name of said child appears upon the roll of new born citizens of the **Creek** Nation as Number **163**.

    The child is now entitled to an allotment, and application therefor should be made without delay at the Land Office for the Nation in which the prospective allotment is located.

    An entire allotment for said child must be selected at the time of the original application.

Applications for Enrollment of Creek Newborn
Act of 1905   Volume III

Respectively,

Commissioner.

BIRTH AFFIDAVIT.

DEPARTMENT OF THE INTERIOR.
COMMISSION TO THE FIVE CIVILIZED TRIBES.

IN RE APPLICATION FOR ENROLLMENT, as a citizen of the CREEK Nation, of George Tiger, born on the 20th day of February, 1905

Name of Father: Dave Tiger   a citizen of the   Creek   Nation.
Name of Mother: NeoSho Tiger   a citizen of the   Creek   Nation.

Postoffice   *(blank)*

AFFIDAVIT OF MOTHER.

UNITED STATES OF AMERICA, Indian Territory,
    WESTERN   DISTRICT.

I, NeoSho Tiger, on oath state that I am thirty years of age and a citizen by blood, of the Creek Nation; that I am the lawful wife of Dave Tiger, who is a citizen, by blood of the Creek Nation; that a male child was born to me on 20th day of February, 1905, that said child has been named George Tiger, and is now living.

                                her
                        Neosho x Tiger
Witnesses To Mark: mark
  Jas Tiger
  J.B. Davis

Subscribed and sworn to before me this 16th day of March, 1905.

                        B.J. Beavers
                        Notary Public.

AFFIDAVIT OF ATTENDING PHYSICIAN OR MID-WIFE.

UNITED STATES OF AMERICA, Indian Territory,
    WESTERN   DISTRICT.

I, Yanah Lynch, a midwife, on oath state that I attended on Mrs. NeoSho Tiger, wife of Dave Tiger on the 20th day of February, 1905; that there was born to

Applications for Enrollment of Creek Newborn
Act of 1905 Volume III

her on said date a *(blank)* child; that said child is now living and is said to have been named George Tiger

                                      her
                             Yanah x Lynch

Witnesses To Mark: mark
{ Jas Tiger
{ J.B. Davis

Subscribed and sworn to before me this 16th day of March, 1905.

                                            B.J. Beavers
                                            Notary Public.

BIRTH AFFIDAVIT.

DEPARTMENT OF THE INTERIOR.
COMMISSION TO THE FIVE CIVILIZED TRIBES.

IN RE APPLICATION FOR ENROLLMENT, as a citizen of the CREEK Nation, of Edward Tiger, born on the 7th day of August, 1902

Name of Father:	Dave Tiger	a citizen of the	Creek	Nation.
Name of Mother:	Neosho Tiger	a citizen of the	Creek	Nation.

                               Postoffice   Coweta, Ind. Ter.

AFFIDAVIT OF MOTHER.

UNITED STATES OF AMERICA, Indian Territory, }
    WESTERN   DISTRICT.   }

    I, Neosho Tiger, on oath state that I am thirty years of age and a citizen by blood, of the Creek Nation; that I am the lawful wife of Dave Tiger, who is a citizen, by blood of the Creek Nation; that a male child was born to me on 7th day of August, 1902, that said child has been named Edward Tiger, and is now living.

                                      her
                             Neosho x Tiger

Witnesses To Mark: mark
{ Jas Tiger
{ J.B. Davis

Subscribed and sworn to before me this 16th day of March, 1905.

                                            B.J. Beavers
                                            Notary Public.

Applications for Enrollment of Creek Newborn
Act of 1905   Volume III

AFFIDAVIT OF ATTENDING PHYSICIAN OR MID-WIFE.

UNITED STATES OF AMERICA, Indian Territory,
    WESTERN   DISTRICT.

    I, Yanah Lynch , a midwife , on oath state that I attended on Mrs. NeoSho Tiger , wife of Dave Tiger on the 7th day of August , 1902 ; that there was born to her on said date a male child; that said child is now living and is said to have been named Edward Tiger

                                                 her
                                         Yanah x Lynch
Witnesses To Mark: mark
{ Jas Tiger
  J.B. Davis

    Subscribed and sworn to before me this 16th day of March , 1905.

                                        B.J. Beavers
                                        Notary Public.

BIRTH AFFIDAVIT.
DEPARTMENT OF THE INTERIOR,
COMMISSION TO THE FIVE CIVILIZED TRIBES.

    IN RE Application for Enrollment, as a citizen of the Creek Nation, of Ernest Beaver , born on the 1 day of *(blank)*, 190*(blank)*

| Name of Father: | John Beaver | a citizen of the | Creek | Nation. |
| Name of Mother: | Ella Beaver | a citizen of the | U. S. | Nation. |

                          Post-Office: Bristow

AFFIDAVIT OF ATTENDING PHYSICIAN OR MID-WIFE.

UNITED STATES OF AMERICA,
    Indian Territory.
    Western   District.

    I, J. W. Bronaugh , a Physician , on oath state that I attended on Mrs. Ella Beaver , wife of John Beaver on the 14th day of December , 1904 ; that there was born to her on said date a male child; that said child is now living, and is said to have been named Ernest Beaver

                                      J. W. Bronaugh, M.D.

WITNESSES TO MARK:
{

Applications for Enrollment of Creek Newborn
Act of 1905 Volume III

Subscribed and sworn to before me this 20th *day of* April, 1905.

       DJ Red
         Notary Public.

BIRTH AFFIDAVIT.

DEPARTMENT OF THE INTERIOR.
COMMISSION TO THE FIVE CIVILIZED TRIBES.

  IN RE APPLICATION FOR ENROLLMENT, as a citizen of the CREEK Nation, of Ernest Beaver, born on the 14 day of December, 1904

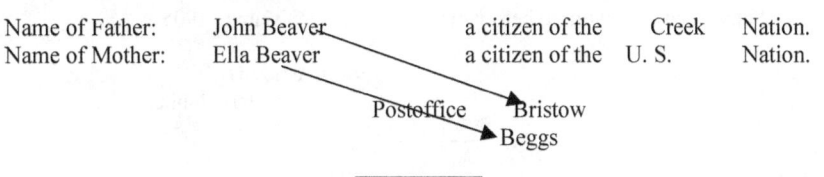

| Name of Father: | John Beaver | a citizen of the | Creek | Nation. |
| Name of Mother: | Ella Beaver | a citizen of the | U. S. | Nation. |

      Postoffice Bristow
          Beggs

Child present – Gr.

AFFIDAVIT OF MOTHER.

UNITED STATES OF AMERICA, Indian Territory,
  WESTERN   DISTRICT.

  I, Ella Beaver, on oath state that I am 23 years of age and a citizen by ----- , of the U. S. Nation; that I am the lawful wife of John Beaver, who is a citizen, by blood of the Creek Nation; that a male child was born to me on 14 day of December, 1904, that said child has been named Earnest[sic] Beaver, and is now living.
          Her
        Ella x Beaver
Witnesses To Mark: mark
 { Irwin Donovan
 { EC Griesel

  Subscribed and sworn to before me this 15 day of March, 1905.

       Edw C Griesel
         Notary Public.

Applications for Enrollment of Creek Newborn
Act of 1905   Volume III

AFFIDAVIT OF ATTENDING ~~PHYSICIAN OR MID-WIFE~~.
Father

UNITED STATES OF AMERICA, Indian Territory, }
WESTERN   DISTRICT.

I, John Beaver, ~~a~~, on oath state that I attended on Mrs. Ella Beaver, wife of myself on the 14 day of December, 1904; that there was born to her on said date a male child; that said child is now living and is said to have been named Earnest Beaver

His
John x Beaver
mark

Witnesses To Mark:
{ Irwin Donovan
{ EC Griesel

Subscribed and sworn to before me this 15 day of March, 1905.

Edw C Griesel
Notary Public.

BIRTH AFFIDAVIT.

DEPARTMENT OF THE INTERIOR.
COMMISSION TO THE FIVE CIVILIZED TRIBES.

IN RE APPLICATION FOR ENROLLMENT, as a citizen of the Creek Nation, of Ernest Beaver, born on the 14 day of Dec, 1904

Name of Father: (Tuskegee)	John Beaver	a citizen of the	Creek	Nation.
Name of Mother:	Ella Beaver	a citizen of the	U. S.	Nation.

Postoffice   Bristow

AFFIDAVIT OF ~~MOTHER~~.   (Child Present)
Father

UNITED STATES OF AMERICA, Indian Territory, }
Western   DISTRICT.

I, John Beaver, on oath state that I am 55 years of age and a citizen by blood, of the Creek Nation; that I am the lawful ~~wife~~ Husband of Ella Beaver, who is a citizen, by ~~blood~~ --- of the Creek Nation; that a male child was born to me on 14 day of Dec, 1904, that said child has been named Ernest Beaver, and is now living.

His
John x Beaver
mark

Applications for Enrollment of Creek Newborn
Act of 1905   Volume III

Witnesses To Mark:
- Jesse McDermott
- EC Griesel

Subscribed and sworn to before me this 19 day of April, 1905.

                                    Edw C Griesel
                                    Notary Public.

BIRTH AFFIDAVIT.

DEPARTMENT OF THE INTERIOR.
COMMISSION TO THE FIVE CIVILIZED TRIBES.

IN RE APPLICATION FOR ENROLLMENT, as a citizen of the Creek Nation, of Alice Berryhill, born on the 12 day of June 1901, 1*(blank)*

Name of Father: Joe Berryhill   a citizen of the   Creek   Nation.
Name of Mother: Sallie Berryhill (Deceased)   a citizen of the   Creek   Nation.

                      Postoffice   Fantress[sic], I.T.

                  AFFIDAVIT OF ~~MOTHER~~. Father

UNITED STATES OF AMERICA, Indian Territory,
Western Judicial District[sic]   DISTRICT.

I, Joe Berryhill   (Father), on oath state that I am 44   years of age and a citizen by Blood , of the Creek   Nation; that I a lawful husband of Sallie Berryhill , who ~~is~~ was a citizen, by   Blood of the Creek   Nation; that a Female   child was born to me on 12th day of June, 1901   , 1*(blank)* , that said child has been named   Alice Berryhill , and was living March 4, 1905.

                                  Joe Berryhill

Witnesses To Mark:

Subscribed and sworn to before me this 16 day of Mch, 1905.

                                  John H. Phillips
                                  Notary Public.

My Commission Expires Sept. 6th 1906.

Applications for Enrollment of Creek Newborn
Act of 1905 Volume III

AFFIDAVIT OF ATTENDING PHYSICIAN OR MID-WIFE.

UNITED STATES OF AMERICA, Indian Territory, }
Western Judicial District[sic] DISTRICT.

I, Semarhitchker , a Mid- Wife , on oath state that I attended on Mrs. Sallie Berryhill (Deceased) , wife of Joe Berryhill on the 12th day of June, 1901 , 1*(blank)* ; that there was born to her on said date a Female child; that said child was living March 4, 1905, and is said to have been named Alice Berryhill

her
Semarhitchker x
mark

Witnesses To Mark:
{ William Jimboy
{ John H. Phillips

Subscribed and sworn to before me this 16 day of Mch, 1905.

John H. Phillips
Notary Public.

My Commission Expires Sept. 6th 1906.

DEPARTMENT OF THE INTERIOR.
COMMISSION TO THE FIVE CIVILIZED TRIBES.

In the matter of the death of Reno Berryhill a citizen of the Creek Nation, who formerly resided at or near Fantress[sic], Creek Nation , Ind. Ter., and died on the 10th day of July, 1905, , 1*(blank)*.

AFFIDAVIT OF RELATIVE.

UNITED STATES OF AMERICA, Indian Territory, }
Western Judicial DISTRICT.

I, Joe Berryhill , on oath state that I am 42 years of age and a citizen by Blood , of the Creek Nation; that my postoffice address is Fantress[sic], Creek Nation , Ind. Ter.; that I am Father of Reno Berryhill who was a citizen, by Blood , of the Creek Nation and that said Reno Berryhill died on the 10th day of July, 1905 , 1*(blank)*

Joe Berryhill

Witnesses To Mark:
{

Applications for Enrollment of Creek Newborn
Act of 1905   Volume III

Subscribed and sworn to before me this 20th day of July, 1905.

John H Phillips
Notary Public.

My Commission Expires Sept. 6th 1906.

AFFIDAVIT OF ACQUAINTANCE.

UNITED STATES OF AMERICA, Indian Territory, }
Western Judicial   DISTRICT.

I, William Jimboy, on oath state that I am 55 years of age, and a citizen by Blood of the Creek Nation; that my postoffice address is Weleetka, Creek Nation, Ind. Ter.; that I was personally acquainted with Reno Berryhill who was a citizen, by blood, of the Creek Nation; and that said Reno Berryhill died on the 10th day of July, 1905, 1*(blank)*

William Jimboy

Witnesses To Mark:
{

Subscribed and sworn to before me this 20th day of July, 1905.

John H Phillips
Notary Public.

My Commission Expires Sept. 6th 1906.

BIRTH AFFIDAVIT.

DEPARTMENT OF THE INTERIOR.
COMMISSION TO THE FIVE CIVILIZED TRIBES.

IN RE APPLICATION FOR ENROLLMENT, as a citizen of the Creek Nation, of Reno Berryhill, born on the 12th day of May, 1904, 1*(blank)*

Name of Father:	Joe Berryhill	a citizen of the Creek	Nation.
Name of Mother:	Hepsie Berryhill	a citizen of the Creek	Nation.

Postoffice   Fantress[sic], I.T.

Applications for Enrollment of Creek Newborn
Act of 1905   Volume III

AFFIDAVIT OF MOTHER.

UNITED STATES OF AMERICA, Indian Territory, ⎱
Western Judicial District[sic]   DISTRICT. ⎰

    I, Hepsie Berryhill , on oath state that I am 31 years of age and a citizen by Blood , of the Muskogee or Creek Nation; that I am the lawful wife of Joe Berryhill, who is a citizen, by Blood of the Muskogee or Creek Nation; that a Male child was born to me on 12th day of May, 1904 , 1*(blank)* , that said child has been named Reno Berryhill , and was living March 4, 1905.

                                           Hepsie Berryhill

Witnesses To Mark:
{

    Subscribed and sworn to before me this 16 day of Mch , 1905.

                                           John H Phillips
                                                Notary Public.

My Commission Expires Sept. 6th 1906.

AFFIDAVIT OF ATTENDING PHYSICIAN OR MID-WIFE.

UNITED STATES OF AMERICA, Indian Territory, ⎱
Western Judicial District[sic]   DISTRICT. ⎰

    I, Hailey Jimboy , a Mid- wife , on oath state that I attended on Mrs. Hepsie Berryhill , wife of Joe Berryhill on the 12th day of May, 1904 , 1*(blank)* ; that there was born to her on said date a Male child; that said child was living March 4, 1905, and is said to have been named Reno Berryhill   her

                                           Hailey x Jimboy
Witnesses To Mark: mark
{ William Jimboy
  John H. Phillips

    Subscribed and sworn to before me this 16 day of Mch , 1905.

                                           John H Phillips
                                              Notary Public.

My Commission Expires Sept. 6th 1906.

Applications for Enrollment of Creek Newborn
Act of 1905   Volume III

COPY of original on file in L.O.
DEPARTMENT OF THE INTERIOR.
COMMISSION TO THE FIVE CIVILIZED TRIBES.

In the matter of the death of   Sallie Berryhill   a citizen of the Creek Nation, who formerly resided at or near Fantress[sic], Creek Nation   , Ind. Ter., and died on the 8th   day of December   , 1902

AFFIDAVIT OF RELATIVE.

UNITED STATES OF AMERICA, Indian Territory, ⎱
    Western Judicial   DISTRICT. ⎰

I,   Joe Berryhill , on oath state that I am 42   years of age and a citizen by Blood , of the   Creek   Nation; that my postoffice address is Fantress[sic], Creek Nation , Ind. Ter.; that I am   Husband   of Sallie Berryhill   who was a citizen, by Blood, of the   Creek   Nation and that said Sallie Berryhill   died on the   8th   day of December, 1902 , 1*(blank)*

                                            (signed) Joe Berryhill
Witnesses To Mark:

(Seal)

Subscribed and sworn to before me this 20th day of July, 1905, 1*(blank)*

                                  John H Phillips
My commission expires Sept 6th 1906   Notary Public.

AFFIDAVIT OF ACQUAINTANCE.

UNITED STATES OF AMERICA, Indian Territory, ⎱
    Western Judicial   DISTRICT. ⎰

I,   William Jimboy , on oath state that I am 55   years of age, and a citizen by Blood   of the   Creek   Nation; that my postoffice address is Weleetka, Creek Nation , Ind. Ter.; that I was personally acquainted with   Sallie Berryhill   who was a citizen, by Blood , of the Creek   Nation; and that said   Sallie Berryhill   died on the 8th   day of December, 1902 , 1*(blank)*

                                      (Signed)   William Jimboy
Witnesses To Mark:

(Seal)

Subscribed and sworn to before me this 8th day of July, 1905.

                                  John H Phillips
My commission expires Sept 6th 1906   Notary Public.

Applications for Enrollment of Creek Newborn
Act of 1905 Volume III

NC-236

DEPARTMENT OF THE INTERIOR,
COMMISSIONER TO THE FIVE CIVILIZED TRIBES.

Muskogee, Indian Territory, November 16, 1905.

In the matter of the application for the enrollment of Fannie Lee Horn as a citizen by blood of the Creek Nation.

Sam Horn, being duly sworn, testified as follows:

EXAMINATION BY THE COMMISSION:
Q What is your name? A Sam Horn.
Q How old are you? A 28.
Q What is your postoffice? A Checotah.
Q What is your father's name? A Sam Horn, a citizen of the Cherokee Nation.
Q What is your mother's name? A Melvin Hughes.

Witness is identified as Sam Horn, on Creek Indian card, field No. 481, opposite Roll No. 1580.

Q Have you two children that have been born in the last four years? A Yes sir.
Q For one you made application as a new-born, name Jessie? A Yes sir.
Q Is she living? A Yes sir.
Q You made affidavit for the enrollment of another child, older than Jessie? A Yes sir.
Q What is its name? A Fannie Lee Horn.
Q How old is Fannie Lee? A She was four years old the 14th of September this year. She was born the 14th of September, 1901.
Q Is Fannie Lee living? A Yes sir.
Q Sure of that? A Yes sir.
Q When did you see her last? A Day before yesterday morning.
Q What is the name of her mother? A Lillie.
Q She is not a citizen? A No sir.

Witness is advised that there is on file in this case the affidavit of Lillie Horn, the mother of this child, and also of the midwife, Melvina Hughes, stating that that child was born September 14, 1901, but we have here no proof that the child was living March 4, 1905, as the new law requires. This Office requires witness to have Lillie Horn, the mother, and Melvina Hughes, the midwife, execute new affidavits setting forth this fact.

INDIAN TERRITORY, Western District.

I, J. Y. Miller, a stenographer to the Commissioner to the Five Civilized Tribes, do hereby certify that the above and foregoing is a true and complete translation of my notes as same appear in my stenographic report of this case.

Applications for Enrollment of Creek Newborn
Act of 1905 Volume III

JY Miller

Subscribed and sworn to before me
this the 16th day of November,
1905.

Edw C Griesel
Notary Public.

BIRTH AFFIDAVIT.

DEPARTMENT OF THE INTERIOR.
COMMISSION TO THE FIVE CIVILIZED TRIBES.

IN RE APPLICATION FOR ENROLLMENT, as a citizen of the Creek Nation, of Jessie Horn , born on the 14 day of November , 1904
(Parents = Sam Horn & Melvina Hughes)

Name of Father:	Sam Horn	a citizen of the	Creek	Nation.
Name of Mother:	Lillie Horn	a citizen of the	U.S.	Nation.

Postoffice   Checotah

AFFIDAVIT OF ~~MOTHER~~. Father

UNITED STATES OF AMERICA, Indian Territory,⎱
    Western   DISTRICT. ⎰

I, Sam Horn , on oath state that I am 28 years of age and a citizen by blood , of the Creek Nation; that I am the lawful ~~wife~~ husband of Lillie Horn , who is a citizen, by ----- of the U.S. Nation; that a female child was born to me on 14" day of November , 1904 , that said child has been named Jessie Horn , and was living March 4, 1905.
                                                                    his
                                                         Sam x Horn
Witnesses To Mark: mark
⎰ Henry G. Hains
⎱ J McDermott

Subscribed and sworn to before me this 16" day of November, 1905.

Henry G. Hains
Notary Public.

Applications for Enrollment of Creek Newborn
Act of 1905 Volume III

BIRTH AFFIDAVIT.

DEPARTMENT OF THE INTERIOR,
COMMISSION TO THE FIVE CIVILIZED TRIBES.

IN RE Application for Enrollment, as a citizen of the Creek Nation, of Fannie Lee Horn , born on the 14th day of September , 1901

Name of Father: Samuel Horn   a citizen of the   Creek   Nation.
Name of Mother: Lillie Horn   a citizen of the United StatesNation.

Post-office   Checotah, I.T.

AFFIDAVIT OF MOTHER.

UNITED STATES OF AMERICA,
    Indian Territory,
Western   DISTRICT.

I, Lillie Horn , on oath state that I am 22 years of age and a citizen by *(blank)* , of the United States   Nation; that I am the lawful wife of Samuel Horn , who is a citizen, by Blood of the Creek   Nation; that a Female   child was born to me on 14th day of September , 1901 , that said child has been named Fannie Lee Horn , and is now living.

her
Lillie Horn x
mark

Witnesses To Mark:
  { A A Smith
    Trevor Faulkner

Subscribed and sworn to before me this 10th *day of* July , *19*02.

    My Commission Expires July 1, 1906.   JB Morrow
Notary Public.

AFFIDAVIT OF ATTENDING PHYSICIAN OR MID-WIFE.

UNITED STATES OF AMERICA,
    Indian Territory,
Western   DISTRICT.

I, Melvina Hughes , a Midwife , on oath state that I attended on Mrs. Lillie Horn, wife of Samuel Horn on the 14th day of September , 1901 ; that there was born to her on said date a   Female   child; that said child is now living and is said to have been named Fannie Lee Horn

her
Melvina Hughes x
mark

Applications for Enrollment of Creek Newborn
Act of 1905 Volume III

Witnesses To Mark:
- A A Smith
- Trevor Faulkner

Subscribed and sworn to before me this 10th *day of* July, *1902.*

My Commission Expires July 1, 1906. JB Morrow
Notary Public.

BIRTH AFFIDAVIT.

DEPARTMENT OF THE INTERIOR.
COMMISSION TO THE FIVE CIVILIZED TRIBES.

IN RE APPLICATION FOR ENROLLMENT, as a citizen of the Creek or Muskogee Nation, of Jessie Horn, born on the 14th day of November, 1904

Name of Father:	Sam Horn	a citizen of the Creek Nation.
Name of Mother:	Lillie Horn	a citizen of the United StatesNation.

Postoffice Checotah, Ind Ter

AFFIDAVIT OF MOTHER.

UNITED STATES OF AMERICA, Indian Territory,
Western DISTRICT.

I, Lillie Horn, on oath state that I am twenty five years of age and a citizen by *(blank)*, of the United States Nation; that I am the lawful wife of Sam Horn, who is a citizen, by blood of the Creek or Muskogee Nation; that a female child was born to me on 14th day of November, 1904, that said child has been named Jessie Horn, and was living March 4, 1905.

her
Lillie x Horn
Witnesses To Mark: mark
- J B Lucas Checotah, I.T.
- Ben D. Gross Checotah, I.T.

Subscribed and sworn to before me this 17th day of March, 1905.

My Commission Expires Oct. 7th, 1906. W R Allen
Notary Public.

Applications for Enrollment of Creek Newborn
Act of 1905 Volume III

AFFIDAVIT OF ATTENDING PHYSICIAN OR MID-WIFE.

UNITED STATES OF AMERICA, Indian Territory, }
    Western   DISTRICT.

I, George W. McGuire , a physician , on oath state that I attended on Mrs. Lillie Horn , wife of Sam Horn on the 14th day of November , 1904 ; that there was born to her on said date a female child; that said child was living March 4, 1905, and is said to have been named Jessie

                                    Geo. W. McGuire

Witnesses To Mark:
  { J B Lucas Checotah I.T.
    J T Ard   "   " "

Subscribed and sworn to before me this 17th day of March , 1905.

My Commission Expires Oct. 7th, 1906.   W R Allen
                                            Notary Public.

BIRTH AFFIDAVIT.

DEPARTMENT OF THE INTERIOR.
COMMISSION TO THE FIVE CIVILIZED TRIBES.

IN RE APPLICATION FOR ENROLLMENT, as a citizen of the Creek Nation, of Fannie Lee Horn , born on the 14th day of September , 1901

Name of Father: Sam Horn   a citizen of the   Creek   Nation.
Name of Mother: Lillie Horn   a citizen of the United StatesNation.

                          Postoffice   Checotah, Ind Ty

AFFIDAVIT OF MOTHER.

UNITED STATES OF AMERICA, Indian Territory, }
    Western   DISTRICT.

I, Lillie Horn , on oath state that I am 26 years of age and a citizen by *(blank)* , of the United States Nation; that I am the lawful wife of Sam Horn , who is a citizen, by Blood of the Creek Nation; that a female child was born to me on 14th day of September , 1901 , that said child has been named Fannie Lee Horn , and was living March 4, 1905.
                                        her
                                  Lillie x Horn
Witnesses To Mark: mark
  { Guy *(Illegible)*
    W.W. Bray   Checotah, I.T.

Applications for Enrollment of Creek Newborn
Act of 1905 Volume III

Subscribed and sworn to before me this 23^{d} day of November, 1905.

My Commission Expires July 1, 1906.   JB Morrow
                                                            Notary Public.

MARRIAGE LICENSE.

United States of America
Indian Territory
Northern District.   SS   No. 361

TO ANY PERSON AUTHORIZED BY LAW TO SOLEMNIZE MARRIAGE GREETING:

You are hereby commanded to solemnize the rite and publish the banns of matrimony between Mr. Sam Horn of Checotah in the Indian Territory, aged 22 years and Miss Lillie Smith of Checotah in the Indian Territory aged 20 years, according to law, and do you officially sign and return this license to the parties therein named.

Witness my hand and official seal at Muscogee Indian Territory this 14 day of Nov A.D. 1899

J. A. Winston
Clerk of the U S Court

By N.S. Young Deputy

Ceritificate[sic] of Marriage

United States of America
Indian Territory
Northern District

I, J.M. Amerson, a minister of the gospel, do hereby certify that on the 20 day of November A.D. 1899, I did duly and according to law as commanded in the foregoing license, solemnize the rite and publish the banns of matrimony between the parties therein named.

WITNESS my hand this 21 day of November A.D. 1899
My credentials are recorded in the office of the Clerk of the United States Court, Indian Territory, Northern District
Book A, page 52 or 57

J.M. Amerson
A Minister of the Gospel

Applications for Enrollment of Creek Newborn
Act of 1905 Volume III

AFFIDAVIT OF DISINTERESTED WITNESSES.

United States of America,
    Indian Territory,
    Western District.

We, the undersigned, on oath state that we are personally acquainted with Lilly Horn, wife of Sam Horn, and that there was born to her on or about the 14th day of September, 1901, a female child; that said child was living March 4, 1905, and is said to have been named Fannie Lee Horn.

We further state that we have no interest in this case.

                                    Sallie Coon

                                    Lizie[sic] Hughes

(2) Witnesses to mark:

_____

_____

Subscribed and sworn to before me this 23[d] day of November 1905.

My Commission Expires July 1, 1906.   JB Morrow
                                            Notary Public.

                                                              NC 236.

                        Muskogee, Indian Territory, July 5, 1905.

Lillie Horn,
    Checotah, Indian Territory.

Dear Madam:

In the matter of the application for the enrollment of your minor child, Jessie Horn, as a citizen of the Creek Nation, you are advised that there is no proof at this office of your marriage to the father of said child, Sam Horn, a citizen of the Creek Nation.

A certified copy of your marriage license or other satisfactory proof of your marriage to said Sam Horn should be forwarded at once to this office.

                                    Respectfully,

                                                Commissioner.

Applications for Enrollment of Creek Newborn
Act of 1905 Volume III

BIRTH AFFIDAVIT.

DEPARTMENT OF THE INTERIOR.
COMMISSION TO THE FIVE CIVILIZED TRIBES.

IN RE APPLICATION FOR ENROLLMENT, as a citizen of the Creek Nation, of Fred Trusler, born on the 8" day of January, 1902

Name of Father:	Frank Trusler	a citizen of the	U.S.	Nation.
Name of Mother:	Phoebe B. Trusler	a citizen of the	Creek	Nation.

Postoffice   Broken Arrow, Ind Ter

AFFIDAVIT OF MOTHER.

UNITED STATES OF AMERICA, Indian Territory,
Western   DISTRICT.

I, Phoebe B. Trusler, on oath state that I am 22 years of age and a citizen by Blood, of the Creek Nation; that I am the lawful wife of Frank Trusler, who is a citizen, by Birth of the United States Nation; that a Male child was born to me on 8" day of January, 1902, that said child has been named Fred Trusler, and was living March 4, 1905.

Phoebe B Trusler

Witnesses To Mark:

Subscribed and sworn to before me this 14" day of March, 1905.

Com Ex 7/3/1906   Robert E. Lynch
                            Notary Public.

AFFIDAVIT OF ATTENDING PHYSICIAN OR MID-WIFE.

UNITED STATES OF AMERICA, Indian Territory,
Western   DISTRICT.

I, Wm H Manes, a Physician, on oath state that I attended on Mrs. Phoebe B Trusler, wife of Frank Trusler on the 8" day of January, 1902; that there was born to her on said date a male child; that said child was living March 4, 1905, and is said to have been named Fred Trusler

William H. Manes, MD

Applications for Enrollment of Creek Newborn
Act of 1905   Volume III

Witnesses To Mark:

{

      Subscribed and sworn to before me this 14" day of March, 1905.

        Com Ex 7/3/1906   Robert E. Lynch
                                                   Notary Public.

COMMISSIONERS:
TAMS BIXBY,
THOMAS B. NEEDLES,
C.R. BRECKINBRIDGE.

WM. O. BEALL
Secretary

DEPARTMENT OF THE INTERIOR,
COMMISSIONER TO THE FIVE CIVILIZED TRIBES.

REFER IN REPLY TO THE FOLLOWING:

Cr NC-237

ADDRESS ONLY THE
COMMISSION TO THE FIVE CIVILIZED TRIBES.

          Muskogee, Indian Territory, June 13, 1905.

Phoebe B. Trusler,
    Broken Arrow, Indian Territory.

Dear Madam:

    In the matter of the application for the enrollment of your minor child, Fred Trusler, as a citizen of the Creek Nation, you are advised that the Commission cannot identify you on its rolls of Creek citizens.

    You are requested to furnish the Commission with your maiden name, the names of your parents, the Creek Indian Town to which you claim to belong, your roll number as same appears on your deeds to land in the Creek Nation, and any other information which will help identify you as a citizen of said Nation.

                        Respectfully,

                        Tams Bixby   Chairman.

N C 237   COPY

I 5415

                        Broken Arrow, I. T. June 16-1905.

Commission to the Five Civilized Tribes.

I Mrs Phoebe B. Trusler will write you that my maiden name wa Phoebe B. Mathewson I belong to Bigspring town and I can not tell you what my roll number is for I appeared before Shepard at Sapulpa to have the restrictions removed of my lands and Mr Shepard has never returned my deeds therefore I can [sic] tell you what my roll number is

Applications for Enrollment of Creek Newborn
Act of 1905   Volume III

(Signed) Thoebe[sic] B. Trusler

BIRTH AFFIDAVIT.

DEPARTMENT OF THE INTERIOR.
COMMISSION TO THE FIVE CIVILIZED TRIBES.

IN RE APPLICATION FOR ENROLLMENT, as a citizen of the CREEK Nation, of Margaret Willison Daily, born on the 21 day of Oct., 1901

Name of Father: Dr. C. E. Dailey[sic]   a citizen of the   U.S.   Nation.
Name of Mother: Lucy S. "   a citizen of the   Creek   Nation.

Postoffice   Muskogee

Child Present Gr.

AFFIDAVIT OF MOTHER.

UNITED STATES OF AMERICA, Indian Territory,
   WESTERN   DISTRICT.

I, Lucy S. Daily, on oath state that I am 28 years of age and a citizen by blood, of the Creek Nation; that I am the lawful wife of Dr C. E. Dailey, who is a citizen, by ----- of the U. S. Nation; that a female child was born to me on 21 day of Oct., 1901, that said child has been named Margaret Willison Daily, and is now living.

Lucy S. Daily

Witnesses To Mark:
{

Subscribed and sworn to before me this 10 day of March, 1905.

My Commission   J. McDermott
Ex July 25" 1907   Notary Public.

BIRTH AFFIDAVIT.

DEPARTMENT OF THE INTERIOR.
COMMISSION TO THE FIVE CIVILIZED TRIBES.

IN RE APPLICATION FOR ENROLLMENT, as a citizen of the Creek Nation, of Margaret Willison Daily, born on the 21 day of Oct., 1901

Name of Father: Dr. C. E. Dailey[sic]   a citizen of the   U.S.   Nation.
Name of Mother: Lucy S. "   a citizen of the   Creek   Nation.

Applications for Enrollment of Creek Newborn
Act of 1905   Volume III

Postoffice   Muskogee

acquaintance
AFFIDAVIT OF ~~MOTHER~~.

UNITED STATES OF AMERICA, Indian Territory, ⎫
      Western   DISTRICT.   ⎭

I, Kate C Mittong , on oath state that I am *(blank)* years of age and a citizen by ----- , of the U.S. Nation; that I am acquainted with Lucy S Daily the lawful wife of Dr. C.E. Daily , who is a citizen, by ----- of the U.S. Nation; that a female child was born to ~~me~~ her on 21 day of October , 1901 , that said child has been named Margaret Willison Daily , and was living March 4, 1905. & that I am no kin and have no interest herein.

Kate C Mittong

Witnesses To Mark:
{

Subscribed and sworn to before me this 14" day of July , 1905.

Henry G. Hains
Notary Public.

acquaintance
AFFIDAVIT OF ~~ATTENDING PHYSICIAN OR MID-WIFE~~.

UNITED STATES OF AMERICA, Indian Territory, ⎫
      Western   DISTRICT.   ⎭

know
I, A. L. Gregory , an acquaintance , on oath state that I ~~attended on~~ Mrs. Lucy S. Daily , wife of Dr. C.E. Daily & on or about the 21" day of October , 1901 ; that there was born to her on said date a female child; that said child was living March 4, 1905, and is said to have been named Margaret Willison Daily & I am no kin nor havr I any interest herein.

A. L. Gregory

Witnesses To Mark:
{

Subscribed and sworn to before me this 14" day of July , 1905.

Henry G. Hains
Notary Public.

Applications for Enrollment of Creek Newborn
Act of 1905   Volume III

AFFIDAVIT

....

UNITED STATES OF AMERICA)
WESTERN JUDICIAL DISTRICT (ss.
INDIAN TERRITORY   )

On this 11th day of March A.D. 1905, before me, a Notary Public. Public within and for the Western Judicial District of the Indian Territory, personally appeared Isabel Cobb of Wagoner, Indian Territory, who being first duly sworn declares and says:

As attending physician I was present at the birth of Margaret Daily, daughter of Lucy Shannon Daily, on the 21st day of October A.D. 1901 at Gibson Station, Indian Territory.

Isabel Cobb M.D.

Subscribed and sworn to before me this 11th day of March A.D. 1905.

My com expires May 7, 1908.   Signa L. Hatfield
                                                       Notary Public.

An exact copy of this instrument
is preserved in the office of
S. L. Hatfield, Wagoner, I. T.

NC 238.

Muskogee, Indian Territory, June 22, 1905.

Lucy S. Dailey,
    Muskogee, Indian Territory.

Dear Madam:
    In the matter of the application for the enrollment of your minor child, Margaret Willison Dailey, as a citizen of the Creek Nation, you are advised that there is on file with the Commission an affidavit executed by the midwife who was in attendance at the birth of said child, in which, proof that said child was living March 4, 1905, is wanting.

You are advised if it is impossible to obtain the affidavit of the midwife relative to said fact, it will be necessary for you to furnish the Commission with the affidavits of two disinterested witnesses as to the birth of said child disinterested witnesses, who can testify as to whether said child was living March 4, 1905. This matter should receive your immediate attention.

Applications for Enrollment of Creek Newborn
Act of 1905 Volume III

Respectfully,

Chairman.

2 BA

DEPARTMENT OF THE INTERIOR,
COMMISSIONER TO THE FIVE CIVILIZED TRIBES.

REFER IN REPLY TO THE FOLLOWING:

NC-239

Muskogee, Indian Territory, **August 4, 1905.**

Ruth Johnson,
    Care Joe Johnson,
        Broken Arrow, Indian Territory.

Dear Madam:

    You are hereby advised that on **July 28, 1905**, the Secretary of the Interior approved the enrollment of your minor child, **George Johnson,**, as a citizen by blood of the **Creek** Nation, and that the name of said child appears upon the roll of new born citizens of the **Creek** Nation as Number **164**.

    The child is now entitled to an allotment, and application therefor should be made without delay at the Land Office for the Nation in which the prospective allotment is located.

    An entire allotment for said child must be selected at the time of the original application.

Respectively,

Commissioner.

BIRTH AFFIDAVIT.

DEPARTMENT OF THE INTERIOR.
COMMISSION TO THE FIVE CIVILIZED TRIBES.

    IN RE APPLICATION FOR ENROLLMENT, as a citizen of the CREEK Nation, of George Johnson, born on the 20 day of Dec, 1903

| Name of Father: | Joe Johnson | a citizen of the ~~Cree~~ U.S. Nation. |
| Name of Mother: | Rutha " | a citizen of the Creek Nation. |

Postoffice   Broken Arrow

Applications for Enrollment of Creek Newborn
Act of 1905 Volume III

(child present)

AFFIDAVIT OF MOTHER.

UNITED STATES OF AMERICA, Indian Territory,
WESTERN DISTRICT.

I, Rutha Johnson , on oath state that I am 26 years of age and a citizen by blood, of the Creek Nation; that I am the lawful wife of Joe Johnson , who is a citizen, by ----- of the U. S. Nation; that a male child was born to me on 20 day of Dec. , 1903 , that said child has been named George Johnson , and is now living.

Rutha Johnson

Witnesses To Mark:

Subscribed and sworn to before me this 15 day of March , 1905.

Edw C Griesel
Notary Public.

DEPARTMENT OF THE INTERIOR,
COMMISSIONER TO THE FIVE CIVILIZED TRIBES.

REFER IN REPLY TO THE FOLLOWING:
NC-240

Muskogee, Indian Territory, **August 4, 1905.**

Chaney Trent,
    Care Jim Trent,
        Wagoner, Indian Territory.

Dear Madam:

You are hereby advised that on **July 28, 1905** , the Secretary of the Interior approved the enrollment of your minor child, **Jesse Trent** , as a citizen by blood of the **Creek** Nation, and that the name of said child appears upon the roll of new born citizens of the **Creek** Nation as Number **165** .

The child is now entitled to an allotment, and application therefor should be made without delay at the Land Office for the Nation in which the prospective allotment is located.

An entire allotment for said child must be selected at the time of the original application.

Respectively,

Commissioner.

Applications for Enrollment of Creek Newborn
Act of 1905   Volume III

BIRTH AFFIDAVIT.

DEPARTMENT OF THE INTERIOR.
COMMISSION TO THE FIVE CIVILIZED TRIBES.

IN RE APPLICATION FOR ENROLLMENT, as a citizen of the CREEK Nation, of Jesse Trent, born on the 24 day of Dec., 1902

Name of Father:	Jim Trent	a citizen of the	U. S. Nation.
Name of Mother:	Chaney "	a citizen of the	Creek Nation.

Postoffice   Wagoner

AFFIDAVIT OF ~~MOTHER.~~ Father

UNITED STATES OF AMERICA, Indian Territory, }
    WESTERN   DISTRICT.

I, Jim Trent, on oath state that I am 41 years of age and a citizen by -----, of the U.S. Nation; that I am the lawful ~~wife~~ husband of Chaney Trent, who is a citizen, by blood of the Creek Nation; that a male child was born to me on 24 day of Dec., 1902, that said child has been named Jesse Trent, and is now living.

                      His
                      Jim x Trent
Witnesses To Mark: mark

Subscribed and sworn to before me this 20 day of March, 1905.

                      Edw C Griesel
                          Notary Public.

BIRTH AFFIDAVIT.

DEPARTMENT OF THE INTERIOR.
COMMISSION TO THE FIVE CIVILIZED TRIBES.

IN RE APPLICATION FOR ENROLLMENT, as a citizen of the Creek Nation, of Jesse Trent, born on the 24 day of Dec., 1902

Name of Father:	Jim Trent	a citizen of the	U. S. Nation.
Name of Mother:	Chaney "	a citizen of the	Creek Nation.

Postoffice   Wagoner

Applications for Enrollment of Creek Newborn
Act of 1905 Volume III

Child Present Gr.

AFFIDAVIT OF MOTHER.

UNITED STATES OF AMERICA, Indian Territory, }
    Western   DISTRICT.

    I, Chaney Trent , on oath state that I am about 40 years of age and a citizen by blood , of the Creek Nation; that I am the lawful wife of Jim Trent , who is a citizen, by ----- of the U.S. Nation; that a male child was born to me on 24 day of Dec. , 1902 , that said child has been named Jesse Trent , and is now living.

                                Her
                            Chaney x Trent

Witnesses To Mark: mark
{ H.G. Hains
  EC Griesel

    Subscribed and sworn to before me this 23 day of Mar , 1905.

                            Edw C Griesel
                              Notary Public.

AFFIDAVIT OF ATTENDING ~~PHYSICIAN~~ OR MID-WIFE.

UNITED STATES OF AMERICA, Indian Territory, }
    Western   DISTRICT.

    I, Margaret Atkin Parks , a Mid Wife , on oath state that I attended on Mrs. Chaney Trent , wife of Jim Trent on the 24 day of Dec , 1902 ; that there was born to her on said date a male child; that said child is now living and is said to have been named Jesse Trent

                            Margaret Atkin Parks

Witnesses To Mark:
{

    Subscribed and sworn to before me this 23 day of March, 1905.

                            Edw C Griesel
                              Notary Public.

Applications for Enrollment of Creek Newborn
Act of 1905   Volume III

NC-241

Muskogee, Indian Territory, May 29, 1905.

Albert Stake,
    Beggs, Indian Territory.

Dear Sir:

    In the matter of the application for the enrollment of your minor child, Missie Stake, as a citizen of the Creek Nation, you are advised that the Commission requires the affidavit of the midwife or physician in attendance at the child's birth; and if the same cannot be secured, the affidavits of two disinterested witnesses as to the birth of said child disinterested witnesses relative to the birth of said child.

    There is herewith enclosed a blank form of birth affidavit, and in executing same care should be exercised to see that all blanks are properly filled, all names written in full and in the event that the person signing the affidavit is unable to write, signature by mark must be attested by two witnesses.

                         Respectfully,

1 B A   Chairman.

NC-241.

Muskogee, Indian Territory, July 26, 1905.

Albert Stake,
    Beggs, Indian Territory.

Dear Sir:

    There are on file in the matter of the application for the enrollment of your daughter Missie Stake as a citizen by blood of the Creek Nation, affidavits of yourself and wife from which it appears that said child was born July 6, 1902, and affidavits of your wife, Sallie Stake, and Sallie Asbury from which it appears that said child was born September 6, 1902.

    You are requested to immediately inform this office as to which of the above dates, if either of them, is the correct date of the birth of said child.

                         Respectfully,

                                        Commissioner.

Applications for Enrollment of Creek Newborn
Act of 1905   Volume III

N C 241

COPY

Beggs, I. T. 8/11-1905

Commissioner to the Five Civilized Tribes
   Muskogee I. T.

Mr. Tom Bixby   Sir

I received your notice consigning[sic] the affidavits of my wife and myself I am sorry of the mistake if its[sic] on my part.   My daughter Missie Stake was born September 6-1902 As I'm your remain

(Signed) Albert Stake
Beggs I. T.

BIRTH AFFIDAVIT.

DEPARTMENT OF THE INTERIOR.
COMMISSION TO THE FIVE CIVILIZED TRIBES.

IN RE APPLICATION FOR ENROLLMENT, as a citizen of the Creek Nation, of Missie Stake, born on the 6" day of September, 1902

Name of Father:	Albert Stake	a citizen of the	Creek	Nation.
Name of Mother:	Sallie Stake	a citizen of the	Creek	Nation.

Postoffice   Beggs, I.T.

AFFIDAVIT OF MOTHER.

UNITED STATES OF AMERICA, Indian Territory,
   Western   DISTRICT.

I, Sallie Stake, on oath state that I am about 30 years of age and a citizen by Blood, of the Creek Nation; that I am the lawful wife of Albert Stake, who is a citizen, by Blood of the Creek Nation; that a Female child was born to me on 6" day of September, 1902, that said child has been named Missie Stake, and ~~was living March 4, 1905~~. is now living.

                                              her
                              Sallie Stake x
Witnesses To Mark: mark
   { A. Liebman, Okmulgee I.T.
    W W Morton   "

Applications for Enrollment of Creek Newborn
Act of 1905   Volume III

Subscribed and sworn to before me this 14 day of July , 1905.

                                       Wm P Morton
                                             Notary Public.

My Com Ex July 23-06

AFFIDAVIT OF ATTENDING PHYSICIAN OR MID-WIFE.

UNITED STATES OF AMERICA, Indian Territory, ⎫
      Western   DISTRICT.   ⎭

    I, Sallie Asbury , a Mid Wife , on oath state that I attended on Mrs. Sallie Stake , wife of Albert Stake on the 6" day of September , 1902 ; that there was born to her on said date a   Female   child; that said child ~~was~~ is now living ~~March 4, 1905,~~ and is said to have been named Missie Stake   her
                                          Sallie x Asbury
Witnesses To Mark: mark
  ⎧ A. Liebman, Okmulgee I.T.
  ⎩ W W Morton   "

Subscribed and sworn to before me this 14 day of July , 1905.

                                       Wm P Morton
                                             Notary Public.

My Com Ex July 23-06

BIRTH AFFIDAVIT.

DEPARTMENT OF THE INTERIOR.
COMMISSION TO THE FIVE CIVILIZED TRIBES.

    IN RE APPLICATION FOR ENROLLMENT, as a citizen of the CREEK Nation, of Missie Stake, born on the 6 day of July , 1902

Name of Father:	Albert Stake	a citizen of the	Creek	Nation.
Name of Mother:	Sallie "	a citizen of the	"	Nation.

                               Postoffice   Beggs

Applications for Enrollment of Creek Newborn
Act of 1905   Volume III

Child Present – Gr.

AFFIDAVIT OF MOTHER.

UNITED STATES OF AMERICA, Indian Territory, ⎫
    WESTERN   DISTRICT. ⎬

I, Sallie Stake , on oath state that I am 35 years of age and a citizen by blood , of the Creek Nation; that I am the lawful wife of Albert Stake , who is a citizen, by blood of the Creek Nation; that a female child was born to me on 6 day of July , 1902 , that said child has been named Missie Stake , and is now living.

                                      Sallie Stake

Witnesses To Mark:
{

Subscribed and sworn to before me this 15 day of March , 1905.

                                      Edw C Griesel
                                          Notary Public.

                              father
AFFIDAVIT OF ~~ATTENDING PHYSICIAN OR MID-WIFE~~.
                           (no midwife present)

UNITED STATES OF AMERICA, Indian Territory, ⎫
    WESTERN   DISTRICT. ⎬

I, Albert Stake , am *(blank)* , ~~on oath state that I attended on Mrs. , wife~~ of Sallie Stake on the 6 day of July , 1902 ; that there was born to her on said date a female child; that said child is now living and is said to have been named Missie Stake

                                      Albert Stake

Witnesses To Mark:
{

Subscribed and sworn to before me this 15 day of March, 1905.

                                      Edw C Griesel
                                        Notary Public.

Applications for Enrollment of Creek Newborn
Act of 1905   Volume III

BIRTH AFFIDAVIT.

DEPARTMENT OF THE INTERIOR.
COMMISSION TO THE FIVE CIVILIZED TRIBES.

IN RE APPLICATION FOR ENROLLMENT, as a citizen of the CREEK Nation, of Mary Wadsworth, born on the 13 day of Feb., 1903

Name of Father: Mitchell Wadsworth   a citizen of the   Creek   Nation.
Name of Mother: Emma   "   (dc'd.) a citizen of the   "   Nation.

Postoffice   Coweta

AFFIDAVIT OF MOTHER.

UNITED STATES OF AMERICA, Indian Territory,
    WESTERN   DISTRICT.

I, Mitchel Wadsworth, on oath state that I am 38 years of age and a citizen by blood, of the Creek Nation; that I am the lawful ~~wife~~ hus of Emma Wadsworth (dc'd), who is a citizen, by blood of the Creek Nation; that a female child was born to me on 13 day of Feb., 1903, that said child has been named Mary Wadsworth, and is now living.

Mitchell Wadsworth

Witnesses To Mark:
{

Subscribed and sworn to before me this 15 day of March, 1905.

Edw C Griesel
Notary Public.

AFFIDAVIT OF ATTENDING PHYSICIAN OR MID-WIFE.
of Wagoner

UNITED STATES OF AMERICA, Indian Territory,
    WESTERN   DISTRICT.

I, G. W. Jobe, a physician, on oath state that I attended on Mrs. Emma Wadsworth, wife of Mitchel Wadsworth on the 13 day of Feb, 1903; that there was born to her on said date a female child; that said child is now living and is said to have been named Mary Wadsworth

G W Jobe M.D.

Witnesses To Mark:
{

Applications for Enrollment of Creek Newborn
Act of 1905   Volume III

Subscribed and sworn to before me this 15 day of March, 1905.

Edw C Griesel
Notary Public.

BIRTH AFFIDAVIT.

DEPARTMENT OF THE INTERIOR.
COMMISSION TO THE FIVE CIVILIZED TRIBES.

IN RE APPLICATION FOR ENROLLMENT, as a citizen of the CREEK Nation, of (-----) Wadsworth, born on the 23 day of Dec. , 1904

Name of Father: Mitchell Wadsworth   a citizen of the   Creek   Nation.
Name of Mother: Emma   "   (d.)   a citizen of the   "   Nation.

Postoffice   Coweta

AFFIDAVIT OF MOTHER.

UNITED STATES OF AMERICA, Indian Territory,
    WESTERN   DISTRICT.

I, Mitchell Wadsworth , on oath state that I am 38 years of age and a citizen by blood , of the Creek Nation; that I am the lawful ~~wife~~ hus of Emma Wadsworth (dc'd), who is a citizen, by blood of the Creek Nation; that a (?) child was born to me on 23 day of Dec. , 1904 , that said child has been named (-----) Wadsworth , and ~~is now living~~. was born dead

Mitchell Wadsworth

Witnesses To Mark:
{

Subscribed and sworn to before me this 15 day of March, 1905.

Edw C Griesel
Notary Public.

NC 242   J.L.D.
DEPARTMENT OF THE INTERIOR,
COMMISSIONER TO THE FIVE CIVILIZED TRIBES.

In the matter of the application for the enrollment of _____ Wadsworth, deceased, as a citizen by blood of the Creek Nation.

. . . .

Applications for Enrollment of Creek Newborn
Act of 1905   Volume III

STATEMENT AND ORDER.

The record in this case shows that on March 15, 1905, application was made, in affidavit form, for the enrollment of _____ Wadsworth, deceased, as a citizen by blood of the Creek Nation, under the provisions of the act of Congress approved March 3, 1905.

It appears that the affidavit filed in this matter that said _____ Wadsworth, deceased, was born dead on December 23, 1904.

The act of Congress approved March 3, 1905, (33 Stats., 1048), provides:
"That the Commission to the Five Civilized Tribes is authorized for sixty days after the date of the approval of this act to receive and consider applications for enrollment, of children, born subsequent to May twenty-fifth, nineteen hundred and one, and prior to March fourth, nineteen hundred and five, and living on said latter date, to citizens of the Creek tribe of Indians whose enrollment has been approved by the Secretary of the Interior prior to the approval of this act; and to enroll and make allotments to such children."

It is, therefore, ordered that the application for the enrollment of said _____ Wadsworth, deceased, as a citizen by blood of the Creek Nation, be, and the same is, hereby dismissed.

Tams Bixby   Commissioner.

Muskogee, Indian Territory.
JAN 4 – 1907

DEPARTMENT OF THE INTERIOR,
COMMISSIONER TO THE FIVE CIVILIZED TRIBES.

REFER IN REPLY TO THE FOLLOWING:
NC-243

Muskogee, Indian Territory, **August 4, 1905.**

Lena Freeman,
       Care of John W. Freeman,
              Henryetta, Indian Territory.

Dear Madam:

You are hereby advised that on **July 28, 1905**, the Secretary of the Interior approved the enrollment of your minor child, **Theodore R. Freeman**, as a citizen by blood of the **Creek** Nation, and that the name of said child appears upon the roll of new born citizens of the **Creek** Nation as Number **166**.

Applications for Enrollment of Creek Newborn
Act of 1905   Volume III

The child is now entitled to an allotment, and application therefor should be made without delay at the Land Office for the Nation in which the prospective allotment is located.

An entire allotment for said child must be selected at the time of the original application.

Respectively,

Commissioner.

BIRTH AFFIDAVIT.

DEPARTMENT OF THE INTERIOR,
COMMISSION TO THE FIVE CIVILIZED TRIBES.

IN RE APPLICATION FOR ENROLLMENT, as a citizen of the Creek Nation, of Theodore R. Freeman, born on the nineteenth day of May, 1904, name of father, John W. Freeman a non-citizen of the Creek Nation, Name of mother Lena Freeman, a citizen of the Creek Nation. Henryetta Indian Territory.

AFFIDAVIT OF MOTHER.

United States of America,   (
Indian Territory,   (ss.
Western Judicial District.   (
   (

I, Lena Freeman, on oath state that I am twenty two, 22, years of age, and a citizen by blood of the Creek Nation; that I am the lawful wife of John W. Freeman, who is not a citizen by blood of the Creek Nation; that a male child was born to me on the 19th, day of May, 1904, that said child has been named Theodore R. Freeman, and is now living.

Lena Freeman

Subscribed and sworn to before me this the 13th, day of March, 1905.

William B. Morgan
My commission expires April, 22nd, 1908.   Notary Public.

Affidavit of Attending Physician.

United States of America,   )
Indian Territory,   (ss.
Western Judicial District.   )

Applications for Enrollment of Creek Newborn
Act of 1905   Volume III

I, Chas E. Scharnegal, a practicing physician, on oath state that I attended on Mrs. Lena Freeman, wife of John W. Freeman, on the 19th day of May, 1904, that there was born to her on said date a male child that said child is now living and is said to have been named Theodore R. Freeman.

C.E. Scharnegal M.D.

Subscribed and Seworn to before me this the 13th, day of March, 1905.

William B. Morgan
Notary Public.

My commission expires April 22, 1908vs.[sic]

BIRTH AFFIDAVIT.

DEPARTMENT OF THE INTERIOR.
COMMISSION TO THE FIVE CIVILIZED TRIBES.

IN RE APPLICATION FOR ENROLLMENT, as a citizen of the Creek Nation, of Peter Wesley, born on the 2^d day of Feb , 1904

Name of Father:	John Wesley	a citizen of the	Creek	Nation.
Name of Mother:	Polly Wesley	a citizen of the	Creek	Nation.

Postoffice   Wetumka, I.T.

AFFIDAVIT OF MOTHER.

UNITED STATES OF AMERICA, Indian Territory, ⎫
    Western   DISTRICT.   ⎭

I, Polley Wesley , on oath state that I am 28 years of age and a citizen by blood, of the Creek Nation; that I am the lawful wife of John Wesley , who is a citizen, by blood of the Creek Nation; that a male child was born to me on 2^d day of Feb , 1904 , that said child has been named Peter Wesley , and was living March 4, 1905.

her
Polly x Wesley
mark

Witnesses To Mark:
  ⎰ Amos King
  ⎱ Louis *(Illegible)*

Applications for Enrollment of Creek Newborn
Act of 1905   Volume III

Subscribed and sworn to before me this 20th day of July, 1905.

J.R. Dunzy
Notary Public.

AFFIDAVIT OF ATTENDING PHYSICIAN OR MID-WIFE.

UNITED STATES OF AMERICA, Indian Territory, }
    Western   DISTRICT.

I, Losannia Scott, a Midwife, on oath state that I attended on Mrs. Polley Wesley, wife of John Wesley on the 2^d day of Feb, 1904; that there was born to her on said date a male child; that said child was living March 4, 1905, and is said to have been named Peter Wesley

                                    her
                            Losannia x Scott

Witnesses To Mark: mark
  { Amos King
    Louis *(Illegible)*

Subscribed and sworn to before me this 20th day of July, 1905.

J.R. Dunzy
Notary Public.

BIRTH AFFIDAVIT.

DEPARTMENT OF THE INTERIOR.
COMMISSION TO THE FIVE CIVILIZED TRIBES.

IN RE APPLICATION FOR ENROLLMENT, as a citizen of the Creek Nation, of Peter Wesley, born on the 2^d day of Feby, 1904

| Name of Father: | John Wesley | a citizen of the | Creek | Nation. |
| Name of Mother: | Polly Wesley | a citizen of the | Creek | Nation. |

                Postoffice   Wetumka, I.T.

AFFIDAVIT OF MOTHER.

UNITED STATES OF AMERICA, Indian Territory, }
    Western   DISTRICT.

I, Polly Wesley, on oath state that I am 27 years of age and a citizen by blood, of the Creek Nation; that I am the lawful wife of John Wesley, who is a citizen, by

Applications for Enrollment of Creek Newborn
Act of 1905 Volume III

blood of the Creek Nation; that a male child was born to me on 2^d day of Feby, 1904, that said child has been named Peter Wesley, and was living March 4, 1905.

            Polly Wesley

Witnesses To Mark:
{

  Subscribed and sworn to before me this 12th day of June, 1905.

            Jeff T. Canard
            Notary Public.

Com Ex Aug 2^d 1906

AFFIDAVIT OF ATTENDING PHYSICIAN OR MID-WIFE.

UNITED STATES OF AMERICA, Indian Territory,
  Western DISTRICT.

  I, John Wesley, a mid wife, on oath state that I attended on Mrs. Polly Wesley, my wife of *(blank)* on the 2^d day of Feby, 1904; that there was born to her on said date a male child; that said child was living March 4, 1905, and is said to have been named Peter Wesley

            John Wesley

Witnesses To Mark:
{

            Jeff T. Canard
            Notary Public.

Com Ex Aug 2^d 1906

BIRTH AFFIDAVIT.

DEPARTMENT OF THE INTERIOR.
COMMISSION TO THE FIVE CIVILIZED TRIBES.

  IN RE APPLICATION FOR ENROLLMENT, as a citizen of the CREEK Nation, of Peter Wesley, born on the 2 day of Feb, 1904

Name of Father:	John Wesley	a citizen of the	Creek	Nation.
Name of Mother:	Polly "	a citizen of the	"	Nation.

        Postoffice Wetumka

Applications for Enrollment of Creek Newborn
Act of 1905   Volume III

child present

AFFIDAVIT OF MOTHER.

UNITED STATES OF AMERICA, Indian Territory, ⎫
    WESTERN   DISTRICT. ⎭

    I, Polly Wesley, on oath state that I am 29 years of age and a citizen by blood, of the Creek Nation; that I am the lawful wife of John Wesley, who is a citizen, by blood of the Creek Nation; that a male child was born to me on 2 day of Feb., 1904, that said child has been named Peter Wesley, and is now living.

                                          Polly Wesley

Witnesses To Mark:
{

    Subscribed and sworn to before me this 15 day of March, 1905.

                                          Edw C Griesel
                                              Notary Public.

                                        father
AFFIDAVIT OF ~~ATTENDING PHYSICIAN OR MID-WIFE~~.
                                                  (no midwife)

UNITED STATES OF AMERICA, Indian Territory, ⎫
    WESTERN   DISTRICT. ⎭

                                                                    husband
    I, John Wesley, am   , ~~on oath state that I attended on Mrs. , my wife~~ of Polly Wesley on the 2 day of Feb, 1904; that there was born to her on said date a male child; that said child is now living and is said to have been named Peter Wesley

                                          John Wesley

Witnesses To Mark:
{

    Subscribed and sworn to before me this 15 day of March, 1905.

                                          Edw C Griesel
                                              Notary Public.

Applications for Enrollment of Creek Newborn
Act of 1905 Volume III

BIRTH AFFIDAVIT.

DEPARTMENT OF THE INTERIOR.
COMMISSION TO THE FIVE CIVILIZED TRIBES.

    IN RE APPLICATION FOR ENROLLMENT, as a citizen of the CREEK Nation, of Tiger Wesley, born on the 31 day of Dec, 1902

Name of Father:	John Wesley	a citizen of the	Creek	Nation.
Name of Mother:	Polly "	a citizen of the	"	Nation.

                      Postoffice   Wetumka

Child Present – Gr.

                    AFFIDAVIT OF ~~MOTHER~~. Father

UNITED STATES OF AMERICA, Indian Territory, ⎫
       WESTERN   DISTRICT. ⎭

    I, John Wesley, on oath state that I am 29 years of age and a citizen by blood, of the Creek Nation; that I am the lawful ~~wife~~ husband of Polly Wesley, who is a citizen, by blood of the Creek Nation; that a male child was born to me on 31 day of Dec, 1902, that said child has been named Tiger Wesley, and is now living.

                              John Wesley

Witnesses To Mark:
{

    Subscribed and sworn to before me this 15 day of March, 1905.

                            Edw C Griesel
                                Notary Public.

BIRTH AFFIDAVIT.

DEPARTMENT OF THE INTERIOR.
COMMISSION TO THE FIVE CIVILIZED TRIBES.

    IN RE APPLICATION FOR ENROLLMENT, as a citizen of the CREEK Nation, of Tiger Wesley, born on the 31 day of Dec, 1902

Name of Father:	John Wesley	a citizen of the	Creek	Nation.
Name of Mother:	Polly "	a citizen of the	Creek	Nation.

                      Postoffice   Wetumka

Applications for Enrollment of Creek Newborn
Act of 1905 Volume III

child present

AFFIDAVIT OF MOTHER.

UNITED STATES OF AMERICA, Indian Territory, }
WESTERN DISTRICT.

I, Polly ~~Tiger~~ Wesley , on oath state that I am 29 years of age and a citizen by blood, of the Creek Nation; that I am the lawful wife of John Wesley , who is a citizen, by blood of the Creek Nation; that a male child was born to me on 31 day of Dec. , 1902 , that said child has been named Tiger Wesley , and is now living.

                           Polly Wesley

Witnesses To Mark:
{

Subscribed and sworn to before me this 15 day of March , 1905.

                           Edw C Griesel
                                Notary Public.

BIRTH AFFIDAVIT.

DEPARTMENT OF THE INTERIOR.
COMMISSION TO THE FIVE CIVILIZED TRIBES.

IN RE APPLICATION FOR ENROLLMENT, as a citizen of the Creek Nation, of Tiger Wesley, born on the 30 day of Jan , 1902

Name of Father:	John Wesley	a citizen of the	Creek	Nation.
Name of Mother:	Polly Wesley	a citizen of the	Creek	Nation.

                     Postoffice   Wetumka I.T.

AFFIDAVIT OF MOTHER.

UNITED STATES OF AMERICA, Indian Territory, }
Western DISTRICT.

I, Polly Wesley , on oath state that I am 28 years of age and a citizen by blood, of the Creek Nation; that I am the lawful wife of John Wesley , who is a citizen, by Blood of the Creek Nation; that a male child was born to me on 30th day of January, 1902 , that said child has been named Tiger Wesley , and was living March 4, 1905.

                                       her
                            Polly x Wesley
                               mark

Applications for Enrollment of Creek Newborn
Act of 1905   Volume III

Witnesses To Mark:
{ Amos King
{ Louis Dunzy

Subscribed and sworn to before me this 20th day of July, 1905.

          J.R. Dunzy
           Notary Public.

AFFIDAVIT OF ATTENDING PHYSICIAN OR MID-WIFE.

UNITED STATES OF AMERICA, Indian Territory,
  Western DISTRICT.

  I, Winey Scott, a Mid-wife, on oath state that I attended on Mrs. Polly Wesley, wife of John Wesley on the 30th day of Jany, 1902 ; that there was born to her on said date a male child; that said child was living March 4, 1905, and is said to have been named Tiger Wesley

              her
          Winey x Scott
Witnesses To Mark: mark
{ Amos King
{ Louis Dunzy

Subscribed and sworn to before me this 20th day of July, 1905.

          J.R. Dunzy
           Notary Public.

BIRTH AFFIDAVIT.

DEPARTMENT OF THE INTERIOR.
COMMISSION TO THE FIVE CIVILIZED TRIBES.

  IN RE APPLICATION FOR ENROLLMENT, as a citizen of the Creek Nation, of Tiger Wesley, born on the 31st day of January, 1902

Name of Father:	John Wesley	a citizen of the	Creek	Nation.
Name of Mother:	Polly Wesley	a citizen of the	Creek	Nation.

        Postoffice Wetumka Ind.Ter.

Applications for Enrollment of Creek Newborn
Act of 1905 Volume III

AFFIDAVIT OF MOTHER.

UNITED STATES OF AMERICA, Indian Territory, }
   Western   DISTRICT.

    I, Polly Wesley , on oath state that I am 27 years of age and a citizen by blood, of the Creek Nation; that I am the lawful wife of John Wesley , who is a citizen, by blood of the Creek Nation; that a male child was born to me on 31st day of January, 1902 , that said child has been named Tiger Wesley , and was living March 4, 1905.

                                  Polly Wesley

Witnesses To Mark:
{

    Subscribed and sworn to before me this 12th day of June , 1905.

                                    Jeff T. Canard
                                    Notary Public.

Com ex Aug 2^d 1906

AFFIDAVIT OF ATTENDING PHYSICIAN OR MID-WIFE.

UNITED STATES OF AMERICA, Indian Territory, }
   Western   DISTRICT.

    I, Winey Scott , a midwife , on oath state that I attended on Mrs. Polly Wesley , wife of John Wesley on the 31st day of January , 1902 ; that there was born to her on said date a male child; that said child was living March 4, 1905, and is said to have been named Tiger Wesley

                                      her
                              Winey x Scott

Witnesses To Mark: mark
{ Lyra Dorter
  Roly Canard

    Subscribed and sworn to before me this 12th day of June , 1905.

                                  Jeff T. Canard
                                  Notary Public.

Com ex Aug 2^d 1906

                                                  NC 244.

                    Muskogee, Indian Territory, June 5, 1905.

Polly Wesley,
    Wetumka, Indian Territory.

Applications for Enrollment of Creek Newborn
Act of 1905 Volume III

Dear Madam:

In the matter of the application for the enrollment of your minor children, Tiger and Peter Wesley, as citizens of the Creek Nation, you are advised that the Commission requires the affidavit of the midwife or physician in attendance at the birth of said child, and if same cannot be procured, the affidavits of two disinterested witnesses as to the birth of said child disinterested witnesses as to the birth of said children should be supplied.

There are herewith enclosed two blank forms of birth affidavits, and in executing same care should be exercised to see that all blanks are properly filled, all names written in full and in the event that the persons signing the affidavits are unable to write, signatures by mark must be attested by two witnesses. Each affidavit must be executed before a Notary Public and the notarial seal and signature of the officer must be attached to each separate affidavit.

Respectfully,

2 BA   Commissioner in Charge.

NC 244.

Muskogee, Indian Territory, June 22, 1905.

Polly Wesley,
    Wetumka, Indian Territory.

Dear Madam:

In the matter of the application for the enrollment of your minor children, Tiger and Peter Wesley, you are again advised that the Commission requires the affidavit of two disinterested witnesses as to their births.

There are herewith enclosed two blank forms of birth affidavits, and in executing same care should be exercised to see that all blanks are properly filled, all names written in full and in the event that the persons signing the affidavits are unable to write, signatures by mark must be attested by two witnesses. Each affidavit must be executed before a Notary Public and the notarial seal and signature of the officer must be attached to each separate affidavit.

Respectfully,

2 BA.   Chairman.

Applications for Enrollment of Creek Newborn
Act of 1905 Volume III

N C 244   HGH

COPY

Muskogee, Indian Territory, July 26, 1905.

John Wesley,
    Wetumka, Indian Territory.

Dear Sir:

    On March 15, 1904 you and your wife Polly Wesley appeared before the Commission to the Five Civilized Tribes Five Civilized Tribes and made application for the enrollment of your minor child, you are advised that the Commission requires further evidence as to the birth of said child. of your son, Tiger Wesley as a citizen by blood of the Creek Nation and at the time submitted your affidavits as to the birth of said child on December 31, 1902. Subsequently you filed with said Commission the affidavits of your said wife Polly Wesley and Winey Scott, midwife, from which it appears that said child was born on January 31, 1902 and from the affidavits of said parties which were sworn to on July 20, 1905 it appears that the said Tiger Wesley was born January 30, 1902.

    You are requested to immediately advise this office as to which, if any, of the above dates is the correct date of the birth of said child.

                                        Respectfully,

                                        (Signed) Tams Bixby,

                                                                                 Commissioner.

The child was born Jan 31st 1902 which is correct

                                        (Signed) John Wesley

                                                                          Cr NC-246

Muskogee, Indian Territory, June 10, 1905.

Simondy King,
    Wetumka, Indian Territory.

Dear Madam:

    In the matter of the application for the enrollment of your minor child, Lucy King, as a citizen of the Creek Nation, you are advised that the Commission requires the affidavit of the midwife or physician in attendance at the birth of said child.

Applications for Enrollment of Creek Newborn
Act of 1905 Volume III

For this purpose, there is herewith enclosed a blank form of birth affidavit. In having same executed, care should be taken to see that all blanks are properly filled, all names spelled in full, and in the event that the person signing the affidavit is unable to write, signature by mark must be attested by two witnesses.

Respectfully,

Chairman.

1 B A

BIRTH AFFIDAVIT.

DEPARTMENT OF THE INTERIOR.
COMMISSION TO THE FIVE CIVILIZED TRIBES.

IN RE APPLICATION FOR ENROLLMENT, as a citizen of the CREEK Nation, of Lucy King, born on the 30 day of Aug, 1903

Name of Father: Amos King   a citizen of the   Creek   Nation.
Name of Mother: Simondy "   a citizen of the   "   Nation.

Postoffice   Wetumka

(child present)

AFFIDAVIT OF MOTHER.

UNITED STATES OF AMERICA, Indian Territory,
    WESTERN   DISTRICT.

I, Simondy King , on oath state that I am 28 years of age and a citizen by blood, of the Creek Nation; that I am the lawful wife of Amos King , who is a citizen, by blood of the Creek Nation; that a female child was born to me on 30 day of Aug , 1903 , that said child has been named Lucy King , and is now living.

                            Her
                    Simondy x King
Witnesses To Mark: mark
  { J McDermott
    EC Griesel

Subscribed and sworn to before me this 15 day of March , 1905.

                    Edw C Griesel
                        Notary Public.

Applications for Enrollment of Creek Newborn
Act of 1905 Volume III

BIRTH AFFIDAVIT.

DEPARTMENT OF THE INTERIOR.
COMMISSION TO THE FIVE CIVILIZED TRIBES.

IN RE APPLICATION FOR ENROLLMENT, as a citizen of the Creek Nation, of Lucy King, born on the 30 day of Aug, 1903

Name of Father: Amos King   a citizen of the   Creek   Nation.
Name of Mother: Simondy   "   a citizen of the   "   Nation.

Postoffice   Wetumka

child present

AFFIDAVIT OF ~~MOTHER~~. Father

UNITED STATES OF AMERICA, Indian Territory, ⎱
    Western   DISTRICT.   ⎰

I, Amos King, on oath state that I am 35 years of age and a citizen by blood, of the Creek Nation; that I am the lawful ~~wife~~ Husband of Simondy Kind, who is a citizen, by blood of the Creek Nation; that a female child was born to me on 30 day of Aug, 1903, that said child has been named Lucy King, and is now living.

                                  Amos King

Witnesses To Mark:
{

Subscribed and sworn to before me this 15 day of March, 1905.

                            Edw C Griesel
                            Notary Public.

BIRTH AFFIDAVIT.

DEPARTMENT OF THE INTERIOR.
COMMISSION TO THE FIVE CIVILIZED TRIBES.

IN RE APPLICATION FOR ENROLLMENT, as a citizen of the Creek Nation, of Lucy King, born on the 30th day of Aug, 1903

Name of Father: Amos King   a citizen of the   Creek   Nation.
Name of Mother: Limonda[sic] King   a citizen of the   Creek   Nation.

Postoffice   Wetumka I.T.

Applications for Enrollment of Creek Newborn
Act of 1905   Volume III

AFFIDAVIT OF MOTHER.

UNITED STATES OF AMERICA, Indian Territory, ⎱
    Western   DISTRICT.   ⎰

I, Simonda[sic] King , on oath state that I am 37   years of age and a citizen by blood, of the Creek   Nation; that I am the lawful wife of Amos King , who is a citizen, by blood of the Creek   Nation; that a female   child was born to me on 30th day of Aug , 1903 , that said child has been named Lucy King , and was living March 4, 1905.

                                                Her
                                    Simonda x King
Witnesses To Mark: mark
  { Louis Dunzy
    Amos King

Subscribed and sworn to before me this 14th day of July , 1905.

                                      J.R. Dunzy
                                         Notary Public.

AFFIDAVIT OF ATTENDING PHYSICIAN OR MID-WIFE.

UNITED STATES OF AMERICA, Indian Territory, ⎱
    Western   DISTRICT.   ⎰

I, Winey Scott , a mid-wife   , on oath state that I attended on Mrs. Simonda King , wife of Amos King on the 30th day of Aug , 1903 ; that there was born to her on said date a   female   child; that said child was living March 4, 1905, and is said to have been named Lucy King
                                        her
                                    Winey x Scott
Witnesses To Mark: mark
  { Louis Dunzy
    Amos King

Subscribed and sworn to before me this 14th day of July , 1905.

                                      J.R. Dunzy
                                       Notary Public.

Applications for Enrollment of Creek Newborn
Act of 1905 Volume III

BIRTH AFFIDAVIT.

DEPARTMENT OF THE INTERIOR.
COMMISSION TO THE FIVE CIVILIZED TRIBES.

IN RE APPLICATION FOR ENROLLMENT, as a citizen of the Creek Nation, of Josephine Nevada Callahan, born on the 15 day of March, 1903

Name of Father:	Walter K Callahan	a citizen of the	Creek	Nation.
Name of Mother:	Alice A Callahan	a citizen of the	Cherokee	Nation.

Postoffice   Owyhee[sic] Nevada

AFFIDAVIT OF MOTHER.

UNITED STATES OF AMERICA, Indian Territory, ⎫
     (blank)   DISTRICT.   ⎭

I, Alice A Callahan, on oath state that I am 26 years of age and a citizen by blood, of the Cherokee Nation; that I am the lawful wife of Walter K. Callahan, who is a citizen, by blood of the Creek Nation; that a female child was born to me on the 15 day of March, 1903, that said child has been named Josephine Nevada Callahan, and is now living.

Alice A Callahan

Witnesses To Mark:
{

Subscribed and sworn to before me this 15th day of March, 1905.

Horton H Miller
Notary Public.
Supt. & Spl. Disbursing Agent.

AFFIDAVIT OF ATTENDING PHYSICIAN OR MID-WIFE.

UNITED STATES OF AMERICA, Indian Territory, ⎫
     (blank)   DISTRICT.   ⎭

I, Walter K Callahan M.D., a Practicing Physician, on oath state that I attended on Mrs. Alice A Callahan, wife of Walter K Callahan on the 15 day of March, 1903; that there was born to her on said date a Female child; that said child is now living and is said to have been named Josephine Nevada Callahan

Walter K Callahan M.D.

Witnesses To Mark:
{

Applications for Enrollment of Creek Newborn
Act of 1905 Volume III

Subscribed and sworn to before me this 15th day of March, 1905.

>Horton H Miller
>Notary Public.
>SUPT. & SPL. DISBURSING AGENT.

DEPARTMENT OF THE INTERIOR.
COMMISSION TO THE FIVE CIVILIZED TRIBES.

POWER OF ATTORNEY.

KNOW ALL MEN BY THESE PRESENTS,

That Alice A. Callahan, of Owyhee Nevada Indian Territory, has made, constituted and appointed, and by these presents does make, constitute and appoint J. O. Callahan, of Muskogee, Indian Territory, her true and lawful attorney for her, and in her name, place and stead, to make application to the Commission to the Five Civilized Tribes Five Civilized Tribes for allotments of lands in the Creek Nation[sic] Nation to herself and minor children, viz: Josephine Nevada Callahan all of whom are citizens of said Nation, fiving and granting unto her said attorney full power and authority to do and perform all and every at and thing whatsoever, requisite and necessary to be done in selecting, designating and obtaining said allotments, as fully to all intents and purposes as she might or could do, if personal present; hereby ratifying and confirming all that her said attorney shall lawfully do, or cause to be done, by virtue hereof.

IN WITNESS WHEREOF, she has hereunto set her hand this 15th day of March, A. D. 1905.

Witnesses To Mark: Alice A. Callahan

United States of America,
 Indian Territory,   } ss.
 (blank)   District.

Be it remembered that on this day personally appeared before me Alice A. Callahan to me personally known to be the person who executed the foregoing power of attorney, and being by me examined separately and apart from her said attorney J.O. Callahan stated and acknowledged that she had executed said instrument as her free and voluntary act and deed, without compulsion or undue influence, and for the purposes therein mentioned and set forth.

Applications for Enrollment of Creek Newborn
Act of 1905   Volume III

In Testimony whereof I have hereunto set my hand and affixed my Notarial Seal this 15th day of March A. D. 1905

        Horton H Miller
        Notary Public.
        SUPT.& SPL. DISBURSING AGENT.

MARRIAGE LICENSE

United States of America ⎫
 Indian Territory   ⎬ ss.   No. 953
Northern ~~Western~~ District ⎭

To Any Person Authorized by Law to Solemnize Marriage---Greeting:

  You are Hereby Commanded to Solemnize the Rite and Publish the Banns of Matrimony between Mr. Walter K Callahan of Wagoner in the Indian Territory, aged 26 years and Miss Alice Reid of Muskogee in the Indian Territory aged 18 years according to law, and do you officially sign and return this license to the parties therein named.

  WITNESS my hand and official seal ~~at Muskogee Indian Territory~~ this 16" day of October A.D. ~~190~~ 1897
          Jas. A. Winston
          Clerk of the U S Court.

By Newton S. Young Deputy.

❦ ❦ CERTIFICATE OF MARRIAGE ❦ ❦

United States of America ⎫
 Indian Territory   ⎬ ss.
Northern ~~Western~~ District ⎭

  I, E. D. Cameron *, a Minister of the Gospel, DO HEREBY CERTIFY* that on the 17 day of Oct A. D. ~~190~~ 1897 did duly and according to law as commanded in the foregoing License, solemnize the Rite and Publish the Banns of Matrimony between the parties therein named.

  WITNESS my hand this 18 day of Oct A. D. ~~190~~ 1897

  My credentials are recorded in the office of the Clerk of the United States Court, Indian Territory ~~Western~~ District Book B Page 120-21

         E. D. Cameron
         A Minister of the Gospel

Applications for Enrollment of Creek Newborn
Act of 1905 Volume III

Note This license and certificate of marriage must be returned to the office of the Clerk of the United States court in the Western District Indian Territory from whence it was issued within sixty days from the date thereof of the party to whom the license was issued will be liable in the amount of the one hundred dollars ($100.00)

Filed and duly recorded, this 18 day of Oct, 1897
    Book F. Page 313   Jas. A. Winston Clerk U.S. Court

CERTIFICATE OF TRUE COPY.

United States of America,
   Indian Territory,   } ss.
   Western District.

I, R. P. HARRISON, Clerk of the United States Court in the Western District, Indian Territory, do hereby certify that the instrument hereto attached is a full, true and correct copy of a Marriage License *as the same appears from the records of my office.*

          WITNESS my hand and seal of said Court at   Muskogee
          in said Territory, this 24" day of June   A. D. 1905

By   John Harlan   R. P. Harrison
         Deputy Clerk   *Clerk and Ex-Officio Recorder.*

                      Book   F   page 131

DEPARTMENT OF THE INTERIOR.
COMMISSION TO THE FIVE CIVILIZED TRIBES.

POWER OF ATTORNEY.

KNOW ALL MEN BY THESE PRESENTS,

     That   Walter K. Callahan, of Owyhee Nevada Indian Territory, has made, constituted and appointed, and by these presents does make, constitute and appoint J. O. Callahan, of Muskogee, Indian Territory, his true and lawful attorney for his[sic], and in his name, place and stead, to make application to the Commission to the Five Civilized Tribes Five Civilized Tribes for allotments of lands in the Creek Nation[sic] Nation to h__self and minor children, viz: Josephine Nevada Callahan all of whom are citizens of said Nation, fiving and granting unto his said attorney full power and authority to do and perform all and every at and thing whatsoever, requisite and necessary to be done in selecting, designating and obtaining said allotments, as fully to all intents and purposes as she might or could do, if personal present; hereby ratifying and confirming all that his said attorney shall lawfully do, or cause to be done, by virtue hereof.

Applications for Enrollment of Creek Newborn
Act of 1905 Volume III

IN WITNESS WHEREOF, __he has hereunto set his hand this 15th day of March, A. D. 1905.

Witnesses To Mark:

Walter K. Callahan

United States of America,
Indian Territory, } ss.
(blank) District.

Be it remembered that on this day personally appeared before me Walter K. Callahan to me personally known to be the person who executed the foregoing power of attorney, and being by me examined separately and apart from his said attorney J.O. Callahan stated and acknowledged that __he had executed said instrument as his free and voluntary act and deed, without compulsion or undue influence, and for the purposes therein mentioned and set forth.

In Testimony whereof I have hereunto set my hand and affixed my Notarial Seal this 15th day of March A. D. 1905

Horton H Miller
Notary Public.
SUPT.& SPL. DISBURSING AGENT.

BIRTH AFFIDAVIT.

DEPARTMENT OF THE INTERIOR.
COMMISSION TO THE FIVE CIVILIZED TRIBES.

IN RE APPLICATION FOR ENROLLMENT, as a citizen of the CREEK Nation, of Josephine Callahan, born on ~~the day of~~ about , 1904

Name of Father:	W. K. Callahan	a citizen of the	Creek	Nation.
Name of Mother:	Alice Callahan	a citizen of the	Cherokee	Nation.

Postoffice   Oyhee[sic], Nevada

AFFIDAVIT OF MOTHER.

UNITED STATES OF AMERICA, Indian Territory, }
WESTERN   DISTRICT.

I, R. A. Evans , on oath state that I am 53 years of age and a citizen by adoption , of the Cherokee Nation; that I am the ~~lawful wife~~ friend of W. K. Callahan, who is a citizen, by blood of the Creek Nation; that a female child was born to ~~me~~

Applications for Enrollment of Creek Newborn
Act of 1905   Volume III

him ~~on   day of~~ about, 1904 , that said child has been named   Josephine Callahan , and is now living.

R. A. Evans

Witnesses To Mark:
{

Subscribed and sworn to before me this 15 day of March , 1905.

Edw C Griesel
Notary Public.

Mrs. Evans expects to have parents file an application themselves, but does this to preserve their rights.

N.C. 247.

Muskogee, Indian Territory, November 12, 1906.

Chief Clerk,
    Cherokee Enrollment Division,
        General Office.

Dear Sir:

    You are hereby advised that the name of Josephine Nevada Callahan, born March 15, 1903, to Walter K. Callahan, a citizen of the Creek Nation, and Alice A. Callahan, an alleged citizen of the Cherokee Nation, is contained in the schedule of New Born citizens by blood of the Creek Nation, approved by the Secretary of the Interior July 28, 1905, opposite Roll No. 167.

Respectfully,

Commissioner.

BIRTH AFFIDAVIT.

DEPARTMENT OF THE INTERIOR,
COMMISSION TO THE FIVE CIVILIZED TRIBES.

IN RE Application for Enrollment, as a citizen of the Creek Nation, of Nixie Clinton , born on the 24 day of August , 1901

Name of Father:	Geo Clinton	a citizen of the	Creek	Nation.
Name of Mother:	Sallie Clinton	a citizen of the	Creek	Nation.

Post-office   Bristow I.T.

Applications for Enrollment of Creek Newborn
Act of 1905   Volume III

AFFIDAVIT OF MOTHER.

UNITED STATES OF AMERICA, Indian Territory,
Northern DISTRICT.

I, Sallie Clinton , on oath state that I am about 30 years of age and a citizen by Birth , of the Creek Nation; that I am the lawful wife of Geo Clinton , who is a citizen, by Birth of the Creek Nation; that a male child was born to me on 24 day of August , 1901 , that said child has been named Nixie Clinton , and is now living.

                                      Her
                              Sallie x Clinton
Witnesses To Mark: mark
   L.M. Wolfe
   H M Carman

Subscribed and sworn to before me this 1st *day of* October, *1901.*

My Commission expires July 23, 1904.   J. D. Rigney
                                              Notary Public.

BIRTH AFFIDAVIT.
DEPARTMENT OF THE INTERIOR.
COMMISSION TO THE FIVE CIVILIZED TRIBES.

IN RE APPLICATION FOR ENROLLMENT, as a citizen of the Creek Nation, of Nixie Clinton , born on the 24 day of August , 1901

| Name of Father: | George Clinton | a citizen of the | Creek | Nation. |
| Name of Mother: | Sallie Clinton | a citizen of the | Creek | Nation. |

                          Post-office   Bristow I.T.

AFFIDAVIT OF MOTHER.

UNITED STATES OF AMERICA, Indian Territory,
Western DISTRICT.

I, Sallie Clinton , on oath state that I am about 30 years of age and a citizen by birth , of the Creek Nation; that I am the lawful wife of George Clinton , who is a citizen, by birth of the Creek Nation; that a male child was born to me on 24 day of August , 1901 , that said child has been named Nixie Clinton , and is now living.

Applications for Enrollment of Creek Newborn
Act of 1905   Volume III

                                            Her
                                    Sallie x Clinton
Witnesses To Mark: mark
{ T.J. Lillard
  D Mays

Subscribed and sworn to before me this 28 *day of* November, *190*2.

My Com Ex July 11th 1906   E W Sims
                                              Notary Public.

AFFIDAVIT OF ATTENDING PHYSICIAN OR MID-WIFE.

UNITED STATES OF AMERICA, Indian Territory, }
    Western   DISTRICT.

    I, Juda Long , a Midwife , on oath state that I attended on Mrs. Sallie Clinton , wife of George Clinton on the 24 day of August , 1901 ; that there was born to her on said date a   male   child; that said child is now living and is said to have been named Nixie Clinton
                                        her
                                  Juda x Long
Witnesses To Mark: mark
{ T.J. Lillard
  D Mays

Subscribed and sworn to before me this 28 *day of* November, *190*2.

                                  E W Sims
                                        Notary Public.
My Com Ex July 11th 1906

BIRTH AFFIDAVIT.
                          DEPARTMENT OF THE INTERIOR.
                COMMISSION TO THE FIVE CIVILIZED TRIBES.

    IN RE Application for Enrollment, as a citizen of the Creek Nation, of Nexie Clinton, born on the 24th day of August , 1901

Name of Father: George Clinton   a citizen of the   Creek   Nation.
Name of Mother: Sallie Clinton   a citizen of the   Creek   Nation.

                                Post-office   Bristow Ind.Ter.

Applications for Enrollment of Creek Newborn
Act of 1905   Volume III

AFFIDAVIT OF MOTHER.

UNITED STATES OF AMERICA, Indian Territory,
  Western   DISTRICT.

I, Sallie Clinton , on oath state that I am about 32 years of age and a citizen by blood , of the Creek Nation; that I am the lawful wife of George Clinton , who is a citizen, by blood of the Creek Nation; that a male child was born to me on 24th day of August , 1901 , that said child has been named Nexie Clinton , and is now living.

                                            Her
                            Sallie Clinton x

Witnesses To Mark: mark
{ L.D. Groom
  Albert Ewers

Subscribed and sworn to before me this 15th *day of* March, *190*5.

                                William L. Cheatham
                                Notary Public.

AFFIDAVIT OF ATTENDING PHYSICIAN OR MID-WIFE.

UNITED STATES OF AMERICA, Indian Territory,
  Western   DISTRICT.

I, Judy Long , a Midwife , on oath state that I attended on Mrs. Sallie Clinton , wife of George Clinton on the 24th day of August , 1901 ; that there was born to her on said date a male child; that said child is now living and is said to have been named Nexie Clinton

                                          her
                            Judy x Long

Witnesses To Mark: mark
{ L.D. Groom
  Albert Ewers

Subscribed and sworn to before me this 15th *day of* March, *190*5.

                                William L. Cheatham
                                Notary Public.

Applications for Enrollment of Creek Newborn
Act of 1905 Volume III

Birth Affidavit.

DEPARTMENT OF THE INTERIOR,

Commission to the Five Civilized Tribes.

IN RE Application for Enrollment as a citizen of the Creek Nation of **Henry Clinton**, born on the **26th** day of **October** 1903, Name of Father **George Clinton**, a citizen of the Creek Nation, Name of mother **Sallie Clinton**, a citizen of the Creek Nation.

Post Office **Bristow Ind. Ter**

Affidavit of Mother.

Indian Territory,
ss
Western District.

I, **Sallie Clinton** on oath state that I am **32** years of age and a citizen by blood of the Creek Nation; that I am the lawful wife of George Clinton, who is a citizen by blood of the Creek Nation, that a male child was born to me on the **26th** day of **October**, 1903, that said child has been named **Henry Clinton**, and is now **Dear, having died Feby. 18th, 1905**

Witnesses to mark:
 L. D. Groom
 Albert Ewers

       her
    Sallie Clinton x
       mark

Subscribed and sworn to before me this the **15th** day of **March** 1905

      William L. Cheatham
       Notary Public.

Affidavit of Attending Physician ot[sic] Midwife.

Indian Territory,
ss
Western District,

I, **Judy Long** a **midwife** on oath state that I attneded[sic] on Mrs. **Sallie Clinton** wife of **George Clinton** on the **26th** day of October 1903 that there was born to her on said date a **male** child; that said child is **Dead** and is said to have been named **Henry Clinton having died Feby. 18th 1905**

       her
    Judy x Long
      mark

Witnesses to mark:
 L. D. Groom
 Albert Ewers

Applications for Enrollment of Creek Newborn
Act of 1905 Volume III

Subscribed and sworn to before me this the **15** day of **March** 1905

William L. Cheatham
Notary Public.

NC 248 JLD

DEPARTMENT OF THE INTERIOR,
COMMISSIONER TO THE FIVE CIVILIZED TRIBES.
....

In the matter of the application for the enrollment of Henry Clinton, deceased, as a citizen by blood of the Creek Nation.
....

STATEMENT AND ORDER.

The record in this case shows that on March 16, 1905, application was made, in affidavit form, for the enrollment of Henry Clinton, deceased, as a citizen by blood of the Creek Nation, under the provisions of the act of Congress approved March 3, 1905.

It appears from the affidavit filed in this matter that said Henry Clinton, deceased, was born October 26, 1903, and died February 18, 1905.

The Act of Congress approved March 3, 1905, (33 Stats., 1048), provides:
"That the Commission to the Five Civilized Tribes is authorized for sixty days after the date of the approval of this act to receive and consider applications for enrollment, of children, <u>born subsequent to May twenty-fifth, nineteen hundred and one, and prior to March fourth, nineteen hundred and five, and living on said latter date,</u> to citizens of the Creek tribe of Indians whose enrollment has been approved by the Secretary of the Interior prior to the approval of this act; and to enroll and make allotments to such children."

It is, therefore, ordered that the application for the enrollment of said Henry Clinton, deceased, as a citizen by blood of the Creek Nation be, and the same is, hereby dismissed.

Tams Bixby Commissioner.

Muskogee, Indian Territory.
JAN 4 – 1907

Applications for Enrollment of Creek Newborn
Act of 1905   Volume III

BIRTH AFFIDAVIT.

DEPARTMENT OF THE INTERIOR.
COMMISSION TO THE FIVE CIVILIZED TRIBES.

IN RE APPLICATION FOR ENROLLMENT, as a citizen of the CREEK Nation, of Addie Gray, born on the 3 day of Sept, 1904

Name of Father:	Siah Gray	a citizen of the	Creek	Nation.
Name of Mother:	Mary "	a citizen of the	"	Nation.

Postoffice   Fame

AFFIDAVIT OF ~~MOTHER~~. Father

UNITED STATES OF AMERICA, Indian Territory,
WESTERN   DISTRICT.

I, Siah Gray, on oath state that I am 45 years of age and a citizen by blood, of the Creek Nation; that I am the lawful ~~wife~~ husb of Mary Gray, who is a citizen, by blood of the Creek Nation; that a female child was born to me on 3 day of Sept., 1904, that said child has been named Addie Gray, and is now living.

Siah Gray

Witnesses To Mark:
{

Subscribed and sworn to before me this 16 day of March, 1905.

Edw C Griesel
Notary Public.

BIRTH AFFIDAVIT.

DEPARTMENT OF THE INTERIOR.
COMMISSION TO THE FIVE CIVILIZED TRIBES.

IN RE APPLICATION FOR ENROLLMENT, as a citizen of the Creek Nation, of Addie Gray, born on the 3rd day of September, 1904

Name of Father:	Siah Gray	a citizen of the	Creek	Nation.
Name of Mother:	Mary Gray	a citizen of the	Creek	Nation.

Postoffice   Fame, I.T.

Applications for Enrollment of Creek Newborn
Act of 1905   Volume III

AFFIDAVIT OF MOTHER.

UNITED STATES OF AMERICA, Indian Territory, } Western DISTRICT.

I, Mary Gray, on oath state that I am Thirty four years of age and a citizen by blood, of the Creek Nation; that I am the lawful wife of Siah Gray, who is a citizen, by blood of the Creek Nation; that a female child was born to me on 3rd day of September, 1904, that said child has been named Addie Gray, and is now living.

                                        her
                                  Mary x Gray

Witnesses To Mark: mark
{ Roley McIntosh
{ David Washington

Subscribed and sworn to before me this 20th day of March, 1905.

                                  Bennie McIntosh
                                  Notary Public.

AFFIDAVIT OF ATTENDING PHYSICIAN OR MID-WIFE.

UNITED STATES OF AMERICA, Indian Territory, } Western DISTRICT.

I, Fannie Laslie, a *(blank)*, on oath state that I attended on Mrs. Mary Gray, wife of Siah Gray on the 3rd day of September, 1904; that there was born to her on said date a female child; that said child is now living and is said to have been named Addie Gray

                                      her
                                Fannie x Laslie

Witnesses To Mark: mark
{ Roley McIntosh
{ David Washington

Subscribed and sworn to before me this 20th day of March, 1905.

                                  Bennie McIntosh
                                  Notary Public.

My commission expires
    May 16th 1908

Applications for Enrollment of Creek Newborn
Act of 1905   Volume III

NC 250.

Muskogee, Indian Territory, July 14, 190*(blank)*

Commissioner to the Five Civilized Tribes,
    Cherokee Enrollment Division,
        Muskogee, Indian Territory.

Gentlemen:

    March 20, 1905, application was made to the Commission to the Five Civilized Tribes for the enrollment of Wiley Jackson Woffard, born April 15, 1904, as a citizen by blood of the Creek Nation. It is stated in said application that the father of said child is Sherley Woffard, a citizen of the Cherokee Nation, and that the mother is Lizzie Woffard, a citizen of the Creek Nation.

    You are requested to inform the Creek Enrollment Division as to whether application was made for the enrollment of said Wiley Jackson Woffard, as a citizen of the Cheroke[sic] Nation, and if so, what disposition has been made of the name.

                Respectfully,

                            Commissioner.

REFER IN REPLY TO THE FOLLOWING:
_____

DEPARTMENT OF THE INTERIOR,
COMMISSIONER TO THE FIVE CIVILIZED TRIBES.

Muskogee, Indian Territory, July 18, 1905.

Chief Clerk,
    Creek Enrollment Division,
        Muskogee, Indian Territory.

Dear Sir:

    Replying to your letter of July 18, 1905, (NC. 250) asking to be advised whether or not any application has ever been made for the enrollment, as a citizen of the Cherokee Nation, of Wiley Jackson Woffard, a child of Sherley Woffard, a citizen of the Cherokee Nation, and Lizzie Woffard, a citizen of the Creek Nation, you are advised that from an examination of the records of the Cherokee Enrollment Division it does not appear that any application has ever been made for the enrollment of said child as a citizen of that nation.

                Respectfully,

GHI.   Tams Bixby Commissioner.

Applications for Enrollment of Creek Newborn
Act of 1905 Volume III

Child present. J. D.

BIRTH AFFIDAVIT.

DEPARTMENT OF THE INTERIOR.
COMMISSION TO THE FIVE CIVILIZED TRIBES.

   IN RE APPLICATION FOR ENROLLMENT, as a citizen of the CREEK Nation, of   Jackson Wiley Wofford , born on the 16 day of April , 1904

Name of Father: Sherley ~~Jackson~~ Wofford   a citizen of the   Cherokee   Nation.
Name of Mother: Lizzie Wofford   a citizen of the   Creek   Nation.

Postoffice

AFFIDAVIT OF MOTHER.

UNITED STATES OF AMERICA, Indian Territory, ⎫
   (blank)   DISTRICT. ⎭

   I, Lizzie Wofford , on oath state that I am 19 years of age and a citizen by blood , of the Creek Nation; that I am the lawful wife of Sherley ~~Jackson~~ Wofford , who is a citizen, by adoption of the Cherokee Nation; that a male child was born to me on   16 day of April , 1904 , that said child has been named Jackson Wiley Wofford, and is now living.

Lizzie Wofford

Witnesses To Mark:
{

   Subscribed and sworn to before me this 20 day of March , 1905.

Edw C Griesel
Notary Public.

Applications for Enrollment of Creek Newborn
Act of 1905 Volume III

BIRTH AFFIDAVIT.

DEPARTMENT OF THE INTERIOR.
COMMISSION TO THE FIVE CIVILIZED TRIBES.

IN RE APPLICATION FOR ENROLLMENT, as a citizen of the CREEK Nation, of Jackson Wiley Wofford , born on the 16 day of April , 1904

Name of Father:	Sherly Wofford	a citizen of the Cherokee	Nation.
Name of Mother:	Lizzie Wofford	a citizen of the Creek	Nation.

Postoffice   Coweta Indian Territory

AFFIDAVIT OF MOTHER.

UNITED STATES OF AMERICA, Indian Territory,
Western   DISTRICT.

I, Lizzie Wofford , on oath state that I am nineteen years of age and a citizen by blood , of the Creek Nation; that I am the lawful wife of Sherly Wofford , who is a citizen, by blood of the Cherokee Nation; that a male child was born to me on 16th day of April , 1904 , that said child has been named Jackson Wofford, and is now living.

Lizzie Wofford

Witnesses To Mark:
{ N.E. Charles

Subscribed and sworn to before me this 23rd day of March , 1905.

B J Beaver
Notary Public.

My commission expires Dec 19-1908

AFFIDAVIT OF ATTENDING PHYSICIAN OR MID-WIFE.

UNITED STATES OF AMERICA, Indian Territory,
Western   DISTRICT.

I, Iny Abbot , a midwife , on oath state that I attended on Mrs. Lizzie Wofford , wife of Sherly Wofford on the 16th day of April , 1904 ; that there was born to her on said date a male child; that said child is now living and is said to have been named Jackson Wofford.

her
Iny x Abbot
mark

Applications for Enrollment of Creek Newborn
Act of 1905   Volume III

Witnesses To Mark:
{ N.E. Charles
{ S. B. Childers

Subscribed and sworn to before me this 23rd day of March , 1905.

B J Beaver
Notary Public.

My commission expires Dec 19-1908

N.C. 250.

Muskogee, Indian Territory, November 12, 1906.

Chief Clerk,
    Cherokee Enrollment Division,
        General Office.

Dear Sir:

You are hereby advised that the name of Jackson Wofford, born April 15, 1904, to Sherly Wofford, an alleged citizen of the Cherokee Nation, and Lizzie Wofford, a citizen of the Creek Nation, is contained in the schedule of New Born citizens of the Creek Nation, approved by the Secretary of the Interior August 22, 1905, opposite Roll No. 265.

Respectfully,

Commissioner.

Index

ABBOT
  Iny 325
ABBOTT
  W D 219, 220
ALBERT
  Eric O 227
ALEXANDER
  Artie 230, 231, 232
  Arty 229
  Mary 229, 230, 231, 232
  Nancy 115, 116, 230, 231, 232
ALLEN
  Jeese 162
  Lizzie 162, 163, 164
  W R 82, 84, 85, 205, 276, 277
AMERSON
  J M 278
ANDERSON
  Charley 96, 97, 98
  Lee Charley 95, 96, 97, 98, 99, 100
  Martha 95, 96, 97, 98, 99, 100
  Thomas 95, 96, 97, 98
APPLEGEET
  Cora F 108, 109, 110
  W F 108, 110
  W R 109
  Zelma Fay 108, 109, 110
ARBUCKLE
  Harriett E 213
ARD
  J T 277
ARNETT
  Albert 134
  Albert W 137, 138, 139
  Iola 134, 135, 136, 137, 138, 139
  Maggie .. 134, 135, 136, 137, 138, 139
  A W 135, 136, 137, 139
ASBURY
  Francis 223, 224
  Sallie 289, 291
ATKINS
  Isabelle 68, 69
  Isabelle M 68
  James P 68, 69
  Jas P 115, 116, 217
  Robert Meagher 68, 69
  W D 115, 116

William D 217
AULTMAN
  Claud L 82, 83
  Claude L 81
  Claude Leon 84
  Fraklin Clyde 81
  Frank B 81, 82, 83, 85, 86
  Franklin B 81, 82, 84
  Franklin C 81, 85, 86
  Franklin Clyde 82
  Millie 82, 83, 85
  Millie W 81, 82, 84
AURD
  F S 180, 183
AUSBORN
  Annie 150

BAILEY
  Charles 110, 112, 113
  Charlie 112
BARD
  Daniel L 171, 172
  Daniel Lee 175
  Daniel N 171, 172, 173, 174, 175
  Emma 172, 173, 174, 175
  Oda May 171, 173, 174
BARNEY
  Albert 183, 184
  Albert Emmet 183, 184
  Bessie 183, 184
  Homer 184
BAUGHMAN
  G L 185, 186, 187, 188, 189
  Gold C 185, 186
  Gold C, Jr 188, 189
  Malvin W 186, 187
  Melvin W 185, 188
  Sarah 185, 186, 187, 188, 189
BEAVER
  B J 35, 36, 37, 198, 263, 264, 265,
  325, 326
  Earnest 266, 267
  Ella 265, 266, 267
  Ernest 265, 266, 267
  John 265, 266, 267
BERRY
  V 69

327

Index

BERRYHILL
   Alice 268, 269
   Hepsie 270, 271
   Jennie 1, 224
   Jenny 1
   Joe 268, 269, 270, 271, 272
   Reno 269, 270, 271
   Sallie 268, 269, 272
   Sarah 43, 44, 109

BEST
   Charles M 112, 114

BIBLE
   David 259, 260
   Lewis 258, 259, 260, 261
   Mulsie 258, 259, 260, 261
   William McHenry 258
   Wm McKinley 261

BIGPOND
   Anderson 162, 163
   John 162, 163, 164, 166, 167
   Nancy ... 162, 163, 164, 165, 166, 167
   Susie 162, 164, 166, 167

BIGPONS
   John 165
   Susie 165

BIXBY
   Tams 5, 17, 34, 38, 49, 58, 88, 222,
      281, 295, 306, 320, 323
   Tom 290

BLACKILL
   Susan B 133

BLACKWELL
   Susan P 132, 133

BONNER
   H R 229, 236, 237

BONNET
   H R 144, 145, 146, 147

BOUDINOT
   Cornelius 198

BOUGH
   Arthur 193, 194, 195
   Emma 193, 194, 195
   Ethel 193, 194
   Henry 194, 195
   Rachel 194, 195

BOYD
   N D 121, 122, 123

BRAY
   W W 277

BRENNAN
   Francis P 113
   Francis R 111, 112, 113, 114, 246

BRIGHT
   Leon Dewitt 247
   Luke O 245, 246, 247
   Mary 235, 245, 246, 247
   Thelma Beatrice ... 235, 245, 246, 247

BRONAUGH
   J W 210, 265
   J W, MD 210, 265

BROWN
   Daniel W 190
   Gold C 190
   Joseph 249
   Neosho P 110, 111, 112, 113
   Zenia 190

BRUCE
   Browder F 191, 192
   Moten 191, 192
   Pheba 191
   Thebe 191, 192

BRUMMET
   Anna 247

BRUNER
   Flora 226, 227
   Jennie 226, 227
   William G 226, 227

BUFORD
   Charles 174, 175, 204, 205

BURGESS
   Ed 256, 257
   Inay 256
   May 257
   Ruby 256, 257

BURLINGAME 54

BUSH
   R B 1
   W H 1

CAIN
   Chas F 202
   Louisa J 202
   W A 202

CALLAHAN

Index

Alice 314
Alice A 310, 311, 315
J O 311, 313, 314
Josephine 314, 315
Josephine Nevada..310, 311, 313, 315
W K 314
Walter K 310, 312, 313, 314, 315
Walter K, MD 310
CAMERON
   E D 312
CAMPBELL
   Jessie 78, 79
   Mattie 79
   Tine Winburn 78, 79
   Tom 78, 79
CANARD
   J T 128
   Jeff T 6, 7, 129, 130, 299, 304
   Lena 215
   Martin 215
   Roly 6, 304
   Simmer 6
CANE
   Charles R 16, 17, 18, 19, 20
   Charley R 21, 22
   Charlie R 16, 18, 20
   Mollie B 16, 17, 18, 19, 20, 21, 22
   Robert C 17
   Robert Carl 16, 17, 19, 20, 21
   William R 21, 22
   Willie I 16
   Willie R 17, 18
CANON
   R B 105
CAREY
   Jessie 225
CARLILE
   Bessie 183, 184
CARMAN
   H M 316
CASTAIN
   E166, 167
CHARLES
   N E 325, 326
CHEATHAM
   William L 318, 319, 320
CHILDERS

S B 326
CHISHOLM
   Rosa 258, 260
CLAWSON
   D D 155
   W R 89, 90, 92, 93, 155, 156
CLINTON
   Geo 315, 316
   George 316, 317, 318, 319
   Henry 319, 320
   Nexie 317, 318
   Nixie 315, 316
   Sallie 315, 316, 317, 318, 319
CLOUD
   Nancy 162, 164, 165
COBB
   Isabel 284
   Isabel, MD 284
COLTER
   Kate 67
COMBS
   J W 133, 134
   John Boyd ... 44, 45, 47, 49, 51, 52, 53
   John W 45, 46, 47, 49, 50, 51, 52
   Katie 44, 46, 47, 49, 50, 51, 52
   Minnie 50, 51
   Mrs 47, 48
   Nettie 50, 51
   Pearl 44, 46, 50
   Pearly 45
   Wesley 46
COMBS, ... 46
COON
   Fred C 204, 205
   Oda M 204, 205
   Sallie 204, 205, 279
COOPER
   Annie 250, 251, 252
   E E 250, 251, 252
   Florence 250, 251, 252
   W G 258, 259, 260, 261
COPPEDGE
   Charles E 112, 114
COSAR
   Sissie 98
COSER
   Sissie 96

Index

COTT
- William M, MD 232
- Wm 159, 160
- Wm, MD 159, 160

COUCH
- Allie B 3
- Amanda 3, 4
- Gertie May 4, 5
- J C 3, 4
- Mary E 3

CRABTREE
- Flora 57, 59

DAGLEY
- Eliza 254

DAILEY
- Dr C E 282
- Lucy S 282, 284
- Margaret Willison 284

DAILY
- Dr C E 283
- Lucy S 282, 283
- Lucy Shannon 284
- Margaret 284
- Margaret Willison 282, 283

DALSAVER
- Missouri 160
- Wm 160

DARLING
- A M 201

DAUCARTOS
- C C 191, 192

DAVIDSON
- Charles A 237
- Chas A 238

DAVIS
- E L 162
- J B 263, 264, 265
- Sam'l C 147, 148
- Samuel C 147

DAWSON
- Cooper 133
- Dessie Lee 133, 134

DEERE
- Hannah 31
- J J 207
- Lawyer 154

Wisey 90, 92

DILLSAVER
- Misouri 160, 161
- Missouri 160, 161
- Mode 160, 161
- Orvel Dean 161
- Robert Lowe 160

DILSAVER
- Missouri 159
- Orvel Dean 160
- Robert Lowe 159
- Wm 159

DIXON
- Bell 176

DONOVAN
- Irwin 131, 184, 266, 267

DORTER
- Lyra 304

DOYLE
- Ada ... 118, 119, 120, 121, 122, 123, 124, 125, 126
- Burris ... 118, 119, 120, 121, 122, 123, 124, 125
- Eva 118, 119, 122, 123, 124, 125
- Walter 118, 119, 120, 121, 125

DUBOIS
- M L 3, 5

DUBOSE
- M L 4

DUNZY
- J R 298, 303, 309
- Louis 303, 309

EARLEY
- Lizzie 184

EDKRIDGE
- C C 240

EISENBERG
- R B 73

ESKRIDGE
- C C 95, 239

EVANS
- J A 202
- James 200, 201, 202, 203, 204
- James, Jr 200, 204
- Mrs 315
- Phidelta Lee 201, 202, 203

Index

R A 314, 315
Stella 200, 201, 202
EWERS
Albert 318, 319

FAULKNER
Trevor 275, 276
FERRY
Ada 162, 165
FIFE
Dawes 248, 249
Sarah 248, 249
Timmie 248, 249
FINLEY
Elmer 210
FLYNN
J W 176
FOSTER
Edward 237, 239
Grace M 239
Grace N 240
J E 237, 238
John W 239, 240
FOYIL
W A 139
FRANCIS
Bettie 242, 243, 244
Jeff 240, 241, 242, 244
Millie 240, 241, 242, 243, 244
Robert 240, 241, 242, 243, 244
FRANKLIN
M C 158
Mrs M C 158
FREEMAN
Chas R 254, 255
Ernie 255
Ernie V 254
John W 295, 296, 297
Lena 295, 296, 297
Rhoda 117
Theodore R 295, 296, 297

GAMBLER
Martin 198
GARDNER
E M 46, 52
Ella 45, 46

Mrs 45, 46, 48
GARNER
Fle 207
GARRIGUES
Anna 96
GAUGHMAN
G L 189
GOAT
Wardley 98
GOODE
George 206, 207, 208
Myrtle M 206, 207, 208
Rowena 206, 207, 208
GRAY
Addie 321, 322
Mary 321, 322
Siah 321, 322
GREENLEAF
Ida 186
Sarah 187
GREGORY
Archie 14
Archie A 13, 15
Florence 14
Florence L 15
Frank Lee 14, 15
Gilbert R 130, 131, 132
Ina 131, 132
A L 283
Rose Ida 130, 131, 132
GRIESEL
E C .. 3, 64, 72, 88, 91, 119, 153, 154,
163, 164, 165, 172, 174, 184, 193,
194, 195, 197, 251, 252, 266, 267,
268, 288, 307
Edw C 2, 3, 4, 5, 7, 14, 18, 20, 21,
33, 42, 43, 49, 55, 61, 64, 68, 71, 72,
77, 79, 83, 85, 86, 88, 89, 91, 102,
104, 110, 119, 123, 149, 150, 151,
153, 154, 157, 172, 173, 174, 177,
178, 179, 182, 183, 184, 188, 189,
190, 191, 192, 193, 194, 195, 197,
208, 211, 219, 251, 252, 257, 259,
261, 266, 267, 268, 274, 286, 287,
288, 292, 293, 294, 300, 301, 302,
307, 308, 315, 321, 324
GROOM

Index

L D 318, 319
GROSS
  Ben D 150, 151, 276
HACKETT
  F J 144, 145
  Sarah E 143, 144, 145, 146, 147
HAINES
  Henry G 96
HAINS
  H G ... 97, 193, 194, 195, 197, 215, 231, 251, 288
  Henry G 74, 128, 274, 283
  Sukey 252
HAMILTON
  J H 162, 165
HARDRIDGE
  E E 230, 231
HARJO
  Lussie 25, 26, 28
HARLAN
  John 313
HARPER
  Carrie C 212
HARRISON
  Geo D 67
  R P 313
HART
  James 112, 114
HASTON
  W S 170, 171
HATFIELD
  S L 284
  Signa L 284
HAYMER
  Frank L 9
HEITZMON
  Chas 103
  Chas W 103
HENDERSON
  S H 1
HENRY
  Allen 43, 44, 109
  Carrie 211, 212, 213
  Edith Clair 214
  Edith Clara 211, 212
  Howard H 211, 214

J P 212
James P 211, 212, 214
HICKS
  C P 115, 116
  Cleveland P 217
  Hettie M 190
HIGHLAND
  Lula N 156, 157, 159
  Lulu N 158
  Pat 156, 157, 159
  Patrick 156, 157, 158
  Patrick, Jr. 156, 159
  Patrick A 158
HILL
  Amanda 23, 24
  James 24, 25, 26, 27, 28, 29, 30, 31, 32
  Jim 24, 30, 31
  Lucy 23, 24, 25, 26, 27, 28, 29
  M E 207
  Mandy 29, 30, 31, 32
  Polley 30
  Pollie 24
  Polly 25, 26, 27, 28, 29, 30, 31, 32
HOLDEMAN
  Orlando U 75
HOLDER
  W W 256, 257
HOLT
  Z I J 9, 181
HOPWOOD
  K F 93
  Kellen F 93, 94
  Mollie 93, 94
  Ora Pearl 93
  Ora Pearle 94
HORN
  Fannie Lee 273, 275, 277, 279
  Jessie 273, 274, 276, 277
  Lillie 273, 274, 275, 276, 277, 279
  Sam 273, 274, 276, 277, 278, 279
  Samuel 275
HOWARD
  H B 22, 23
  Mattie 22, 23
  Maxie 22, 23
HUFFINE

Index

Mary 256
HUGHES
  Elsie 54, 55, 56, 57, 58
  Ethel 54
  Evalie 55
  Eveley 53
  Lena Ethel 54, 55, 58, 59, 60
  Lizie 279
  Lizzie 53, 56, 57, 58, 59, 60
  Lona Ethel 53
  Melvin 273
  Melvina 273, 274, 275
  Minnie Ethel 55
  Robert 53, 54, 57, 58, 59, 60

INGRAM
  Catherine F 15
INSCHO
  Hattie 247

JACKSON
  J J 56
  N J 56
JACOB
  Newman 96
JACOBS
  Ella L 169
  Jennie C 169
  John A 169
  Newman 95, 96, 97
  Newman F 169
  William R 169
JEROME
  J E 1, 2, 20
JIMBOY
  Hailey 271
  Peggy 6, 7
  Wiley 6, 7
  William 269, 270, 272
JOBE
  G W 229, 236, 293
  G W, MD 229, 237, 293
JOHNSON
  Annie 33, 34, 36, 37, 38, 41, 42
  Annie C 36
  Annie Childers 35, 36
  Arena 35, 36, 38, 39

Aurena 40
B P 223, 224
George 285, 286
I F 221, 222
Isaac 221, 222, 223, 224
Isac 220
Joe 285, 286
Miley 220, 222, 223, 224
Nicey 221, 222, 223, 224
Rena   32, 33, 34, 37, 38, 39, 40, 41, 42
Robert F   34, 35, 36, 37, 38, 39, 40, 41, 42
Robert H 33, 37
Ruth 285
Rutha 285, 286
Scott 221, 222
JONES
  E R 103

KERR
  Arcenoe 73, 75
  Arcenoe M 71, 74
  Arsyno 71, 72, 74
  Arsyno M 75
  Arsynos 70, 72, 73
  Commodore, Jr 71, 74, 75
  Ethel 70, 71, 72, 73, 74, 75
  Henry 71, 72, 73, 74, 75
KILMER
  C E 214
KING
  Amos 297, 298, 303, 307, 308, 309
  Limonda 308
  Lucy 306, 307, 308, 309
  Simonda 309
  Simondy 306, 307, 308
KINYON
  J A 219

LASLIE
  Fannie 322
LEIBER
  John G 73
LEWIS
  E E 233, 234
LIEBER

John G 73, 166, 167
LIEBMAN
   A 290, 291
LILLARD
   T J 317
LINDSAY
   Mary 177, 178
LONG
   Juda 317
   Judy 318, 319
   Katie 96
   Kizzie 154
LOVETT
   Annie 215
   Kizzie 23, 215
LOWE
   Canuky 152, 153, 154, 155
   Joe 152, 153, 154, 155
   Toche 153, 154
   Tuche 155
LOWREY
   R 202
LUCAS
   J B 276, 277
LUMPKIN
   C W 223, 224
LYFORD
   H O 248
   H O, MD 248
LYNCH
   Robert E 147, 148, 227, 280, 281
   Yanah 263, 264, 265

MCDERMOTT
   J   10, 11, 12, 13, 23, 26, 27, 28, 29,
      30, 35, 80, 88, 91, 93, 97, 129, 140,
      153, 160, 161, 163, 164, 165, 196,
      213, 215, 216, 221, 223, 232, 234,
      241, 243, 251, 268, 274, 282, 307
   Jesse...24, 40, 95, 128, 149, 163, 164,
      165, 195, 196, 231, 249
MCGILBRA
   Hepsey 199
MCGILBRAY
   Captain 196
   Hepsey 195, 196
MCGIRT

Isaac 128
MCGUIRE
   C F 144, 147
   C F, MD 144
   Geo W, MD 79, 141
   George W 141, 277
MCINTOSH
   Alice 150, 151
   Annie Lila 150, 151, 152
   Arsynos 70
   Bennie 322
   D N, Jr 150, 151, 152
   Edith Louise 60, 61
   Freeland B 60, 61
   Kate 60, 61
   L G 31
   Lula N 156
   Lulu N 158
   Roley 322
   Roley C 174
   Susan 70
   Susan B 70
   Susan D 72, 73
MCKELLOP
   Betsey 1, 2
   Betsy 2
   Louisa 1, 2
   Peter 1, 2
MCKILLOP
   Peter 2
MCKIM
   R A 247
   W A 247
   William 247
MCQUEEN
   Miss 45, 47
   Sabra 48
   Sage 45
MANES
   William H, MD 280
   Wm H 280
MANN
   Luther 225, 226
MANVILLE
   M F 238
MARTAIN 63
   Jesse 62

Index

T M 62
MARTIAN
   Anna 64, 65
   Leona 64, 65
   Tom 64
MARTIN
   Anna 62, 63, 64, 65, 66, 67
   Jesse 62, 66, 67
   Johnson 35, 38, 39
   Leona 63, 64, 66
   Thomas 62, 63, 64, 66, 67
   Tom 65
   William T 67
MATHEWSON
   Phoebe B 281
MAXEY
   Eugen 111
   Eugene 110, 111, 112, 113, 114
   Eugene Willie 110, 111, 112
   Neosha P 112
   Neosho P 110, 111, 112, 113, 114
   Simeon C 111, 112, 113, 114
   Simeon C, Sr 112, 113
MAY
   Minnie 16, 18, 20, 21, 22
MAYS
   D 317
MERRICK
   Edward ...   120, 124, 125, 127, 128, 131, 132
   Lona 49
MICCO
   Harry 230, 231
MIKEY
   Josiah 116, 117, 118
   Lewis 116, 117, 118
   Lizzie 116, 117, 118
MILES
   Jennie 108
   Jennie Murrell..   100, 101, 102, 106, 107
   Louisa 107
   Rosalee 100, 101, 102, 104
   Rosalie 102, 103, 104, 105, 106, 107, 108
   Vivian 102, 103, 104, 105, 106, 107, 108

W J 106
W S 102, 104, 108
William S 102, 103
Wm S 100, 101
MILLER
   Eugene 76, 77, 78
   Horton H 310, 311, 312, 314
   J Y ..   23, 25, 54, 55, 62, 64, 72, 76, 135, 172, 174, 196, 273, 274
   L M 78, 169, 170
   Lillie 77, 170, 171
   Louis M 170, 171
   Nora F 76, 77, 78
   Sam H 169
   Sam'l H 77
   Samuel H 76, 77, 78
   Samuel H, Jr 170, 171
MINTON
   Ada 80
   Ada Ethel 79
   Amelia 80, 140
   Annie 80, 140, 142
   Chanie 80
   Choney 79
   Ida 79
MITCHNER
   Dr 119
MITTONG
   Kate C 283
MOORE & NOBLE 126
MORGAN
   William B 211, 212, 296, 297
MORON
   Joseph C 186, 187
MORRISON
   S H 101, 103, 105
MORROW
   J B ..   50, 51, 52, 56, 57, 59, 80, 133, 134, 136, 138, 141, 143, 275, 276, 278, 279
MORTON
   W W 290, 291
   Wm P 291
MOTT
   M L 52
MOUNDS
   Bettie 94

NAHAKEY
   Moses 149
NAHARKEY
   Martha 147, 148
   Messer 147
   Mille 148
   Millie 147, 148
   Mooser.. 148
   Mosser 148
NARHAHKAY
   Martha 149
   Millie 149
   Mose 149
   Moses 149
NEWMAN
   Wm C 230, 231

O'REILLY
   E J 158
OVERSTREET
   John W 191, 192

PARKER
   Charles Edward 224, 225
   Jessie..................................... 224, 225
   William E 224, 225
PARKS
   Margaret Atkin 288
PARRISH
   Zera E 25, 54, 62, 76, 119, 135
   Zera Ellen 23, 33, 71, 157, 249
PATE
   D M 50
   D M, MD 50
PERRIN
   Mahala 192
   Mahaley 192
PERRYMAN
   George 218, 219, 220
   George B 219
   John 35
   Okema 218, 219, 220
   Ophia 218, 219, 220
   Pheba 191
   Sile... 35
PHEGLEY
   Mary 121, 122, 123

PHILLIPS
   John H 268, 269, 270, 271, 272
PIKE
   Edna 232, 233, 234
   Fay 232, 233, 234
   James B 198
   Vester 232, 233, 234
POLK
   C A 237, 238, 239
   Cinda 242, 244
POLLARD
   A J 180, 181, 183
   A J, MD 180, 181, 183
PORTER
   Elsie 10, 11, 12, 13
   Lewis 10, 11, 12, 13
   McKinley 10, 11
   P 247
   Pleasant 12
   Plesent 13
POSEY
   Alex 25, 26, 154, 242, 244
   Hugh F 235, 236
   John M 235, 236
   Laura E 236
   Mary L 145, 146, 228, 229
   Terry O 228, 229
   Walter 228, 229
PRATT
   Cassius L 65, 66
PRESSGROVE
   Aaron 142, 143
   Joseph 142, 143
   Lizzie 142, 143
PRICE
   Leila 140, 141
PURYEAR
   Emma H 208, 209, 210
   Frank M 208, 209, 210
   William H 208, 209, 210
   Wm H 210

RAABE
   Celia 177, 178
   Chris 175, 176, 177, 178
   Ida May 175, 176, 177, 178
   Stella 175, 176, 177, 178

Index

RAGAN
Sarah Jane 17, 19
RED
D J 209, 210, 266
Martha 149
REID
Alice 312
REYNOLDS
Clarence 79, 140, 141
Lea 79
Leila 140, 141
Oscar 140
Oscar Lee 140, 141, 142
RICE
T 132
T J 15, 16
RICHARD
Mary 247
RIDER
Chas 98
RIGNEY
J D 316
ROBERTS
Cora 136
ROBERTSON
J W 233
J W, MD 234
ROBISON
Adeline Belle 114, 115
Joe S 114, 115, 116
Mattie 114, 115, 116
Newman Joseph 115, 116
ROGERS
Augusta 179, 180, 181, 182, 183
John 181, 182, 183
William P 182
William Penn 181
Wm P 180, 181, 182, 183
Wm Penn 179, 182
Woods C 180
Woods Cooper 179, 180, 181
RUSSELL
Clemmie 42, 43, 44
James 42, 43
James W 43
Mary A 42, 43

SANGER
Stella 200, 201, 202
SARTY
Emanuel 198
Hapsy 197, 198
Hepsey 196, 197, 199
Hepsie 198
Jasper 214
Lena 214
Manuel 195, 196, 197, 198, 199
Retta 214
Roley 197, 198
Rolley 196
Rollie 196, 197, 198, 199
Susan 198, 199
SATTERBEE
Grace M 237
Mrace M 238
SCHARNAGEL
Charles E 211
Chas E, MD 212
SCHARNEGAL
C E, MD 297
Chas E 297
SCHOOLES
A 1
SCOTT
Losannia 298
Winey 303, 304, 306, 309
SEMARHITCHKER 269
SHANNON
Mary D 65
SHANON
Mary D 66
SHARP
Kate 175
SHELBY
David 149
SHEPARD
Dr T E 220
Mr 281
T E 220
SIMMONS
Charley 35, 36, 39
Harley 38
SIMPSON
Rose M 19, 21, 22

SIMS
 E W 117, 317
SKAGGE
 Drennan C 244
SKAGGS
 D C 26, 242, 244
 Drennan C 29, 242
SKAGS
 Drennan C 28
SKELEERE
 A V 69
SMITH
 A A 59, 205, 254, 255, 275, 276
 Lillie 278
 Maggie 134
 Mose 11, 13
 A R 143
 Sarah 227
 Toche 153
SNELSON
 A J 200
 A J, MD 200
STAKE
 Albert 289, 290, 291, 292
 Millie 292
 Missie 289, 290, 291
 Sallie 289, 290, 291, 292
STANCLIFT
 George W 246
STEWART
 Lucy 217
STONE
 J C 159, 161, 230, 231
 J O 232
STORMS
 Sarah A 239, 240
STRAWHUN
 Ella 9

TAYLOR
 Malvina 84
 Mrs Malvina L 84
TEAGUE
 Lizzie 246
THOMAS
 J D 9
 Mr 46

THOMPSON
 Roy 246
 Sarah 10, 12
 W H 219
THORNSBERRY
 Rachel 174
TIGER
 Barney 216, 217
 Dave 262, 263, 264, 265
 Edward 262, 264, 265
 Ewnah J 216, 217
 George 262, 263, 264
 Jas 263, 264, 265
 Katie 216, 217
 NeoSho 263
 Neosho 264
 NeoSho 265
 Peggy 5
 Pinar 6
 Sissie 5, 6
 Sissy 7
TRENT
 Chaney 286, 287, 288
 Jesse 286, 287, 288
 Jim 286, 287, 288
TRUSLER
 Frank 280
 Fred 280, 281
 Phoebe B 280, 281
 Thoebe B 282
TURNBOW
 Aaron 252, 253, 254, 255
 Charlie 253, 254, 255
 James Henry 252, 253, 254
 Katie 252, 253, 254, 255
 Mtilda 255

VANDERPOOL
 J M 136, 139
 J M, MD 139
VAUGHAN
 J W 165

WADSWORTH 295
 Emma 293, 294
 Mary 293
 Mitchel 293

Mitchell 293, 294
WALLACE
   Ella 167, 168
   Jannison 196
   Tully Mae 167, 168
   W A 167, 168
WALRAND
   Z T 200
WALROND
   Z T 201, 203
WASHINGTON
   Divid 322
WELLS
   Lizzie 142
   Lydia 134, 143, 204, 205
   Martha 133, 134
WESLEY
   John .   297, 298, 299, 300, 301, 302, 303, 304, 306
   Peter 297, 298, 299, 300, 305
   Polley 297, 298
   Polly   297, 299, 300, 301, 302, 303, 304, 305, 306
   Tiger 301, 302, 303, 304, 305, 306
WEST
   Geo W, MD 168
   George W 168
WIGGINS
   N E 117
WILLIAMS
   Henryetta 143, 144, 146, 147
   John F 145, 146
   John H 144, 145, 146
   Sarah E 144, 145, 146, 147
WILLIFORD
   Joe Brown 8, 9
   Lou 8, 9
   Lou Brown 8
   M M 8, 9
WILSON
   S M 94
WINSTON
   J A 212, 213, 278
   James A 213
   Jas A 213, 312, 313
WISDOM
   Edgar 94

WOFFARD
   Lizzie 323
   Sherley 323
   Wiley Jackson 323
WOFFORD
   Jackson 325, 326
   Jackson Wiley 324, 325
   Lizzie 324, 325, 326
   Sherley 324
   Sherly 325, 326
   Wiley Jackson 324
WOLFE
   L M 316
WRIGHT
   J G 101
   J G, MD 101
YAHOLA
   Celia 87, 88, 89, 90, 91, 92
   Chapley 128
   Clarence 128
   Houston 86, 87, 88, 89, 92
   Jackson 86, 87, 88, 89, 90, 91, 92
   Roman 86, 87, 89, 90, 91
   Wisey 128
YARGEE
   Annie 171
YARHOLAR
   Chapley 126, 127, 129, 130
   Clarence 126, 127, 128, 129, 130
   Wisey 127, 129
YORGEE
   Haina 90, 92, 93
YOUNG
   Sarah F 82
   W P 212, 213

www.ingramcontent.com/pod-product-compliance
Lightning Source LLC
Chambersburg PA
CBHW020243030426
42336CB00010B/594